For Ralph Gabriel,
my teacher, catalyst,
Friend: how can I ever
thank him enough?
Devotedly,
Marshall Fishwick
XI-20-54

AMERICAN HEROES: MYTH AND REALITY

American Heroes

MYTH AND REALITY

By Marshall W. Fishwick

Introduction by Carl Carmer

Public Affairs Press, Washington, D. C.

Copyright, 1954, by Public Affairs Press
2162 Florida Avenue, Washington 8, D. C.

Printed in the United States of America
Library of Congress Catalog Card No. 54-12693

Preface

Why are the American people hero-worshippers? By what process are our heroes chosen? How are they elevated and by whom? Are heroes everywhere basically the same or is there a distinctively American variety? Why do truth and poetry get so quickly and inextricably mixed? What is the significance of the hero in American culture?

In seeking the answers to these questions I have explored a good many biographies, but have found in them little about the nature of the heroic process. Even those which purport to be "true" generally fall heir to much fancy in their search after facts.

As a result, I have tried to devise a new way of analyzing our great men, putting special emphasis on a behind-the-scenes group which I call the hero-makers. The reader will have to judge for himself how successful I have been. Perhaps I have not gone far— but far enough, I hope, to suggest that here is a largely uncharted, vastly significant new area of American history.

Believing that debunkers have had little permanent effect on American reputations, I have not adopted their methods or poses. However, I have tried frequently to cross the fence in order to get a better look at the sacred cows which graze in our legendary pastures.

In a little book called *The Mythifying Theory, Or Abraham Lincoln a Myth* (1872), D. B. Turner took for granted a principle that I shall try to document: that as far as heroes are concerned, the line between myth and reality is very narrow, and apt to disappear. "In a period of less facility of printing," Emerson wrote, "Lincoln would have become mythological in a very few years." Books like Roy Basler's *The Lincoln Legend and* Lloyd Lewis' *Myths After Lincoln* indicated that the printing press did not put on the brakes.

The faculty for myth and hero-worship is, of course, universal

v

in the human race. It grows out of man's refusal to accept a mechanistic universe and his own human limitations.

Please do not look, in the ensuing chapters, for "the final truth" about American heroes. Look, rather, for clues to the proposition that the last truth can never be told; and that even if it could, we would find such a truth much less satisfactory than that which, for very legitimate reasons, we choose to believe.

*   *   *

It should be noted that shorter versions of some of the chapters have appeared in the *Saturday Review, Yale Review, Western Folklore, Social Education, The Filson Club History Quarterly*, and the *Virginia Magazine of History*, and are used here with permission.

The Humanities Division of the Rockefeller Foundation generously provided summer grants-in-aid which made research for this volume possible.

So many people have given of their time and thought during its preparation that it is impossible to acknowledge my debt to them all. But since they were, at different stages, instrumental in my even attempting it, I feel I must pay specific tribute to three men— Ralph H. Gabriel, James G. Leyburn, and M. B. Schnapper. I only wish the book could have been worthy of such support.

Marshall W. Fishwick

Washington and Lee University
Lexington, Virginia

Introduction

Popular concepts of a national hero are built of many materials. The incontrovertible facts of a biography documented by the agreement of friendly and hostile contemporaries are but the pedestal on which the great figure is raised for the generations to admire. The figure itself, as the public receives it, is molded from a mixture of honest but always fallible interpretations, colorful but undependable folk-lore, enthusiastic efforts at mass-hypnotism, and sometimes plumb dishonest hornswoggling.

Professor Fishwick has focused an inquiring eye upon the sculptors who have created in the general mind its gallery of hero-statues and has subjected both the artists and their materials to a lively going-over. It has already been discovered from his lectures and from occasional appearances of his articles in the public prints that he elicits from his hearers and readers either excited camp-meeting shouts of "Amen!" or more excited and often horrified cries of "Oh, *no!*" Indications of indifference have not been reported.

The word "de-bunk" has lately come to mean in the minds of many to present derogatory materials in a prejudiced or dishonest manner. In this sense of the word Professor Fishwick is no de-bunker. He believes, however, as does every honest historian, that where "bunk" exists it should be exposed for what it is. Objective appraisal is his goal and he has found occasion in this volume to de-bunk sometimes the de-bunkers of heroes, sometimes the heroes themselves, sometimes the wild idolators, the partisan politicans, the selfish coat-tail riders.

American scholars have in recent years placed strong emphasis on the realization that the reporting of changes in popular attitudes of mind, of development and decline of fads and folk-fancies, of the shadings and nuances of the communal imagination, is quite as important to the understanding of our past as the presentation of the facts of military and political history. This book is a worthy example of this kind of thinking. It is a gratifying reward of the logic that has caused the burgeoning of an increasing number of departments of "American Studies" in our colleges.

Marshall Fishwick has done the college he serves and his profession honor by writing in spirited and stimulating fashion a volume which will both give information and provoke controversy. This, I believe, is the surest test of the true educator. The book goes beyond this goal, however, for it serves to introduce to the general reading public a writer whose mind teems with challenging ideas and whose prose has compelling interest.

CARL CARMER

Table of Contents

"The best literature is always the result of something far greater than itself—not the hero, but the portrait of the hero."

Walt Whitman, *November Boughs*

"Who cares what the fact was, when we have made a constellation of it to hang in heaven an immortal sign?"

Ralph Waldo Emerson, *Journals*

"Watch a child with his toy guns and you will see: what most interests him is not (as we so much fear) the fantasy of hurting others, but to work out how a man might look when he shoots or is shot. A hero is one who looks like a hero."

Robert Warshow, *The Westerner*

PART I

Giants in the Land

CHAPTER 1

Clio's Favorites

*"Great men seem to have only one purpose in
life—getting into history. That may be all they
are good for."*—Will Cuppy, *The Decline and Fall
of Practically Everybody*

As they did for so many things, the Greeks had a word for it—
heros, the superior man, embodiment of composite ideals—first
used in connection with the deified dead. The *heros*, or hero, had
and has a reputation directly related to the social and political
structure of his society. No one knows just when and why he
comes. The gift of heaven, he is a force sent by destiny.

Different ages and cultures vary the heroic personality, but all
heroes are true to their age. Whatever their situation, the motives
they urge are elementary, the morality they advocate is obvious.
History is not very effective without people, and people are in-
effective without leaders. The search for heroes is inherent in
human nature. Pre-literate societies allow men, heroes, and gods
to stand on a footing of tolerable equality. In remote areas of
the world men are still deified in their own lifetime. The idea
of aloofness in super-human power comes late in history.

To the historian the hero is one who shapes the course of events;
to the philosopher, one who alters the thinking of his times; to the
folklorist, one who evokes legends and songs. Messiah, emanci-
pator, founding father, preserver, creative genius: these are all
related terms for one whose influence or personality captivates
the people. The personification of predominating ideals, the hero
emerges at a moment when men's emotions are deeply stirred, and
appeals to both the imagination and the reason.

The flux of history is often compared to the course of a river. Like a stream, history moves in one direction for a time, then angles off in another. It gains momentum, washes away old banks, and makes unpredictable turns. This provides the hero with his golden moment. If he can convince others that he caused the turn, he will be a public idol.

Yet that public creates the hero only in the sense that a knight is made by the king when he gives the accolade. The reason for the accolade is independent of the king, and existed before the man became a knight. So a hero is created by public recognition of his worth; but the merit is independent of the recognition. Always susceptible to legend, a hero becomes superhistorical in myth.

His essential qualities are hard to identify and isolate. Each hero is emphatically himself. Many who temporarily qualify— political favorites, matinee idols, sports champions — disappear soon like a flash flood. While they last, however, they benefit from the maxim, "Winner take all." We quote and misquote them with equal ease. Erudite scholars find no indication that they said or did many things attributed to them. But they should have said and done them. That is enough.

In classical times heroes were god-men; in the Middle Ages they were God's men; in the Renaissance universal men; in the eighteenth century enlightened gentlemen; in the nineteenth century self-made men. In our own time we are seeing the common man become heroic.

All cultures invent, in some form or other, an Olympus like that of the imaginative Greeks. To this realm went certain human beings adjudged worthy of immortality. Such a one was Heracles, or, as the Romans called him, Hercules. Celebrated in sculpture by such artists as Myron, Scopas, Polyclitus, Praxiteles, and Lysippus, and worshipped in sacred shrines dotting the Hellenic world, this Heracles was actually a petty ruler in Tiryns, subject to the order of a superior king at Argos. To his known exploits the Greeks added mythical stories over the years. Finally he emerged as the embodiment of the Greek Happy Warrior, whose strength of will, social mission, friendship, and morality won universal praise. He became, as Socrates pointed out in the *Gorgias*, a figure that served the psychological needs of the Greeks.

When Athens rose to power she craved a hero of her own, more closely tied to her destiny than was Heracles; so Theseus was elevated. Previously he had ranked with, but not above, other heroes of pre-Trojan War days. In the *Iliad* he was a fighter and seducer, strong in battle "for rich-haired Helen's sake." Now the Athenians made him Ionian in spirit, fond of dancing and music. He became more circumspect in his love affairs. City officials deleted from Hesiod's works verses referring to Theseus' passion for Aegle. Pisistratus embarked on a deliberate campaign to glorify Theseus. In this he was followed by Cimon, who brought Theseus' bones to Athens from Scyros, buried them in the heart of the city, and formally established his cult. His popularity grew until it rivalled that of Heracles.[1]

In time Theseus came to represent democratic Athens and its brilliant intellectual flowering. He figured prominently in plays by Aeschylus, Sophocles, and Euripides. As the people matured, so did he, becoming more deliberate, lofty, and selfless. In contemplating him Athenians found courage and faith. Thucydides called him "a king of equal insight and power." On Hadrian's Arch was inscribed *Athens, formerly the city of Theseus.* The Athenians did not respect him because he was Theseus; he was Theseus because they respected him.

While Rome held sway many of the old gods declined, but new ones, and new religions, took hold. A pagan Olympus was supplanted by a Christian Heaven, where saints dwelt in glory everlasting. It is well to remember that in Christ's time, Messiahs could be found preaching on many street corners; but by the second century, with the martyrdom of Saint Polycarp, the method of Christian veneration had crystallized, and gained acceptance in a sizable portion of Europe.[2] The many saints' legends, which can be seen working in the same terms as primitive mythology, provide a primary source for studying the process of hero making. Saints perform generally the same heroic offices as did classical gods. They render the services of intercession and prediction, and provide the focus for relic worship and canonization. The last of these processes became an effective instrument for socializing the saintly idea and perpetuating the group values of the Church.[3] In short, heroes got haloes.

Since the flowering of the saint, there has been a succession of occidental paragons. For the most part the modern hero has lost his ritualistic setting. The nearest contemporary approach is the awarding of military medals or special honors. While such secularized heroism does not appeal to as many as did the saintly heroism of the Middle Ages, it does dignify human action. The heroic ideal is still being met. Contemporary America is not so sophisticated, nor is the history of the United States so short that we can defy it. Ours, too, is the land of the hero.

*　　　　*　　　　*

What end do great men and great reputations serve? Each meets certain specific functions, depending on the era and place in which he lives; satisfies emotional and psychological needs of his admirers; and reflects commonly held hopes and beliefs. Public opinion, and hence reputations, change quickly. In one period there exists the tendency to dehumanize in order to exalt; in another, the hysteria of depreciation. Generally the expectations of the hero-seeking multitude is inordinately high. When disappointment follows, the victim is shunted off into limbo.

Of course, fallen heroes may rise again, for there are cycles in their popularity. In this century Washington is losing, and Lee gaining ground. The "ring-tailed roarers" of the last century's western frontier have gone into eclipse with the disappearance of that frontier. Reputations may see-saw with rivaling ones, as do Jefferson's and Hamilton's. This uneven evolution is by no means an exclusively American phenomenon.

Great men are more apt to be solid than subtle. Their aims are plainly put. They act while others think. Henry Adams, Charles Peirce, and Willard Gibbs have been America's intellectual giants. How many school children have even heard of them?

Eventually public idols are accepted and venerated on faith; their myth and their reality merge. They supersede mere facts. Every truth is a reshaping of life impressions. Hence, in the final analysis, it is a free creation of the human intellect. History's real bailiwick is not so much events as opinions. Most of us constantly overlook laws of evidence. We make what we would *like* to have happened into what *did* happen. To miss this point is to render the study of the heroic process impossible. "Who cares what the fact was," observed Emerson, "when we have made a constellation of it to hang in heaven an immortal sign?"

Thought is the alternation between collecting and interpretating data. But we believe many things that cannot be demonstrated, or fully documented. Some of these things we tag "legends." Legends can be more faithful and useful to the human heart than facts; many illustrations of this are contained in later chapters. Although scholars cannot endorse the notion that history is a pack of lies agreed upon, they realize there is truth in the quip about its being the propaganda of the victorious.

The reoccurrence of themes and traits in heroes has convinced some there is a magic formula.[4] Joseph Campbell contends that all myths and worlds redeemed are alike. David Malcomson maintains that all heroes are contained in ten heroic types — namely, the Persevering Tortoise, Futile Searcher, Cinderella, Sly Fox, Escapist, Returning Prodigal, Golden Fly, Ugly Duckling, Patient Griselda, and Inconstant Lover. Other scholars have noted that six episodes are usually presented in Greek tragedy—the *agon* or struggle of hero and villain; the *pathos* or defeat of the hero; the description of death by a messenger; the lamentation; the recognition of the hero; and the *theophany* or insight which is the hero's epiphany.

In many Western European sagas the hero has a distinguished origin, and a birth surrounded by mysterious circumstances. Threats are made on his life, but he escapes and returns to win victories and fame. Tragedy, rather than comedy, dogs his life.[5]

Undoubtedly, all heroes stand on somewhat common ground. The tall tales of America and the miracle tales of the Middle Ages have marked similarities. Comic books utilize situations as old as Homer or Beowulf. The favorite setting for heroes remains the battlefield, which provides the clearest test of strength and decision; but the testing ground may just as well be a country store, a lumber camp or the Yankee Stadium. Lincoln's walking miles to return a penny, Paul Bunyan's straightening out a river, and Babe Ruth's pointing to the bleachers where he intended to knock

a home run are so many ways in which Americans have fulfilled
their heroic roles.

World reputations swing between the poles of the saint (Buddha,
Christ, St. Francis) and the soldier (Alexander, Napoleon, Washington). The former stresses meekness, self-denial, renunciation;
the latter aggressiveness, domination, and affirmation. Activistic
America has honored the soldier more than the saint. The strong
cult of individualism in America has affected our choice of heroes.

There is a difference between the eventful and the event-making
man. The one is in the right place at the right time; anyone with
a finger could have plugged the dike, as did the Dutch boy. Event-
making people act so as to change existing conditions. Not everyone in Russia could have substituted for Lenin in the 1917 Revolution. Both types have a mission and acquire admirers. They are,
in Thomas Carlyle's words, "the modellers, patterns, and in a
wide sense creators of whatsoever the general mass of men con-
trives to do or attain." To say they are always true to their age
is not to say that their standard of values is ageless. "Reputations
of the nineteenth century," said Emerson, "will one day be quoted
to prove its barbarism."

Our heroes have become symbols, just as have Old Glory, the
log cabin, and the skyscraper. Washington symbolizes the Revolution, Boone the Westward Trek, Lincoln the Restored Union, Lee
the Lost Cause. Around them legends flourish—sometimes, as we
shall see, involving supernatural power and insight. This situation
emphasizes that, although they must have surface appeal, great
men must also have large stores of inner power. "For behold,"
Jesus said, "the Kingdom of God is within you." The hero must
turn within himself for the support and solutions he needs. Then,
like the boonbringer, he can return to the outside world and aid
those in it. The hero is a man first of self-achieved submission
and then of action. His path is like that represented in the rites
of passage: separation, initiation, and return. This cycle is exemplified in the careers of Prometheus, Buddha, and Aeneas, as well
as of many who have followed them.

The inward development of personality allows the hero to perform creative acts, and thus help human societies to grow. Before
mastering the macrocosm he overcomes the microcosm. Tackling

the outer world, he is faced by the inertia of his fellow-men; up-setting the social equilibrium inevitably brings conflict. Either his triumph or his defeat will restore the social equilibrium. As Henri Bergson says in *The Creative Mind*, the hero is one whose soul has marked the attainment of a certain point by the evolution of life, and has manifested in an original form a love which is the very essence of the creative effort.

Creative geniuses are "no more than a leaven in the lump of ordinary humanity; and this ordinary humanity is not different in nature from the human type which is typical of primitive socie-ties."[6] In trying to get the uncreative majority to follow him, the hero may use either force or mysticism. The mystic's soul passes out of action into ecstasy, then back into action again. This withdrawal-and-return is frequent in world mythology, as in the stories of Persephone, Adonis, and Osiris. It may be discerned in the spiritual life of mystics, the physical life of the vegetable kingdom, and in human speculation on immortality; in the lives of saints, statesmen, philosophers, and poets, as well as in the histories of nations.

Napoleon Bonaparte's empire has crumbled, his code is out-moded, but his legend survives. His own self-portrait of unblem-ished beauty fostered it. He did not hesitate to order the Pope to Paris for his coronation as Emperor in 1804. His appearance on battlefields was a masterpiece of heroic planning—the silhouette of the great general, on whom Fate hung, sitting on his charger. Wearing his two-cornered hat, he held the chart of the General Staff in one hand and a telescope in the other. He consciously shaped his reputation along lines that best satisfied him. French poets, patriots, and dramatists have done much to perpetuate the legend of Napoleon. An astute French historian has even demon-strated just how and why this has been done.[7]

Following in Napoleon's wake have been such figures as Stalin, Mussolini, and Hitler, erstwhile modern messiahs. Like American leaders of our time, they have been swept into prominence by the Big Build-Up.[8] For reasons no more explicable than why lightning strikes one particular tree, the subject becomes a marked man. Newspapers, columnists, commentators, national magazines, radio, and television concentrate on him. Overnight a new star appears.

Whatever else it has done, technology has accelerated the build-up immeasurably. Publicizing big men is big business.

The most spectacular recent flare-up of hero-worship was occasioned by a woman in a relatively inconsequential nation: Eva Peron, first lady of Argentina. Born out of wedlock in a small provincial village, she was a dancer before marrying Juan Peron. As Secretary of Labor she developed and explained her "mission" so well that when in 1952 she died at 33, Argentina was thrown into despair.[9] Business stopped, and even foreigners were required to go into mourning. A petition was cabled to the Pope in Rome asking for Eva's formal canonization. She had already become a saint at home, to be re-embalmed for "absolute corporeal permanence." Many walked across one or more provinces for a glimpse of the woman who spoke of herself as "just a sparrow in the midst of a great flock of sparrows." Churches displayed her picture in niches formerly reserved for the Virgin Mary. No one can study the "Evita" worship, even at a distance, without realizing its power as it swept over the Pampas.

*   *   *   *

Poets best understand the name and nature of heroes. Only they can create one out of thin air—as Whittier did with Barbara Fritchie. In his *Examination of the Hero in a Time of War*, Wallace Stevens reminds us that, as we fret in our atomic dilemma, we need not depend on reason to create a new Man of the Hour:

> *"The hero is a feeling, a man seen*
> *As if the eye was an emotion,*
> *As if in seeing we saw our feeling*
> *In the object seen and saved that mystic*
> *Against the sight, the penetrating,*
> *Pure eye."*

The hero's appeal stems from something that is basic, even primitive, in every human being:

> *"If the hero is not a person, the emblem*
> *Of him, even if Xenophon, seems*

To stand taller than a person stand, has
A wider brow, large and less human
Eyes and bruted ears: the man-like body
Of a primitive.   He walks with a defter
And lither stride.   His arms are heavy
And his breast is greatness.   All his speeches
Are prodigies in longer phrases."

But his real prowess lies in the clarity and relevance of his thoughts; his ability to hear the "innate music"—

"His thoughts begotten at clear sources
Apparently in air, fall from him
Like chantering from an abundant
Poet, as if he thought gladly, being
Compelled thereto by an innate music." [10]

The historical sequence or coincidental themes already alluded to are not nearly so important as the hero's continuing existence. His destiny, wherever he dwells, is to be enthroned on rainbows. The hero comes by chance, the merest riding of the wind.   In him the culture unites.   He must be, Wallace Stevens insists, even if we have to fashion him ourselves:

"Unless we believe in the hero, what is there
To believe? Incisive what, the fellow
Of what good?   Devise.   Make him of mud,
For every day."

This is the place of the hero in history, and these are some of the notions that have been advanced about the heroic role.   Now we face our primary task: to analyze American heroes, and the way in which myth and reality blend in them.   Perhaps we shall also discover who actually did the blending, and why.

CHAPTER 2

Columbia's Darlings

"As Americans, we have no half-fabulous, legendary wealth, no misty, cloud-enveloped background."—Horatio Greenough

On a hot July 1952 afternoon, thousands of people crowded the streets of Chicago. The Republican National Convention was underway and presidential hopefuls were arriving. Word spread that Candidate Robert Taft was about to appear. His campaigners passed out song sheets which demonstrated the light in which American hero-makers want their subjects to appear. Included were "Battle Hymn of the Republic," "Onward Christian Soldiers," and "When the Roll is Called Up Yonder."

Ovations for favorites have been heard frequently in America. Many are forgotten almost as soon as the acclamation is over. Like all countries, America has had its Cagliostros, who blaze momentarily and then fade. The happy tears shed for Admiral Dewey, who avenged the sinking of the battleship Maine, could have floated a ship of the line. Practical businessmen swooned when Jenny Lind hit high C. So did their wives when Buffalo Bill entered the ring on his white horse. Otherwise respectable ladies collected Rudolph Valentino's cigarette butts and hid them in their bosoms. A cordon of policemen had to stop women from taking his buttons as his body lay in state.

In June, 1927, Charles Lindbergh received 3,500,000 letters, 14,000 parcels, and 100,000 telegrams. The New York *World* got two bushels of Lindbergh poetry. While he was having dinner in New York, a woman broke through his guards to peer into his mouth and determine for herself whether he preferred green beans or green peas.[1] The Hoboes of America proclaimed a thirty-day mourning period when Will Rogers died. Fifty thousand people followed the funeral procession of Sacco and Vanzetti through Boston. Over 7,500,000 pushed into the streets when General MacArthur moved across the country in April, 1951.

Well-fed Americans are starved for the pomp and ritual of older nations. We even have to improvise a pathetic little twenty-minute ritual for the inauguration of our president, the most important official in the world. Our academic rituals are dull and uninspiring, and parades (such as Mardi Gras or the Mummers) have to suffice us as a people. Those who want more form have to get it from ritualistic churches or lodges. There are no prescribed ceremonies for our Independence Day, July 4, or the birthday of the Father of our Country, February 22. Robert's Rules of Order give us about the only national rituals we have.

Such poverty explains the enormous nostalgia for Europe in America, and the mass exodus to Queen Elizabeth's crowning in 1953. For while we are proud of the democratic strain in our heroes, we want them to be as grand as those of other lands. Thus Herman Melville referred to Hercules as "that antique Crockett and Kit Carson."

As foreigners keep telling us, America has lacked many things. Yet no one can say that our people have been deficient in great memories. Without the symbols, heraldry, inherited titles, and traditions which Europeans exalt and revere, Americans have concentrated their affection on a few men. Ralph Waldo Emerson wrote, "If the companions of our childhood should turn out to be heroes, and their condition regal, it would not surprise us." He found public idols pivotal in American life, running out threads of relation through everything, fluid and solid, material and elemental. Because it answers an urgent need, hero worship is an integral part of American life.

We identify ourselves with greatness by means of a signature in an album, a lock of hair, a photograph, or a baseball that has scored a home run; we haunt stage doors and locker rooms; we pursue our favorites with candid cameras and sound recorders. Such scientific gadgets put only a thin veneer over the streak of credulity that goes through an America where over 10,000 rabbit feet are still carried in pockets, and 3,300,000 four leaf clovers are bought annually. P. T. Barnum noted almost a century ago that in the United States a sucker is born every minute; and the time ratio hasn't changed perceptibly since then.

Consider, for example, the "American Goliath," that wonderful ten and a half foot petrified giant "discovered" in Onandaga County, New York in 1896. Planted by George Hull near Cardiff, the gypsum hoax spent a year buried in the portion of New York state that had been the scene of the discovery by Joseph Smith of the Tablets of Moroni; the Spirit Rappings of the Fox Sisters; and the rantings of the End-of-the-World Millerites, the Shakers, and the Publick Universal Friend Jemima Wilkinson. Hull eventually hired two workmen to dig the giant up. One of them, Gideon Emmons, made the observation: "Jerusalem, Nichols, it's a big Injun!" Tens of thousands paid to see it. The giant still attracts many visitors at the Farmer's Museum in Cooperstown, New York. Faith, as well as work, has made America what it is.

A trinity of culture heroes presides over the nation—Washington, Jefferson, and Lincoln. The personification of our Revolution, Washington achieved in his own day as much prestige as the federal government. With his quiet faith in his fellow Americans, and his insistence on the primacy of civil authority, he represents ideals which will not be unseated, in spite of the forbidding portraits and togaed statues. On his two-hundredth birthday there were thousands of "Washingtons" on the map. The national capital, a state, 33 counties, 121 cities and towns, 257 townships, 1140 streets, and uncounted lakes, schools, mountains, and forts bore his name—a tribute which had been paid to no other man, in any country.

Thomas Jefferson, the "Sage of Monticello," is the second member of the triumvirate. Many of his contemporaries were opposed to his ideas and ascendancy. When the 1811 convention met to name what became Louisiana, a delegate from Attakapas threatened to blow up the building if Jefferson's name were even introduced as a possibility. When Jefferson was elected president, Timothy Dwight warned the good ladies of New Haven to stay off the green—because, said the New Englander, they might now be attacked publicly. Jefferson's embargo almost precipitated a

Northern secession movement decades before the South left the Union. He received little veneration in the predominantly Republican decades between the Civil War and the Great Depression.

When the Democrats finally took over in 1932, they revived Jefferson's reputation. The giant Mount Rushmore face, the Jefferson postage stamp and nickel, the Jefferson Memorial in Washington, D.C., and Roosevelt's Monticello speeches were some of the devices used. By World War II, Jefferson had become a symbol for our endangered democracy, and the Democratic party in power. A century and a quarter after his death, scholars carefully collected and edited his literary remains. Thus finally he was given a high place on Olympus.

The last member of the triumvirate is Abraham Lincoln, about whom Richard Stoddard wrote:

> *"The People, of whom he was one*
> *No gentleman, like Washington*
> *(Whose bones, methinks, make room*
> *To have him in their tomb!)"*

Lincoln's career, from log cabin to White House and to martyrdom, personified the times in which he lived. Had Lincoln not lived, it would have been necessary to invent him. Even when the Confederates poked fun at Abe, they acknowledged his democratic appeal:

> *"Jeff Davis is our President*
> *Abe Lincoln is a fool,*
> *Jeff Davis rides a big gray horse*
> *While Lincoln rides a mule."*

History definitely favors unpretentious men on mules. The Roman emperors rode about on white horses. Christ, who entered a minor Roman provincial city on an ass, conquered the world. Richard the Lion-Hearted galloped proudly into battle. We forget it when we read of gentle mule-mounted Saint Francis, talking to the birds. Stephen Douglas spouted magnificent phrases; Abe Lincoln preferred to tell little stories. He said God must have liked the common people, since He made so many of them. Common people appreciated that.

Despite his humble background, Lincoln was much like Jefferson. Both understood the ethical nature of democracy, and of party politics. Both believed in the goodness of human nature; but Jefferson didn't reach as many levels of society as did Lincoln. Not only did the Virginian lack the common touch; he also missed the opportunity to do anything so dramatic as preserving the Union, and the chance to die a martyr's death.

John Wilkes Booth killed Lincoln on April 14, 1865—Good Friday. That he died on the day Christians were celebrating the martyrdom of their Lord was an analogy few ministers missed. Protestant America had acquired a saint. Only five days before the slaying, Lee had surrendered at Appomattox. Congress had ratified the Thirteenth Amendment, and the slaves were free. Then the Savior who had made it all possible was called back to heaven. Lincoln's apotheosis, and Booth's damnation, are central in our heroic history.

Perceptive and ambitious, a master of the American idiom, Lincoln pointed his career along the paths of glory. Devoted admirers pleaded his cause, and historical chance completed the job. For his contemporaries he was a dying god to rank with Osiris, Adonis, or Arthur. Secretary of War Stanton spoke for the nation when he said at the death bed, "Now he belongs to the ages." Walt Whitman called his assassination "one of those climax moments on the stage of universal time, the historic Muse at one entrance, the tragic Muse at the other." In 1954, every car that traveled with an Illinois license plate proclaimed to the world that it came from the "Land of Lincoln." No one can spend an American penny without passing on his image.

To slay a hero is bad business. John Wilkes Booth's act set off a reign of terror in the United States. A brigade of infantry, and uncounted horsemen and detectives, pursued the injured Booth southward after his miraculous escape from the scene of his crime. The federal government offered $100,000 for his capture. Papers and posters stressed that "Everyone should consider his own conscience charged with his solemn duty, and rest neither day nor night until Booth is dead." The hatred shown towards Booth merely indicated the adoration accorded the man whom he martyred. Today, Lincoln is probably the most admired American who has ever lived.

Some think that Franklin D. Roosevelt will turn our trinity into a quartet. Already more has been written about him that any other man since Napoleon. A Franklin D. Roosevelt Association flourishes, and its members collect books, pennants, and buttons featuring their idol. Hyde Park, with over half a million visitors annually, rivals Mount Vernon and Monticello as a tourist attraction. Foreign esteem fostered the re-naming of a main boulevard in Paris, the erecting of a Roosevelt statue in London, and the issuing of commemorative stamps in twenty-three nations.

What explains this admiration of the most controversial figure in our political history is the fact that he (along with Winston Churchill) symbolized the struggle against totalitarian tyranny. F. D. R. is an extension of the Jefferson symbol. With the return of the Republican party in 1952, revisionist historians began to hack away at his reputation and maintain that he had "planned" Pearl Harbor.[3] Only time can determine where the swinging pendulum will come to rest.

*   *   *

Most American heroes have historic prototypes. Cinderellas in all ages move from obscurity to fame, or, as we say, from rags to riches. Our self-made men include Abraham Lincoln, Henry Ford, and Al Smith. Cincinnatus emerged in a time of crisis to save the state. So did Washington, Lincoln, and Wilson. Europeans found no better example of the Enlightment's "natural man" than Daniel Boone. Kit Carson, Andy Jackson, and Buffalo Bill continued the tradition. Yet in each case there is a flavor, a twist, which is distinctively American. The species is the same; but there are American mutations.

Another major influence working upon American heroes has been regionalism. "The Federal sphere will accommodate the statesmen, but not the hero, in the epical and tremendous sense," Donald Davidson has observed.[4] Regions, and within them localities, are the well-springs of our heroes. Our problem is to venerate our regional heroes without disturbing the national equilibrium. Thus we have Paul Revere, Old Stormalong, and Daniel Webster in the Northeast; Daniel Boone, Davy Crockett, and Andy Jackson on the Appalachian frontier; John Calhoun, R. E. Lee, and the Southern Colonel in the South; Billy the Kid, Bigfoot

Wallace, and the Cowboy in the West. Sometimes a dispute over
a hero can open up old sectional wounds, as we shall see in the
next chapter when we discuss Captain John Smith.

Different ages and ethnic groups select their own favorites: a
third major limitation placed on American heroes. The adolescent's choice, used as a model to foster virtues of one sort or
another, is directed toward the matinee idol, the movie and television star, and the sports champion. Motivation for these choices
varies from sublimated sexual satisfaction, to transfer of personality, to vicarious achievement. The exploitation of personalities,
continuous in our history, has been accelerated by modern technology and spectator sports.

Consider George "Babe" Ruth, and the Yankee Stadium often
called "the House that Ruth Built." When big league baseball
suffered from the disgrace of the Black Sox scandal, publicists
diverted attention to a big rollicking kid with a contagious grin
and a definite tendency to knock baseballs over fences. Though
not especially intelligent, he was colorful; his rise from a Baltimore charity school was a modern Cinderella story. Over the
years the home runs, and the Ruth legends, increased. Finally
Ruth felt he was the raw material for a new Paul Bunyan. Team
mates like "Lefty" Gomez were not so sure. Referring to Ruth's
weakness for alcohol Gomez said, "He's the only man in the
United States that if you took a pint of blood, it would need a
revenue stamp." But his was a champion's blood, and no one ever
thought of draining off a pint.

Such charges damaged neither his fame nor his income. Ruth
made $80,000 a season, even during hard times. Always a show-
man, he bought a $5,000 car, gave a more modest one to a priest,
and ate eleven hotdogs in one afternoon. In six months he auto-
graphed 1100 bats. Feature writers pictured him in a vacant lot
with small boys, showing them how to hit. The sick received his
special attention, and a paralyzed boy "raised himself" in the
excitement over seeing the Bambino hit a home run.

Psychologists subjected Ruth to a "psycho-technical test" which
proved his eyes functioned twelve times as quickly as the average
man's. They also demonstrated that he outdid 499 out of 500
men in "the responsiveness of his nerves." He was the Sultan

of Swat; Beowulf at bat; a miracle worker who hit three World Series homers in one wild afternoon.

After his retirement, people continued to idolize Ruth and eat a candy bar named after him. They spoke of the "first Homeric swat" of May 6, 1915, and recalled that four years later he hit the longest home run then recorded, 508 feet. With two strikes on him in the 1926 World Series, he pointed to a distant spot and yelled at the hooting fans, "I'll knock it out there for you!" He did. It was the longest home run ever made at Wrigley Park.

Mrs. Babe Ruth helped the legend by telling what he said that evening when someone praised him for the uncanny stunt: "God was with me, or I couldn't have done it." Gods always help heroes.

One of Ruth's last appearances was with the "All-Time Great" team invited to Baseball's Hall of Fame in Cooperstown, New York. Historian Louis Jones wrote of it: "When the Bambino himself stood with the others the crowd, which had loved him and would continue to love him, let out a roar you could hear in the next town. When he spoke it was to the kids who are the backbone of the game. As always, the Babe had stolen the show."

Babe's story is typically American in its enormous gusto and good humor. Our legends are less apt to exalt wisdom or subtlety than brawn and buffoonery. They are full of bears and cyclones and hard liquor. Believing they can do any damn thing once they set their minds to it, our idols don't like fences. One of their inalienable rights is raising hell in their own particular fashion. Blackbeard the pirate illustrated this. Rejected in marriage, he got his revenge by cutting off his rival's hand, throwing him in the sea, and sending the hand to his fiancee in a silver casket; an unorthodox, but effective gesture.

Many assume without much evidence that our legendary heroes have folk origins. Paul Bunyan, Pecos Bill, and Joe Magarac were fostered by writers who are still alive. So far, these heroes stand on a burlesque, rather than an epic, level. Some have distinguished creators. Annie Christmas sprang from the brains of Roark Bradford and Lyle Saxon. Daddy Joe was aided by Stewart Holbrook, Pecos Bill by Edward O'Reilly, Daddy Mention by B. A. Botkin, Big Mose by Herbert Asbury, and Strap Buckner by Florence Barns. Owen Francis championed Joe Magarac; Paul

Beath, Febold Feboldson; Charles E. Brown, Whiskey Jack; Jeremiah Diggs, Bowleg Bill; J. Harris Cable, Antoine Barada; Louis Jones, Bill Greenfield; and Mary Montague, Tony Beaver. Many are created, but few survive.

Historical heroes have their backers too. A few, like Parson Weems and Jim Farley, are well known. More often they are anonymous. Admirers of Captain John Smith can seldom identify W. W. Henry or Charles Poindexter, who revived Smith's fame in the twentieth century. Hundreds who praise Buffalo Bill don't know that his stories may be traced to the work of Prentiss Ingraham and John Burke.

Almanac writers who had never seen Davy Crockett made him our greatest ring-tailed roarer. Charles Francis Adams, a Yankee whose family represented the quintessence of New Englandism, convinced America that the Confederate General Lee was a great man. A tenderfoot lawyer from the East (Emerson Hough) and a veteran Texas cowpoke (Charles Siringo) made Billy the Kid our favorite desperado. It is time the story of such hero-makers be told. They give a new dimension to our history.

Occasionally a reticent subject appears. While most men are delighted to be the subject of tales and rumors, the godly Peter Cartwright was perplexed by them. "Almost all those various incidents that have gained currency throughout the country concerning Methodist preachers," he complained in 1856, "have been located in me. When they came to hear me in Boston, the people expected little else than a bundle of eccentricities and singularities. When they did not realize according to their anticipations, they were disappointed." [5] Most potential heroes do not disappoint the people; instead, they act out the part others have created for them.

As conditions change, so does the heroic guise. In times of crisis we seek the solidarity of a Lincoln or Wilson. When we are complacent and bored we turn to a Buffalo Bill or Al Capone. We even idolize mediocre men, like U. S. Grant or Warren G. Harding, when they suit their ages. Our special form of settlement, institutions, and development gave us our particular American heroes—men with a local habitation and a name.

Fashions change methodically in heroes. The standard formulas in the days of Buffalo Bill and the penny dreadfuls would never work in this day of science fiction and supersonic sound. David Riesman has observed that children now graduate from animal stories like *Bugs Bunny* to invincible heroes like *Superman* and eventually to heroes like *Batman* who, human in form, are vulnerable, though of course never conquered.[6] Children themselves are aware of the progression, and scorn playmates who don't advance on schedule.

So great is the competition among comic strip artists that they must engage in what Mr. Riesman calls "marginal differentiation" to get their trade mark. Bodies by Al Capp must be as easily recognized as bodies by Fisher. Situations that formerly took many pages must be compressed into a few cartoons. The medium and the paragon must be adjusted to the age.

Film heroes change too. The frantic activism of "Doug" Fairbanks in the 1920's gave way to the homespun wit of Will Rogers in the 1930's, and the casual friendliness of Bing Crosby in the 1940's. All Americans, but especially children, are affected by this evolution in comics and shadowland. In 1950 Lawrence Averill conducted a poll of a thousand teen-agers to find out whom they most admired.[7] Only a third chose historical figures. (In a similar survey made in 1898 by Estell Darrah, 90 per cent came from history.) At the top were baseball's Ted Williams, Hollywood's Gene Autry, and comic-land's Joe Palooka. Four times more boys chose Gene Autry than Jesus Christ. As many named Jack Benny as all priests, scholars, and missionaries combined. In telling whom we like best, we tell what we ourselves are like.

Many are alarmed by our new idols who emerge from ball parks, movies, and comic books. They say the "good old days" of truly impressive American heroes and myths are gone forever. "Good old days" are always gone—this is one of history's truisms. But not the heroic process, which is communal faith channeled to specific cultural purposes, and which grabs up Babe Ruth or Superman as avidly as Samson or Hercules.

Nature has, of course, lost much of its significance for the modern urbanite. Once feared and worshipped, it is now controlled by a flick of the thermostat. Hence it is not from realms of nature and religion, but politics and economics, that many of our heroes arise. Not thunderstorms and snowdrifts, but strikes and inflation, drive us to our knees. New problems demand new kinds of solutions—and new solvers.

What is the thread that holds together the sequence of American heroes? Only a magician who could conjure up the hidden unity of American character would dare give a simple answer. Those of us who fear to try can only search for clues, themes, and leads. Since in this sprawling, diverse land of not very united states it is easier to focus on a figure than an abstract idea or principle, we shall study certain representative heroes and hope they will point to a larger pattern. To master the whole mosaic we shall attempt to remove some of the pieces. If we choose wisely, we may find those on which the lesser pieces depend, and from which they get their shape and values. By dividing the problem of American heroes, perhaps we can make a start towards conquering it.

PART II

Paths of Glory

CHAPTER 3

O Brave New World: John Smith

> *" 'Tis ever thus, when in life's storm*
> *Hope's star to man grows dim,*
> *An angel kneels, in woman's form*
> *And breathes a prayer for him."*
> —George Morris, *Pocahontas.*

On the threshold of American history stands one of our most controversial heroes. Although he barely had a toe hold on the New World, he has not been budged by the heaviest scholarly attacks. So enmeshed was colonial America in European folkways that we could hardly have expected an enduring hero before Plymouth Rock was settled. Yet we have Captain John Smith. One of the most fascinating American heroines, Pocahontas, comes with him.

Subjugator of nine-and-thirty kings, by his own say-so, John Smith aroused derision as easily as he made legends. "It soundeth much to the dimunition of his deeds," Thomas Fuller wryly complained, "that he alone is the herald to publish and proclaim them." More recently, Professor Walter Blair irreverently noted that "Smith could hardly go for a walk without saving a beautiful damsel, or having one fall head over heels in love with him." But Smith's admirers have not been fazed. "To set him down as an arrant braggadocio would seem to some critics," observed historian John Fiske, "essential to their reputation for sound sense." A. G. Bradley found in the Smith saga "nothing to strain the credulity of anyone with a tolerable grasp of historical and social progress." Hero or faker, Captain John Smith has held the popular imagination so firmly that he and Pocahontas are our best known colonial couple.

Smith's checkered career was distinctly susceptible of the heroic. He spent so much of his life acting the part of the swashbuckler that he came to play the role expertly. Son of a prosperous English tenant farmer, he left home in 1596 at sixteen to seek Adventure. If his own account can be trusted, he performed marvelous deeds in the Mediterranean and the Near East. He served with the Austrians against the Turks in 1602, saw duty on the Hungarian border, and was still young when he set out for the New World in 1607. After spending two and a half years in Virginia he was returned to England. Chagrined by the treatment he had received and embittered by those who had ejected him, he induced influential enemies of the men in control of Virginia to sponsor his "authentic" account of the New World. His not too ulterior motive was to prove that the actions of certain Englishmen interfered with colonial enterprise, and that the colonies prospered more under royal control than under corporate management.

The spectacular Pocahontas rescue story (whether or not is was true)was a means of bringing the Captain back into the limelight he so enjoyed. In consequence, when Pocahontas arrived in England in 1616, she got much attention. As Lady Rebecca she cut quite a figure, and of a style the Elizabethans appreciated. In his *Generall Historie* (1624), Smith recorded that "In the utmost of many extremities Pokahontas, the great King's daughter of Virginia, oft saved my life." People of his day wanted to believe it; people of ours do too. Adopting a hero is basically an act of faith.

The literature about the English adventurer is so extensive that it forms a separate chapter in American historiography.[1] Although his contemporaries had some doubts about Captain John Smith's veracity, his role as savior of the Virginia colony, and Pocahontas's action at the execution block were widely accepted up to the mid-nineteenth century. In 1791 Noah Webster included Smith's story in *The Little Reader's Assistant*. "What a hero was Captain Smith! How many Turks and Indians did he slay!" Seven years after Webster's book appeared, John Davis, an English traveler, made his first voyage to the New World to gather material for his highly laudatory books entitled *Captain John Smith and Princess Pocahontas*, and *The First Settlers of Virginia*. Smith's story, it should be noted, is immortalized in bronze on the west door of the entrance to the Capitol rotunda in Washington. A painting conspicuously displayed inside the building shows "The Baptism of Pocahontas at Jamestown." No one has objected to their being there or doubted their justification.

Traveling through Virginia in 1817, the Knickerbocker poet James Kirke Paulding observed, "Fortitude, valor, perseverance, industry, and little Pocahontas . . . [are] tutelary deities." George Washington Parke Custis, whose loyalty to things colonial was unsurpassed, wrote *Pocahontas*, a play first produced in Philadelphia in 1830. This was followed by Robert Owen's *Pocahontas* (1837), John Brougham's *Po-ca-hon-tas, Or the Gentle Savage* (1855), and other plays built around the Indian rescue plot.[2] Pocahontas poems appeared in many pre-Civil War journals. Those by Mary Webster Mosby, Lydia H. Sigourney, Margaret Junkin Preston, and William Waldron were especially popular. Even William Thackeray wrote one, to the gratification of Americans who revered English literature.

By the Civil War, most Americans looked upon John Smith and Pocahontas as splendid representatives of their colonial times. If Smith, who had shown little sympathy towards Yankees (their "humorous ignorancies," he observed, "caused the Plymouth Pilgrims to endure a wonderful deale of misery,") found his chief admirers in the South, he at least had few defamers in the area he himself had named New England.

In 1863 a Boston merchant and historian, Charles Deane, commenced the attack on John Smith. He called the colorful captain a notorious liar and braggart who had invented his dramatic rescue after the lapse of many years. Deane insisted that none of Smith's contemporaries knew of the Pocahontas episode and he concluded there was little truth in it. But the North and the South were then too busy fighting each other to notice Deane. Sectional bitterness still ran high when in 1867 another New Englander, youthful Henry Adams, leveled at John Smith a much more telling blow. Scion of one of America's most tactless family of worthies, Adams had just returned from the seminars of Germany and was anxious to gain attention. His article on Smith in the *North American Review* (January, 1867) set off a war of words which echoed down the corridors of the twentieth century.

In his article Adams printed parallel passages from Smith's *A True Relation* and his *Generall Historie* for textual comparison. He found the Pocahontas rescue story spurious and labeled Smith incurably vain and incompetent. The readiness with which Smith's version had been received Adams found less remarkable than "the credulity which has left it unquestioned almost to the present day." While the *Nation* doubted "if Mr. Adams' arguments can be so much as shaken," the *Southern Review* thought historians dealing in black insinuations were "little worthy of credit, especially when their oblique methods affect the character of a celebrated woman." The *Southern Review* proceeded to place the Smith-Pocahontas fight on a sectional plane where it stayed for a half century: "If Pocahontas, alas! had only been born on the barren soil of New England, then would she have been as beautiful as she was brave. As it is, however, both her personal character and her personal charms are assailed by at least two knights of the New England chivalry of the present day."

The Yankee knights had only begun their attack. Noah Webster's account for school children gave way to Peter Parley's, which drew as a moral from Smith's escapades "that persons, at an early age, have very wicked hearts." Moses Tyler, John Palfrey, and Edward Channing saw in Smith more bluster than greatness. In his 1881 biography of Smith, Charles D. Warner of Connecticut observed that the Captain's memory became more vivid as he was farther removed by time and space from the events he described. Edward D. Neill's *Captain John Smith, Adventurer and Romancer* was devastating. It discredited the Turkish adventures, pronounced Smith's coat of arms a forgery, found the Pocahontas rescue story laughable, and called Smith's literary works "published exaggerations." A second study by Neill, *Pocahontas and Her Companions*, flatly stated that her marriage to Rolfe was a disgraceful fraud. North of the Potomac the rescue story began to be called the Pocahontas legend.

Southerners rallied to the defense of their dashing Captain— and of Southern honor. Their counter-attack was so effective that by the middle of the twentieth century Captain John Smith and Pocahontas were generally thought of as human embodiments of epic colonial heroism.

Since Smith, a figure of masculinity and firmness, made an admirable partner for the Indian Princess whose femininity and softness conquered two continents, it is not surprising that their stories were blended into one. The tyranny of historical facts crumbled before the demands of popular fancy and the literary weapons of William Wirt Henry, Wyndham Robertson, Charles Poindexter, and John Esten Cooke.

No one was in a better position to express regional indignation than William Wirt Henry. Patrick Henry's grandson, he was born in 1831 on a plantation in Charlotte County, Virginia. Lawyer and historian, he served as county attorney, state legislator, president of the Virginia Historical Society, and president of the American Historical Society. To his fellow Southerners he personified the Tidewater planter-aristocrat. At the 1882 Virginia Historical Society meeting, he read a paper called "The Settlement of Jamestown, with Particular Reference to the Late Attacks upon Captain John Smith, Pocahontas, and John Rolfe." He came directly to the point: "The more generous task of making their defense will be mine." With care and ingenuity he evolved explanations for the questionable parts of their stories. In a flourish that honored his grandfather's memory, Henry concluded, "We need not pursue this charge of inconsistencies further, as time would fail us to notice every inconsistency charged by the numerous and ill-informed assailants of Smith."

To Henry there was no doubt whatsoever that the success of the Virginia Colony had depended on the Captain. "The departure of Smith changed the whole aspect of affairs. The Indians at once became hostile, and killed all that came in their way." To the Indian Princess Pocahontas he assigned a religious role and mission. She was, in Henry's opinion, "a guardian angel [who] watched over and preserved the infant colony which has developed into a great people, among whom her own descendants have ever been conspicuous for true nobility." On that exalted note, the defense rested.

Equally qualified to fight for "Captain Jack" was Wyndham Robertson, who was raised on a plantation near Petersburg, Virginia. Educated in Richmond and Williamsburg, he became Virginia's twentieth governor. Northern attacks on John Smith disturbed him so much that he prepared a detailed study: *Pocahontas and Her Descendants*. Taking the marriage of Pocahontas and Rolfe in 1614 as a focal event, Robertson traced the subsequent family to "its seventh season of fruitage." His work was unabashedly presented as "the vindication of Captain John Smith and Pocahontas against the unfriendly strictures of modern critics." Because Pocahontas' descendants were so notable, so was she; this simple *a posteriori* argument ran through the whole book. Among those who turned out to be related to her were the Bollings, Branches, Lewises, Randolphs, and Pages — the very cream of Virginia.

How, asked Robertson, could anyone speak lowly of the Princess when the King of England and the Bishop of London were her devotees? Her natural charm had captivated Mother England. Leaders of society competed for her favor; she had a special seat when Ben Jonson's *Twelfth Night* masque was staged at Whitehall; her portrait revealed a truly aristocratic countenance. "With festival, state, and pompe" the Lord Mayor of London feted her before death cut short her dazzling career. "History, poetry, and art," wrote Robertson, "have vied with one another in investing her name from that day to the present with a halo of surpassing brightness." His argument by association, like that of descent, was persuasive. To ridicule Pocahontas was to deny the importance of family and ancestry in society. Most Americans and practically every Southerner were not prepared to do so.

Charles Poindexter, a more scholarly defender of Smith, was educated at the University of Virginia; he joined the Richmond Howitzers during the Civil War. Long interested in Old Dominion heroes, he published in 1893 *John Smith and His Critics*. At the time he was State Librarian in Richmond. It was in a distinctly fresh light that he viewed the colonial controversy: "Smith's *History* has been standard reading for 250 years, acknowledged and practically unquestioned, unless by some in these latter days. We may be a simple and uncritical people, but when our belief and judgment as to an historical character are challenged, and we are told our admiration has been wasted on a charlatan, whose boasting has deceived us, then may we raise a question as to the amount of wisdom behind the critic's utterance."[3]

Poindexter explained that Smith was engaged in "a piece of work of transcendent interest and importance, as we know now—namely, the founding of the Commonwealth of Virginia." The whole controversy could never be decided by documents and scholarship. "And yet they tell us, the legend must go; but when it goes it will be time for this people to be gone; to be driven from this fair portion of God's earth, made sacred by that brave man's heroism, and by the gentle pity of that Indian maid . . . Smith's *History* has established itself as a tradition in the popular mind more lasting and potent than any written page or printed book." Poindexter saw plainly that Smith had moved beyond mere documentary fact.

John Esten Cooke, one of the South's most popular novelists, promoted Smith vigorously. Born in Winchester, Virginia, Cooke wanted "to do for the Old Dominion what Cooper has done for the Indians, Irving for the Dutch Knickerbockers, and Hawthorne for the weird Puritan life of New England." He buried his spurs at Appomattox when Lee surrendered—a gesture in the tradition of Captain Smith. Cooke's *My Lady Pokahontas* (1885) is still the best novel about the lady. Purporting to be writing in the seventeenth century, he furnished "notes" to a *True Relation of Virginia, Writ by Anas Todkill, Puritan and Pilgrim*. Todkill revealed how Smith fell in love with the Virginia Princess, converted her to Christianity, and strolled hand in hand with her along the James. The lovers decided it was best that they not remain together. In England with her husband John Rolfe, later on, Pocahontas attended the Globe Theater, where William Shakespeare's *The Tempest* was opening. She promptly recognized herself as Miranda.

What Cooke did in *My Lady Pokahontas* was to superimpose trappings of a Victorian romance on the story. It is a landmark in the literary treatment of Pocahontas and of the American Indian. In pre-Civil War America the only good Indian was a dead one. As long as the aboriginal was an active threat to settlement and progress, he was given little consideration. For Pocahontas to be a heroine this attitude had to change, and the savage had to become the vanishing American. In the generation after the Civil War this transition took place. A few years later came Helen Hunt

Jackson's *A Century of Dishonor,* which called our record in Indian relationships "a shameful one of broken treaties and unfilled promises." Like *Uncle Tom's Cabin,* the book's effect was far out of proportion to its literary merit. *A Century of Dishonor* and the ascendancy of the Pocahontas legend coincided.

The influence of Cooke's interpretation of Pocahontas was both direct and indirect. Southern text books adopted his colonial romance; subsequent writers have turned to it nostalgically. Partly through his own books but more particularly through his influence, Cooke fostered the popular conception held by many today.

William Henry gave Pocahontas a religious mission; Robertson set up a patriotic affront; Poindexter put the legend above the documents; Cooke made of it a Victorian romance.   Smith and Pocahontas returned to high standing.

In 1907 came the much publicized Jamestown Tercentennial. In preparing for the festivities, the Pocahontas Memorial Association undertook a program of glorification which included a poem by Paulding suggesting Pocahontas' religious role:

> *"Sister of charity and love,*
> *Whose life blood was soft pity's tide.*
> *Dear goddess of the sylvan grove*
> *Flower of the forest, nature's pride,*
> *He is no man who does not bend the knee*
> *And she no woman who is not like thee!"*

Jamestown Tributes and Toasts contained seven Smith-Pocahontas poems. Little had been done to commemorate the grave of "Rebecca Wrothe, wife of Thomas Wrothe, gent, a Virginia lady born" at Gravesend, England.   So the Society of Colonial Dames donated memorial windows to the tiny church in which Pocahontas was buried. At Jamestown, William Ordway Partridge's statue of the Indian princess was erected, flanked by a bronze Captain John Smith.

Lyon G. Tyler unveiled a new Pocahontas tablet at Jamestown, and asked: "What words must I use to express my feelings on this occasion? Her memory brightens with the years and comes to us today as a soft, clear light that shines from a distant shore, where all else is shrouded in darkness." As he spoke, the audience gazed at the statue of the princess provided by the Pocahontas Memorial Association—her hands outstretched to aid the starving Virginia colonists, her eyes appropriately looking toward heaven.

*   *   *

If the preliminary plans for the 1957 celebration of the three hundred and fiftieth anniversary of the settling of Jamestown come to fruition, Smith's reputation will continue to rise, for he is to be the hero of the program. Another, less ephemeral, multi-million dollar enterprise, only a few miles from the place where the Captain first set foot on the New World, has kept green the memory of seventeenth century things in contemporary America. This is Colonial Williamsburg. While it has not been directly concerned with promoting Smith, his renown has benefited directly and enormously therefrom. The Rockefeller fortune has salvaged reputations as well as buildings.

Dr. W. A. R. Goodwin, late rector of Williamsburg's Bruton Parish Church and incidentally an admirer of John Smith, is generally credited with having persuaded John D. Rockefeller, Jr. to reconstruct the colonial capital.[5] No restoration in history has received such elaborate and painstaking research; none in America is so frequently visited. Representing an expenditure of over $45,000,000 and a yearly operating budget of $2,000,000, Colonial Williamsburg by 1954 had a staff of 1,000 and plans for further capital outlays exceeding $15,000,000. No one could have foreseen such expansion and such influence. The restoration found itself in the position of Lord Byron's teacher:

> *"She taught the child to read, and taught so well*
> *That she herself, by teaching, learn'd to spell."*

Rockefeller himself realized that the project would reawaken interest in those he called "great patriots of our American past." Many of the hundreds of thousands of visitors who come every season make the short pilgrimage to Jamestown, to see "the spot where the Anglo-Saxon history of America begins." They find on the small island, which was saved from disintegration only by a seawall put up for the Jamestown Tercentennial, nothing so elaborate as Colonial Williamsburg. But they do view the statue of a handsome, dashing adventurer, whose hand rests near his sword and whose eyes look out on the vast expanses of America. They see Captain John Smith; and they carry him away in their memories as the first great American.

Though the Captain's account does not appear to be based upon undiluted historical fact, it is not totally false. Whether or not Pocahontas really saved Smith at the execution block, and whether or not they actually fell in love, Pocahontas unquestionably visited Jamestown while he was there. These visits ceased after Smith had departed. She evidently took some interest in him and he in the girl he called "the nonpareil of Virginia." Still, it is hard to believe that Smith, who considered the aboriginals as inferior savages that blocked Britain's path, ultimately would have married her. His deportation (resulting from the return of Ratcliffe and Archer, who allied themselves with Smith's enemies Percy and West) ended abruptly any ideas he might have had of a future life with Pocahontas. In his attitude towards the Indians, as in so many things, Smith revealed his English heritage. Always strongly Anglo-Saxon, Virginians have not found it difficult to give him the benefit of their doubts.

Smith's was no crafty, subtle mind. Contemplation was not his forte; he usually acted first and thought afterwards. If he had any philosophy, it was to meet things as they came. His egocentric world was unmarred by indecision, weakness, or indifference. He saw strange seas, dreamed of empires, and lived through an epic. Whatever one thinks of some of his actions and accusations, one must admire the loyalty and enthusiasm he displayed while exploring the New World. He loved Virginia as "my wyfe, to whom I have given all." No matter how much he exaggerated on occasions, he was telling the truth when as a dying man he wrote, "All the dangers, miseries, and incumbrances and losse of other employments while in Virginia I endured gratis."

After his deportation from Virginia, Smith was dogged by constant failure. In 1615 he convinced Sir Ferdinando Gorges to outfit him for another try at colonizing the New World, but his two small vessels were driven back by storms. Again he set sail, with only a small barque of sixty tons at his command. This time he was captured by pirates, wrecked off La Rochelle, and returned home penniless. When he died he was a poor, weary man, leaving only eighty pounds, twenty of which (in a typical gesture) he directed to be spent on his funeral. The only relatives mentioned in his will were a cousin and the widow of his brother. London's Great Fire of 1666 wiped out St. Sepulchre's Church, in which his body was buried, and his epitaph with it. The last earthly trace of John Smith is gone forever.

The New World for which "Captain Jack" fought has adorned his memory with honor more enduring than all the treasure won by others on the Spanish Main. For many Americans he is today the last of the Knight-Errants, a cross between the medieval crusader and the Jacobite Cavalier. Because his pageantry seemed so incongruous in the vast wilderness of the New World, there is a Don Quixote-like pathos about him. Had he not been so earnest about his schemes of colonization, they would have been ludicrous. He never doubted, up to his dying day, that he could accomplish the impossible. His ambitions were so lofty that inability to consummate them did not destroy their appeal. With all his faults, he set the heroic pattern in colonial America.

Smith has been at the core of controversy; John Rolfe, who actually married the Indian Princess Pocahontas, has not. Little is said of this gentleman of moderate means who came to Virginia in 1609, experimented with the growing and curing of tobacco, and perfected the plant which was the foundation of Virginia's economy. His marriage to a native brought peace at a time when the Indians might have driven the colonists into the sea. But he did not catch the popular imagination, and he did not become a hero.

That Pocahontas, an Indian girl who died at twenty-two, became a legendary figure is extraordinary. Virginias are proud to have her blood in their veins. But they would hardly admit to a drop from any other member of her race. What is it about her that has so appealed to posterity? Not the savage, but the feminine quality. She is the fairy-tale princess come to life; a flesh-and-blood Cinderella in Indian disguise. Her story is full of romance and excitement. She rescued Smith by risking her own life. After a sad separation from him, she was wooed by a white knight from overseas, John Rolfe. She brought peace to the struggling colonists. Best of all, Little Wanton went as a princess to the Mother Country, where she outshone all the celebrated English beauties. Virginia, loyal to Charles I when even England rejected him, thrilled at this. Finally, she suffered a premature and unexpected death. What more could a romantic heroine's story contain? In November, 1952, a "Chapel of Unity" was opened to her memory at Gravesend, England. It has already become a pilgrimage spot.[6]

Attacks on John Smith and Pocahotas have become fewer and less bitter in recent years. Dr. Charles Andrews, the New England colonial historian, supported the rescue story. The 1927 biography of Smith by E. K. Chatterton, and the 1929 book by John Gould Flecther, revealed a far greater man than earlier accounts. Admittedly "Captain Jack" was given to far-fetched phrases, and to veering off the narrow road of truth. But most of us forgive him. After all, this was his prerogative in the Age of Elizabeth. The same tendencies can be found in other colorful figures of the period —Sir Walter Raleigh, Sir Francis Drake, Kit Marlowe, and William Shakespeare.

The John Smith-Pocahontas story, with its epic quality and scope, has appealed to us because it re-affirms the validity of the American experience. Aided by an Indian Princess, John Smith founded a great nation, and made the dream of a permanent English colony a reality. O brave new world, that has such people in it!

Occasionally a skeptic comes forth claiming that Smith's story (in a phrase of his contemporary Will Shakespeare) has "a very ancient and fish-like smell." But the furor that accompanied the Deane-Adams articles has passed. In 1951 George F. Willison argued (in *Behold Virginia: The Fifth Crown*) that Smith's surviving his almost incredible follies was the real miracle of his life; that the Virginia records reach "almost to the point of madness, as in Captain John Smith's account of his exploits and accomplishments in that colony, which, so he came to believe, he had founded and sustained almost singlehandedly." The Historical Society of Manatee County, Florida, has challenged historians to prove the truth of Pocahontas's rescue. The story, it was suggested, was probably devised by a press agent of an earlier day. The Indian maiden Hirrihgua, who saved the life of Juan Ortiz in Manatee County, has—or should have, it would appear—a much better claim to fame.

Americans have ceased to worry about the absence of historical authenticity in this matter. The Captain and the Indian Princess have been accepted. No mere documents can unseat them. As James Branch Cabell contemplated them in their aloof majesty, he remarked: "And yet, to the judgment of the considerate, Captain John Smith's *True Relation* does not in any way affect the ranking of Pocahontas in the official history of Virginia; her legend, the more thanks to Virginia's good taste in mythology, has been made immortal." [7]

CHAPTER 1

E Pluribus Unum: George Washington

"My pa ain't like Washington's pa.
When I cut down our cherry tree,
And said I did, pa walloped me.
And I went up to bed and cried
And golly, how I wished I'd lied!"
        —"Life," February, 1904

Did anyone ever see Washington, the Father of our Country, nude? Nathaniel Hawthorne felt impelled to pose the question and answer it categorically: "It is inconceivable. He had no nakedness, but was born with his clothes on, and his hair powdered, and made a stately bow on his first appearance in the world." Horatio Weld felt rather strongly about a child's first reference to him. "The first word of infancy should be mother, the second father, the third Washington." Artemus Ward chose carefully from his misspellings and described Washington as "a human angil in a 3 kornered hat and knee britches." None of them suggested that under the britches was a human body.

Perhaps, as some contend, Mom is becoming harder and harder to handle; but America is still a man's land, and George Washington remains our symbolic Father. The millions of tourists who visit his grave at Mount Vernon sense this deeply. They go to revere not a man, but a demigod. In death, as in life, Washington has a niche no other American can occupy. If one man can be said to have knit together the American union, and earned its acclaim richly, his name is surely George Washington.

Though disillusioned by some events and perplexed by others, modern Americans have not discarded their Father. "He, personally, was 90% of the force which made of the American Revolution a successful issue," states William Carlos Williams. "Know the intimate character of Washington himself, and you will know practically all there is to understand about the beginnings of the American Republic." Few would say 90% was too high. Certainly not those who knew the living Washington and may have heard him say he had inherited "inferior endowments from nature." And surely not those who went through the Revolution with him, quite aware that he lost a great many more battles than he won.

Washington was born on the family estate in Westmoreland County, Virginia, in 1732, and raised in a rural environment. After his father's death in 1743, he was guided largely by his half-brother, Lawrence, who got him a job as surveyor. In 1753 George had his first military experience in a foray against the French and Indians in the Ohio country. At Great Meadows (near present Pittsburgh), he built Fort Necessity, but was forced to retreat when French pressure mounted. After his participation in the unsuccessful attack on Fort Duquesne led by General Braddock (1755), he served as commander of the Virginia forces on the western frontier for two years. Experience, not theory, was the basis of his insight and leadership.

When still a youth, Washington's countrymen marked him for greatness. In a 1755 sermon Samuel Davies, later president of Princeton, talked of "that heroic youth, Colonel Washington, whom I cannot but hope providence has hitherto preserved in so signal a manner, for some important service to his country." Like most colonials, Davies had marveled when he heard that during Braddock's rout Washington had had two horses shot from under him and that four bullets had pierced his clothes. From such tales legends grew. Some were so exaggerated that Washington had to write home to deny "a circumstantial acct. of my death and dying speech."

When Washington was chosen to head the American Revolutionary forces, all sorts of stories about him began to make the rounds of the Continental Congress. Had you heard that Washington had offered to recruit a thousand soldiers at his own expense, and march them to Boston? Of course you had. And of course

you didn't put any credence in the report that there had been no
such offer. For you, like most Americans of your day, were
hungry for a living symbol of your revolt, and quick to see one
in Washington.

So you joined in the celebrations of his birthday while he was
still the harassed commander of a lank, losing army. You may
have helped mob a New Jersey printer, William Goddard, when
he dared publish Charles Lee's version of his run-in with the
idolized General. And you certainly read some of the popular
broadsides about Washington, which sold for twopence. You
never thought about it, but you were helping to create a national
hero.

Charles Lee, who was relegated to the villain's dungeon when
he crossed Washington, was among the first to note the rise of
the Washington cult. "He has long been in this state of divin-
ity," Lee wrote his sister in the summer of 1782, "but of late the
legality of his apotheosis begins to be called in question." Lee
was right about the apotheosis, wrong about its legality. Never
was an apotheosis so legal in the court of final appeal. The
people's judgment was practically unanimous. Overnight Washington became one of the few men in history big enough to fill
the vacuum when no symbol existed for a major revolution. His
prestige after Cornwallis' surrender was even greater than that of
the government of the United States. When he died in 1799, a
symbol and a tradition, as well as a human body, was buried at
Mount Vernon.

Washington's appeal did not come after time had minimized his
bad traits and magnified his good ones. His own generation lionized him. Parson Weems confidently called him "our demigod"
in 1800. In the same year a Pennsylvania German farmer wrote
Washingtons Ankunft in Elisium, in which Washington strolled
around heaven chatting with Brutus and Columbus. Even though
he led a successful rebellion against British authority, Englishmen
praised him as extravagantly as the most uncritical of his American admirers. Few men have aroused such high regard from
those against whom they rebelled.

Did Washington pass over to Valhalla at any particular moment? Probably not; only Hollywood can simplify the his-

torical process to that extent. But if Washington had a finest hour, it came in 1797 when he voluntarily left the Presidency. His conduct in war, as leader of the Revolution, won him fame, but his conduct in peace, as first helmsman of the new Republic, won him immortality. In youth he craved war; in maturity he wisely avoided it. Rather than indulge in the popular practice of twisting the lion's tail, he sanctioned Jay's Treaty with England, which won precious years of peace for the wobbly young democracy.

"I heard the bullets whistle, and believe me, there is something charming in the sound," Washington wrote his half brother after a skirmish at Great Meadow in 1753. But the Washington of 1790 saw through the pomp and power of warfare; he would rather be on his farm than be made emperor of the world. When defeated men shun the ways of war, they show reconciliation; when victorious men abjure them, they show greatness.

Washington even resisted the powers of peace, which as king or dictator, he could have enjoyed in the vaguely united states. Like Cincinnatus, he not only wielded authority but relinquished it. Having the key to unlimited power challenged but did not corrupt him. Thomas Jefferson recorded an interesting remark of Washington's after a stormy cabinet session in which Jefferson and Hamilton worked over each other's backs with verbal daggers. Washington said, Jefferson reported, "he had never repented but once then having slipped the moment of resigning his office, and that was every moment since; that by God he had rather be in his grave than in his present situation." Here was a man who knew what Ecclesiastes meant when he talked of vanity and chasing after winds.

Why was Washington immortalized during his lifetime? The answer is complex, but at least four factors contributed. He was capable, aristocratic, commanding; he had the look and manner of greatness. He lived at a time, and participated in events, which aroused the heroic. His incredible patience and tenacity personified the colonies' noble but difficult cause. And he refused to usurp either military or civilian power; when the times that tried men's souls were past, he returned to the land.

The Revolution was America's baptism by fire. Those who

saw the licking flames were well aware that souls were being tried. Under Washington's leadership petty jealousies were squelched and England was humbled. Through it all Washington never lost his vision—or aloofness. They never called him George. History, biography, oratory, journalism, poetry, art, and fiction all demonstrate that he is today, as in the past, just what Light Horse Harry Lee said he was in a well-turned metaphor: first in the hearts of his countrymen.

To judge by all the works written about him, one would conclude that Washington was a demigod who came to us flawless, to perform one of God's worthy and inspired projects, then to return to heaven.[1] Paul Svinin, European visitor in 1815, observed that "Every American considers it his sacred duty to have a likeness of Washington in his home, just as we have the images of God's saints." Such adoration is even more amazing when one considers that Washington lived in the Age of Reason, dedicated to a rationalistic view of nature and humanity.

Adulation of Washington has, of course, risen and fallen with the changing times, as is true for any hero; but three massive peaks are clearly discernible. The first came with General Lafayette's visit to America in 1824, which reawakened all the revolutionary glow and reactivated the tongues of veterans who in all ages become more heroic as they are further removed from the battlefield. Lafayette's long and dramatic triumphant tour, which belonged to the poetry of history, evoked a flood of Washington worship. "I cannot write or speak the name of Washington without a contraction and dilation of the heart, if I do it irreverently," confessed John Neal.

The second peak was in 1847-48. America was at war with Mexico, fighting blood was bubbling, and newsstands were hawking Revolutionary thrillers and paper-backed Washington biographies. Coinciding with the war hysteria was the laying of the cornerstone of the capital's Washington Monument in 1848. Catherine Maria Sedgwick admitted his name conjured up a sentiment "resembling the awe of the pious Israelite when he approached the ark of the Lord." The Reverend J. N. Danforth compared Washington with Jesus, and his mother with Mary. The pronoun "Him" was capitalized in many accounts of Washington's life. Only the Protestant ethos saved him from canonization.

Part of this upsurge crystallized into the crusade to "save" Mount Vernon, which had become weedy in the generation after Washington's death.   Ann Pamela Cunningham worked hard for this, as did the orator Edward Everett, who delivered his famous Washington oration 129 times between 1856 and 1860, trading his warmed-over words for cold cash.   Mount Vernon was saved.   It became, and still is, a public shrine.   For a while, however, it looked as if Mount Vernon would be on the boundary of two nations instead of in the center of one.   In the arguments leading to secession Washington's name was evoked by both sides; Northerners and Southerners were equally sure that a live Washington would have fought with them.   When finally the split occurred, the Confederates chose George Washington to appear on their great seal, and a collateral descendant, Robert E. Lee, to lead them.

Washington's bicentennial year, 1932, was the tallest peak of all.   Then America was brimming with nostalgia for the Father. The printed report of the Bicentennial Commission alone filled five huge volumes averaging 700 pages each.   Over 16,000 celebrations were staged, featuring 4,760,245 separate programs.[2]   The man most responsible for all this, Representative Sol Bloom, we shall discuss presently.

Washington-worship, be it noted, has not been limited to America.   It has jumped boundaries and oceans with ease.   In France, Napoleon Bonaparte ordered a week of national mourning when Washington died.   Alfieri and Botta in Italy, Byron and Thackeray in England, and Kosciuszko in Poland knelt from afar, looking toward the Washington shrine.   Translations of the *Farewell Address* flooded South America and Washington's picture was displayed beside Simon Bolivar's frequently.   The modest squire of Mount Vernon had become a world hero. In time, revolutions in far away places paid him homage.   The well-laid foundations of the Washington legend today support a structure international in design and craftsmanship.

*   *   *

Who were the chief architects of this structure?   Parson Mason Weems, John Marshall, Jared Sparks, Gilbert Stuart, Jean Antoine

Houdon, and Sol Bloom. Without their words, pigment, stone, and strategy Washington's reputation would have been different from what it now is. The name of Weems heads the list. The nineteenth son of a Scotch immigrant, he never lost his hungry look; what he lacked in veracity he made up in daring. Minister, bookseller, fiddler, sentimentalist, keeper of the public pulse, Weems emerged in literature as the poor man's Plutarch. He helped create, as Stewart Holbrook reminds us, a mythical Washington, "fantastically bloodless and good, who in spite of much corrective writing largely endures to this day. That is the way it is with folklore, and history good or bad can do little but dent it here and there, and gnaw away at the edges." [3]

Whatever his shortcomings, Parson Weems was an ingenious writer and clever publicist. Best known for his life of Washington, he also did biographies of Benjamin Franklin, William Penn, and Francis Marion. Studying great men made his "bosom heave with emotions unutterable, while the tear of delicious admiration swelled in my eyes." When he got to Washington, the tears became a torrent. His temperament and experience were highly susceptible. He took naturally to praising famous men fervently in his sermons and stump speeches. While he probably had met the General and had been a collector of Washington items, this hardly justified his conferring upon himself the rectorship of Mount Vernon Parish, particularly since there was none of that name. He just was not the type of man to be bound by the tyranny of facts, even when they were covered with clerical garb.

When Washington died suddenly in 1799, hundreds of sketches and sermons came from the presses. The one that most clearly set the future pattern of eulogy was Weems' *History of the Life, Death, Virtues, and Exploits of General Washington*, published in 1800. It was seldom a hard book to come by. Responsive to the law of supply and demand, Weems revised and fattened his work frequently; the fifth edition issued in 1806 had 250 pages. Sales continued strong long after Weems passed to the land of no revisions. In 1921 the seventy-ninth successful edition appeared.

Anticipating Horatio Alger, Weems made the Washington saga a formalized success story. "Here was a proper rise for you," he gloated when Washington snared the rich widow Custis. In the fifth edition he introduced the cherry tree story (the most persistent single legend in American history), the cabbage story, and the wild colt story. Granting that many of his tales were concocted, one feels that scientific historians have been unduly severe to this mixer of mythology, musket-balls, and the back-woods. Shame on Allan Nevins for saying, as he does in the *Encyclopedia of Social Science,* that Weems "long exercised a deplorable influence upon popular history."

Weems worked in the super-historical realm. There were and are two Washingtons. Weems concerned himself with the invented one. Of course his Washington was very different from the one born and reared in Virginia; he was bound to be. Americans of yesteryear who read Weems weren't concerned with the accuracy of the portrait. They read with their hearts. Many cried when they came to the account of Washington's death:

"Swift on angel's wings the brightening Saint ascended; while voices more than human were warbling through the happy region and hymning the great procession towards the gates of heaven. His glorious coming was seen from afar off; and myriads of mighty angels hastened forth with golden harps, to welcome the honoured stranger."

Let those who question such zeal bow their heads in silence.

No attempt at subtlety lurks in Weem's words. His essential achievement can be stated in three words. He got across. He made intelligible the type of hero young America craved, and he had a virtue thoroughgoing historians lacked—he was readable; and the common man appreciated this. So when Weems died they made up legends about him, just as he had done about Washington. Tall tales concerning his life are still going the rounds in the South.

*　　　*　　　*

Chief Justice John Marshall and historian Jared Sparks turned the flesh and blood Washington into marble. The great jurist did not start out with this end in view. In the winter of 1800 Bushrod Washington, nephew and literary executor of the General, asked the judge to do an official biography. Marshall, then heavily in debt, was delighted. Four or five volumes properly sold, he calculated, should bring in $50,000. Besides, had he not served with Washington throughout the Revolution? Was he not a fellow Virginian and patrician, keenly appreciative of Washington's heritage?

An enormous amount of material (it now comprises thirty printed volumes) was made available to the Justice. The mass of paper did not digest easily, but Marshall set doggedly to work and wrote two volumes by 1804. In the first one, which opened with John Cabot's voyage and ended with the French and Indian War, Washington's name appeared only twice; volume two managed to reach the battle of Trenton. Volume three dragged through 1779, and four barely managed to get Washington back home after the war. The fifth and best volume covered the presidential years and Federalist politics. John Adams described the finished product as a mausoleum 100 feet square at the base and 200 feet high. The demigod Washington now had a place to rest in peace. Parson Weems, who probably never read all of Marshall's volumes, thought of an apt descriptive title. He called them the Washingtoniad.

The work of Jared Sparks raises fundamental questions. How much should historic truth be doctored to encourage heroic legend? Where does obligation to truth stop and poetic license begin? Should we attribute to great men what they actually said or did, or what they should have said and done? How deep should the editor's pencil dig? Jared Sparks is the Pontius Pilate of American historians.

Raised on a small Connecticut farm, Sparks (1789-1866) soon displayed a brilliance that eventually made him president of Harvard and a Washington scholar almost literally beyond compare. He read Virgil at the rate of a hundred lines a day after less than eight weeks' schooling. When Harvard's President Kirkland reviewed his college record he concluded, "Sparks is not only a man, but a man and a half." After a try at the ministry, Jared worked on the *North American Review*. There he developed a concern for history and documents that affected the rest of his life. He became our first highly efficient collector and editor of documents. The face of Washington he moulded into a death mask of perfection.

After years of historical writing, Sparks secured permission to remove the Washington papers from Mount Vernon to Boston, where he could study them at leisure. "I hear you are the richest, the busiest, and the happiest man in New England, perhaps the world," Miss A. G. Storrow, a friend, wrote him. No one could have been more ecstatic about Washington's papers than he; eventually he produced twelve volumes from them.

This earnest New Englander thought of himself as a portrait painter in words and a moralist in interpretation. History-as-it-is did not interest him nearly so much as history-as-it-ought-to-have-been. "He thought," John Bassett tells us, "that a sacred halo surrounded the life of a great man, which profane hands should not break lest ordinary men should lose their proper reverence for authority, and for the noble ideals which were embraced in the higher specimens of the race. He could not make up his mind to paint Washington with small faults, and so altered his language." [4]

With his assistant Samuel A. Eliot, Sparks made many changes and deletions in the Washington manuscripts. He altered, for example, "Old Put" to General Putnam, and deleted comments on certain New England officers whom Washington thought were "nearly of the same kidney" as cowardly privates. The English historian Lord Mahon was taken aback. "I am bound to think Mr. Sparks has printed no part of the correspondence precisely as Washington wrote it; but he has greatly altered, and as he thinks corrected and embellished it," he noted with polite restraint.

The "Sparks Controversy" was on. The details need not concern us. Nor need we debate whether Sparks was justified in making alterations. What matters here is what he did to the Washington image. Certainly he crystallized the priggish Washington that Parson Weems and Chief Justice Marshall had already begun to form. The Washington Sparks bequeathed to the nineteenth century was aptly described by a twentieth century historian: "He had no vices; he had no temper; he was completely unselfish. Is it any wonder that he became so strongly entrenched in the American mind that modern history and biography are condemned

—generally unheard—when they present their views of the man as he really was?" [5]

In *Four in America* the cryptic Gertrude Stein summed up the incredible situation in a line. "She is very sleepy, George Washington."

*   *   *

In seeking to immortalize Washington, most artists have actually dehumanized him. Glance at a Washington portrait and you will see how true this is. Done after Washington acquired his poorly-fitting wooden false teeth, most of them picture a dour man with a letter-box mouth.

No one knows how many people have come to think of Washington as looking like the Gilbert Stuart likeness, but their number must run into the millions. His Lansdowne and Athenaeum portraits stare out at us from books, stamps, tablets, advertisements, even bills. The former work, done for the Marquis of Lansdowne, represents Washington standing by a table, his right hand extended. The latter, purchased for the Boston Athenaeum in 1832, depicts only the head. Stuart copied it so many times when he needed money that he called it his hundred dollar bill. If his copies showed signs of haste, they were not admired any the less. Seeing one in England, Nathaniel Hawthorne wrote, "I am proud to see that noblest face and figure here in England; any English nobleman would look like common beef or clay beside him." Stuart's portrait, Emerson insisted, showed an Allegheny-like calm which contrasted sharply with the hysteria of later politicians. In 1932 the Athenaeum portrait was given over to the assembly line; the Washington Bicentennial Commission set out to place a poster-size reproduction in every American school. Hardly a child could have avoided seeing it several times a day. During the Bicentennial, Stuart's Washington was the official portrait; Congress authorized 750,000 reproductions. For better or worse, it is the one most Americans know.

The French sculptor Jean Antoine Houdon devoted much of his long creative life to heroic statues. None had more effect than that of George Washington. Statues of Europeans like Rousseau, Diderot, Moliére, Napoleon, and Lafayette, or of

Americans like Franklin, Fulton, Jones and Jefferson may be better as art; but Houdon's Washington has made a more enduring popular impression.

In 1784 the State of Virginia voted to have a Washington statue made. Thomas Jefferson and Benjamin Franklin, then in Europe, selected Houdon to execute it. He traveled to Mount Vernon to study Washington. Like everyone else, he was deeply impressed by the man's qualities. Patiently he watched for the right moment, to catch it in stone; it came one day when Washington, like an aging defiant eagle, scornfully dismissed a horse trader who suggested a dishonorable advantage. Completed in Paris and returned to Virginia in 1796, the statue has an inscription in keeping with the nobility of the work: "Fait par Houdon, citoyen Français, 1788."

Houdon realized that the Washington idolized by the people was a modern Cincinnatus. So he showed him with a civilian's cane in his right hand, a column of thirteen rods under his left hand, and the mold board of a plow under the column. The forthrightness gave it a strength found only in great sculpture. Virginia eventually insured the statue for a million dollars and put an iron fence around it.

As with Stuart's portrait, reproductions help explain the Houdon vogue. A private company and a public committee—the Gorham Manufacturing Company and the Washington Bicentennial Commission—motivated many of them. The former secured permission to make bronze copies, which now appear in museums and cities around the world. Thanks to Gorham enterprise, visitors to London's Trafalgar Square, Chicago's Art Institute, and Tokyo's Embassy Gardens daily encounter Houdon's Washington. Countless reproductions were made during the 1932 celebrations. As one of its schemes, the Bicentennial Commission distributed plaster copies to public schools from coast to coast. Here was a three-dimensional Washington to see, admire, and carry away in one's memory. Reproductions in books and on posters defy counting. Small wonder that it is one of the best-known statues of modern times.

*   *   *

The last of our hero-makers, Representative Sol Bloom, took

to George Washington the way a spring salmon takes to the Columbia River. By the time Bloom left Congress, Washington was almost better known than Mary Pickford.

The son of Polish Jewish immigrants, Sol began his career in a San Francisco brush factory. Subsequently he became ticket agent, show manager, producer, hootchy-kootchy inventor, music publisher, and backer of the first ferris wheel. When the Spanish-American War broke out, he demonstrated that he was more than equal to the occasion. The same day that news of the Maine disaster broke he completed and published a tune called, "The Heroes who Sank with the Maine." If you gave Sol an idea, he could make it go.

Feeling he had gone far enough, Sol Bloom retired in 1923 a millionaire, and proceeded to devote himself to public service. Tammany Hall backed him for Congress in the plush Riverside Drive district of Manhattan. He managed to get seated in a con-tested election, and to stay until his death in 1949.

However, Bloom's bizarre bills and fist fights in Congress were nothing as compared to his hero-making. In 1930 he became associate director of the George Washington Bicentennial Com-mission. His coequal on the Commission, U. S. Grant III, grand-son of the General who made a name for himself by sticking it out on a battleline all winter, did not persist like his namesake. He left Bloom in sole control. The new commander not only filled the breach, he spilled all over the wall. Before Congress knew what had happened, he organized a nine months' celebration, nailed down an appropriation of $338,000, and hired a staff of 125. During the legislative recess he devoted fifteen hours a day to George in one way or another. Millions of printed pieces jammed the nation's letter boxes. Tons of Washington badges, buttons, and busts went on sale. Sol even took over, with Wash-ington's help, Mother's Day, Memorial Day, Independence Day, and Goethe's birthday. Finally he set up his own radio station, with antenna on top of the Washington Monument. Never, but never, has one man said so much about Washington to so many. As Will Rogers wrote in a letter to the Congressman, "You are the only guy who ever made a party run nine months, and you did it in dry times, too. You made the whole country Washington conscious."

A newspaper cartoon pictured Sol in a Continental uniform, with the caption, "First in War, first in Peace, first in Bicentennial publicity." One columnist thought he was getting to look more and more like Washington. A Republican Senator replied there was little cause for alarm just as long as Washington didn't start to look like Sol Bloom.

To no one's surprise, Sol's offer of $500 for any suggestion to publicize Washington that had escaped him went unclaimed. Sol knew why. "I have taught more real American history in the last twenty years to more students than anyone in the United States," he claimed. Even those who would quibble with the Congressman's definition of "real American history" must concede that no one else has ever done more for Washington. Weems, Marshall, Sparks, Stuart, and Houdon will have to move over and make room for Sol Bloom.

*   *   *

"It is a dangerous business to involve Washington in the machinery of a work of fiction, for he is in no way a fit subject for satire," John R. Thompson warned William Thackeray in 1858. Americans have got so used to the remote Washington that to see an intimate literary portrayal irritates them. Putting so high a figure in a trivial situation smacks of blasphemy. It is as if a Japanese were asked to portray the Mikado in a sequel to the Gilbert and Sullivan opera (which, incidentally, caused an international incident).

To date, none of the novels in which Washington figures has fully satisfied the public. A gallant, aloof, and unreal first president steps gingerly through the pages of novels by Fenimore Cooper, Maria Sedgwick, John Neal, and John Esten Cooke. They were all writing in the manner of Sir Walter Scott, who set the pattern for the nineteenth century historical romance; but they lacked the master's touch.

Playwrights have found it hard to put the Father of their Country on the boards. Samuel Shirk studied Washington dramas, and summarized their mediocrity. Of the 75 plays and pageants on Washington written since 1875, none was a real success.   Only five—August Thomas' *Colonel George of Mount Vernon*, Percy MacKaye's *Wakefield*, Maxwell Anderson's *Valley Forge*, Sidney Kingsley's *The Patriots*, and Paul Green's *Faith of our Fathers*— have been even moderately well received.   The quiet integration of Washington's personality and the scarcity of startling dramatic situations work against portraying him convincingly.

Washington's reputation has of course declined in some periods. When the Jeffersonians were forming the party that swamped the Federalists, the President was one of their primary targets. Freneau, Bache, Madison, and many others attacked him; the Jay Treaty of 1795 brought strong protests.   Another low point occurred after the Civil War.   Lincoln emerged after his martyrdom as the national symbol of unity and greatness.   The South found a new idol in the defeated yet untarnished Lee.   Washington was temporarily discarded.   The most serious attack came in the 1920's, when smartness and light took over.   William E. Woodward's *George Washington: The Image and the Man* (1926) was the debunker's major sally, portraying a vain, ordinary, and undemocratic man, "almost as impersonal at the top of the government as a statue on top of a monument would have been." Strange that Woodward, aware of this haughty impersonality, should launch a pea-shooter attack against a marble man.

His ammunition did not penetrate.   Cal Coolidge, whose monosyllabic granite-block answers made him something of a folk hero in his own right, disposed of the debunkers in a few words.   When asked if they could destroy George Washington, he looked out of the White House window.   "Washington's Monument is still there," he said.

Washington's aloofness preserves his reputation, but it also minimizes his warm-blooded, human side.   There was fire and venom and drama enough in the real Washington.   Think of Washington at Newburgh in 1783 when fronted by the impetuous document of his officers who felt mistreated by the Continental Congress.   "Gentlemen, you will permit me to put on my spectacles, for I have not only grown gray, but almost blind in the service of my country," he said.   Not a man felt, after the simple statement, that he should complain.

Recall the directions Washington's step-grandson gave a visitor at Mount Vernon. "You will meet with an old gentleman riding alone, in plain drab clothes, a broad-brimmed white hat, a hickory switch in his hand, and carrying an umbrella with a long staff, which is attached to his saddle bow. That is General Washington."

Legends are the slowly perfected fruit from a shoot of imagination grafted onto a tree of fact; a blur and blend of what was and what should have been. Some of Washington's can be attributed to specific sources. We know that Parson Weems invented the cherry tree story, and the one about a Quaker named Potts finding Washington praying fervently in the snow-covered woods near Valley Forge. But historical research (which proved that Weems first used the Valley Forge prayer story in the *Federalist* for March 12, 1804) cannot kill the image. The praying Washington remains fixed in the stone of the New York Sub-Treasury Building and indelible in millions of postage stamps. All the scholars put together cannot erase the prayer legend.

To no single source can be attributed the notions that Washington, like Saul of Old, stood head and shoulders above most of his countrymen (actually he was shorter than Thomas Jefferson, whom we seldom think of as tall); that he was a man apart, with no real friends, and too heavy a burden to smile; that he concealed a deep unrequited passion for a haughty colonial beauty; that he carved his initials on Natural Bridge and a score of other landmarks; or that he slept in almost every house of eighteenth century America.

More elaborate are stories of Washington's miraculous escapes from danger. One has an Indian chief turning to his men during the Braddock rout and saying, "Mark yon tall and daring warrior? He is not of the red coat tribe. He hath an Indian's wisdom and his warriors fight as we do—himself alone is exposed. Quick, let your aim be certain, and he will die!" But no Indian bullet can find him. "It is in vain," concludes the chief. "The Great Spirit protects that man and guides his life." What miracle story of medieval times could be more marvelous?

Some legends flatly insist that Washington was protected by the gods. His mother is said to have had a prophetic dream in which young George saved the house (symbolically the Republic) from destruction by flames. Like other favorites of the gods, Washington allegedly had a sword with special properties. Samuel Wood-worth asserted in *The Champion of Freedom* (1816) that this blade would bring forth a message from beyond the grave, that in times of crises it would "flash and brandish itself, arousing the living characters to action."   Just as King Arthur is supposed to turn up to announce the millennium, just as Charlemagne is sched-uled to reappear when his great white beard thrice encircles the stone table before him in Untersburg, so Washington is expected to make a return engagement in order to fulfill legendary require-ments.

In all these tales Washington epitomizes the traits of which young America was fondest: virtue, idealism, and piety. His flaws seem pale when held up against this central proposition; he was willing to stake his life and fortune on his high principles, to take up without question a task others could not perform. This is the basis of his real fame and "second fictional life." The South was particularly proud of this Virginia aristocrat, who became the model for the ante-bellum planter class. "How much more delight-ful to an undebauched mind," Washington wrote to Arthur Young in 1788, "is the task of making improvements on the earth than all the vain glories which can be acquired from ravaging it." Even the Republicans, out of sympathy with Federalist policies, were in accord with Washington's agrarian sympathies. Thomas Jefferson, so unlike Washington in many ways, nevertheless appre-ciated his true stature. "Washington's justice was the most inflexi-ble I have ever known, no motives of interest or consanguinity, of friendship or hatred, being able to bias his decision," Jefferson wrote to Dr. Walter Jones on January 2, 1814. "He was indeed, in every sense of the words, a wise, a good, and a great man."

Robert E. Lee grew up under Washington's shadow, and took his life as a model for his own. When he joined the Confederate forces he must have recalled that Washington too had led a revolu-tionary force against established authority. The Washington-Franklin Roosevelt parallel is also worth noting at this point. Not since the Virginia dynasty had there been a president who was so much a country squire as Roosevelt; Washington was the model squire. Like the first president, Roosevelt was an aristocrat who

loved tradition, attracted subordinates easily, and exhibited an
Appalachian strength in adversity.

But we should not forget that Washington's cult flourished most
during those years when Queen Victoria sat on the British throne
and Britannia ruled taste as well as the waves. Washington made
a most admirable Victorian hero. He was a "code man," proper,
pure, and personable; a man of property and substance; a man
who would have appreciated Tennyson's poems, Galsworthy's
novels, and Rogers' figurines. This is not to say he was a prig
or a kill-joy. In him there burned a mad hell which, on the few
occasions when it was freed, seared the souls of those who stood
in its path. He was the General who wanted "news on the spur of
speed, for I am all impatience," and who had no sympathy with
his routed troops when they ran "like the wild bears of the mountains." No one could have been more gallant with the ladies when
circumstances permitted. Once he danced for three hours without a pause. When it came to Madeira wine, he was an acknowledged epicure. His stories about jackasses were decidedly Rabel-
aisian. There was hotter blood in Washington's veins than this
century dreams of. His real strength lay in his controlled gentle-
ness. He played his part as if he knew exactly what the fifth
act would be like.

Instead of revering the Washington of Madeira, clay pipes,
thundering oaths, and jackass jokes, we admire the one Brumidi
painted on the dome of the National Capitol in Washington. "The
Apotheosis of Washington" depicts the distant demigod, with Freedom at his right and Victory at his left. Here is a Washington for
the ages, a leader who symbolizes the finest qualities our nation
can produce. To contemplate his character has given millions of
Americans a sense of achievement and promise. Even when lifted
out of reality and temporarily overshadowed by dazzling but
ephemeral stars in the hero heaven, he manages to keep his place.
History has affirmed the people's opinion of George Washington.
He remains the greatest of great Americans.

CHAPTER 4

Westward Ho: Daniel Boone

*"Boone's was one of the most fully realized
lives ever lived in modern times, and for that
reason we cannot be sorry for him, no matter
what ill fortune came his way. It was also
one of the most credible; he was the American
Ulysses."* —J. Donald Adams, *Literary Fron-
tiers*

Daniel Boone's place in American history is unique and secure.
He set the general pattern which later western heroes followed,
personified the epic move westward, and "Kilt a bar" that became
a myth. The prototype for Davy Crockett, Kit Carson, Paul
Bunyan, and the American cowboy, he has not been outshone by
more spectacular or successful adventurers. Boone was the
American Moses who led us into the Promised Land.

That he was also a modest man who claimed to have killed
only one Indian, an illiterate man who had difficulty writing his
own name, and an unsocial man who drifted westward in search
of elbow-room, only heightens his achievement. It also raises the
question: how is it that Boone has been exalted, more than such
equally brave companions as Squire Boone, Harrod, McAfee,
and Logan?

His fame rests both upon the quality of his life and acts, and
upon historical circumstances. Boone had the good fortune to
be active when many writers and intellectuals, influenced by Jean
Jacques Rousseau, dreamed of the noble savage who was free
from the shackles of society and convention. Despite its coonskin
trim and backwoods flavor, Boone's image is modeled after the
Enlightenment "natural man." John Filson's biography (trans-

lated into French in 1785 and into German in 1790) spread
Boone's fame. Here was the innately good man of the forest; a
rustic Ben Franklin. His very weaknesses (aggressive individualism, mania for solitude, non-conformity) appealed to his admirers. Even Lord Byron was impressed, as his Boone tribute in
Don Juan shows. He sums up Boone's life, to which he devoted
seven stanzas of Canto Eight, thus:

> "*Boone lived hunting up to ninety;*
> *And what's still stranger, left behind a name*
> *For which men vainly decimate the throng*
> *Not only famous, but of that good fame*
> *Without which glor, 's but a tavern song,—*
> *Simple, serene, the antipodes of shame,*
> *Which hate nor envy e'er could tinge with wrong.*" [1]

Later, Boone made an admirable hero for the Jacksonian Democrats of the 1830's. He remains today the unsurpassed path-
finder of a nation which no longer has a western frontier.

The elevation of Boone was the triumph not only of the times,
but of five Americans who fostered his reputation. John Filson,
Timothy Flint, James Fenimore Cooper, Lyman Draper, and Dan
Beard were largely instrumental in establishing him as a major
American hero. He would probably have achieved high status
even had lesser men championed his cause, though he himself did
little to publicize his exploits. Not to discredit Boone (who was a
sterling man) nor to make heroes of his publicists (who were less
heroic) is this analysis made; but to illuminate the relationship
between the great man and those who revere him.

Boone was born near Reading, Pennsylvania, in 1734, the
sixth son of Squire and Sarah Boone. The promise of religious
freedom had caused Daniel's grandfather to leave England and
settle twelve miles north of Philadelphia. Eventually he moved
to Oley Township, now Berks County, Pennsylvania. The Boones
were born wanderers, always answering the call of that something
which manages to stay just beyond the ridge. Young Daniel got
little education even for that place and time. Later he made
some attempt to further his training and improve his highly individualistic handwriting. Uncle John Boone tried to guide Daniel

in bookish ways, but gave up because Daniel lacked interest. To
John Boone, Squire Boone made the much-quoted (probably
apocryphal) statement in defense of his son: "Let the girls do
the spelling, and Dan will do the shooting." Daniel was early
exposed to the wilderness, and became familiar with wild life in
the dense Pennsylvania woods. He learned his forest lore while
caring for his father's cattle on twenty-five acres located miles
from the main farm. That task he neglected, and the herd was
usually left to wander at will.

Dan Boone was fifteen when his parents left home and headed
for the Valley of Virginia. For a year and a half they lived
near Harrisonburg before moving to Rowan County, North
Carolina. (A nearby Virginian neighbor was John Lincoln; his
great-grandson would share America's top heroic honors with
George Washington, whose ancestors were by then well established
on the Northern Neck.) Daniel Boone married young after having
almost shot his wife-to-be while "fire-hunting" for deer. In those
days, the hunter would flash a torch until he attracted a curious
deer; light reflected in the animal's eyes revealed his target.
Boone once caught sight of gleaming eyes and raised his long
rifle to shoot, but discovered just in time the figure of Rebecca
Bryan. She rushed home to tell her father she had been chased
by a panther. Later on, at the proper moment, she rushed into
the panther's den.

The young couple had been married three years when Boone
took his wife and two children to Virginia to avoid the Indian
uprising brought about by wanton killings of Cherokees. They
settled in Culpeper County, where he made a living hauling tobacco
to Fredericksburg. But this was no life for a man of Boone's
temperament; so he sold his property and left with six families
and forty men for Kentucky. The party was attacked by Indians
near Cumberland Gap. Six were killed, including Boone's son
James, who was in the rear of the main party. Such memorable
tragedies as this merely added to Boone's fame. Virginia's governor chose him to warn the surveyors in the Kentucky territory of
the impending uprising. Boone and "Big Mike" Stone covered
eight hundred miles in sixty-two days, going as far as the Falls
of the Ohio. After that Daniel was placed in command of Moore's

Fort in the Clinch River Valley. In 1775, he was commissioned
by Colonel Richard Henderson to hack out the Wilderness Road to
Boonesborough, where he built the fort that has been re-built for
plays and movies a thousand times.

Here he and his companions resisted several savage attacks and
rescued Jemima Boone and the Calloway girls, who had been
kidnapped by the Indians. Later Daniel himself was captured at
Blue Licks, adopted as a son by the Shawnee Chief, Blackfish, and
given the tribal name, "Big Turtle." The following year he
escaped in time to warn his comrades at Fort Boone of an Indian
raid. These were ideal episodes for the legend-makers, who found
good hunting in the tales of the Dark and Bloody ground.

In later life Boone's chief concern was contesting the loss of
land which he had improperly entered. Ejectment suits deprived
him of his holdings. Dismayed, the old hunter left the Kentucky
that later considered him its special saint, and moved west. Eventually he reached what is now Missouri, where his son Daniel
lived. There he became magistrate of the district. Once again
his holding was voided, this time by the United States land com-
missioner; but in 1814 Congress confirmed his claim. He traveled
back to Kentucky to pay off his debts and (says tradition) ended
up with fifty cents. He stayed only long enough to transact his
business. Then he headed west again to spend his last years with
his son Nathan. Admirers traveling into the wilderness to see the
frontier sage wondered why he preferred to live his life out on
the cutting edge of the frontier. His supposed answer was in
keeping with Rousseau's natural man. "It was too crowded back
East. I had to have more elbow-room."

Boone's uneventful later years did not dull his earlier achievements, nor diminish the respect with which Americans viewed him.
James Audubon recorded after interviewing him: "The stature and
general appearance of this wandered of the western forests approached the gigantic. The very motion of his lips brought the impression that whatever he uttered could not be otherwise than
strictly true." This appraisal is all the more remarkable when we
note that Boone was only five feet eight inches tall. Audubon
viewed Boone as more than a historical figure. The component
parts of the myth were recognizable even then: a Promised Land

beyond the mountains; land-hungry families who considered it a
new Eden; someone leading the people westward; a lone wanderer
guiding his generation on a God-sanctioned mission.

That scores of people had preceded Boone in Kentucky—Cou-
ture, Walsh, Nairns, Morgan, Finley, and Stone, for example—
served but to enhance the Boone saga. Their achievements were
laid at his feet. Some have lamented this and seen it as a gross injustice. Actually it is a normal process with heroes; their lives
polarize many of their contemporaries' feats and accomplishments.
Certainly in Boone's case, as Clarence Alvord put it, "popular
fancy was granted opportunity for unrestrained imagination in
creating myth, which age so hallowed that even well trained historians have hesitated to submit it to the violet rays of scientific
analysis."[2]

Boone himself tried in vain to discredit the idea that he never
relished civilization. Actually he got along reasonably well with his
neighbors, and sought companionship, particularly in his old age.
Boone was no sulking misanthrope. With his native capacity for
leadership and decision, his enduring stoicism despite setbacks,
and his love of the outdoors, he epitomized the unmachined men of
our frontier. These qualities are particularly appealing in our own
twentieth century, now that science and technology have brought
on perplexing problems. Americans look with nostalgia at the image
of a man most happy when farthest away from multiple gadgets,
factories, and smokestacks of civilization. An apt epitaph for Boone
is Mark Twain's last line of *Huckleberry Finn*: "But I reckon I
got to light out for the territory ahead of the rest, because Aunt
Sally she's going to adopt me and civilize me, and I can't stand it.
I been there before." So had Daniel.

The first writer to perceive epic qualities in the Boone story, and
to record them, was an early schoolmaster and explorer named John
Filson. Born on a southeastern Pennsylvania farm in 1747, Filson
was struck by the vision of frontier adventure. At the close of the
Revolution he moved west, spent a year in Kentucky as a school
teacher, and secured several thousand acres of land. He wrote *The
Discovery, Settlement, and Present State of Kentucky*. The appen-
dix, called "The Adventures of Col. Daniel Boone," is the first
authentic sketch of Boone. Florid and pedantic, it purports to be

an autobiography, though meditations in "sylvan shades" about "the ruins of Persepolis or Palmyra" were about as familiar to the real Boone as discussions of the latest coiffures at Versailles.

Only Daniel's illiteracy saved him the shock he might have got from reading such a line as this: "The diversity and beauties of nature I met with in this charming season expelled every gloomy thought . . . At a vast distance I beheld the mountains lift their venerable brows and penetrate the clouds." Small wonder that the book made much more of an impression at Versailles than it did at Boonesborough. The 1785 translation couched in Chateaubriand-like prose, became popular among French writers and courtiers. Though later scholars have considered Filson's story pompous and inaccurate, it was endorsed by Boone himself, both as being the best account of his life, and as "not having a lie in it."

The book's popularity can be gauged by the number and variety of editions it enjoyed. Five years after the first printing in Wilmington, Delaware, it appeared in Paris as *Histoire de Kentucke, Nouvelle Colonie a l'ouest de la Virginie;* in Philadelphia as the *Adventures of Colonel Daniel Boone, One of the Original Settlers of Kentucke;* and in Leipzig as *Reise nach Kentucke und Nachrichten von dieser neu Angebauten Landschaft in Nordamerika.* After that, excerpts and paraphrases cropped up almost continuously.

Among Filson's other accomplishments were the publishing of the *Kentucky Gazette,* and the laying out of Losantville, which grew into Cincinnati. There was an ironic as well as a tragic note to his death. The man whose pen had caused so many Indians to bite the dust was himself tomahawked while traveling up the Little Miami River in October, 1788. And there was no Daniel Boone to save him.

In 1934 Kentucky's Filson Club celebrated its semi-centennial and the sesquicentennial of the Filson volume, which the club's president called "one of the most important in American pioneer history, the foundation of Boone's reputation." Filson was following the great trail blazer through the unpredictable realm of Public Acclaim. To Timothy Flint, as to Parson Weems before him, history was a means of conveying moral ideas and edifying stories, not a scientific recounting of past events. When Weems finished

describing Washington, and Flint Boone, their subjects had haloes.
Born near North Reading, Massachusetts, Timothy Flint graduated
from Harvard in 1800. Sharing the fate of most of his classmates,
he became a preacher. Soon he agreed with his congregation that
his was not the theological bent. While supposedly preparing sermons, he was reading Chateaubriand. While thinking of Biblical
analogies, he was dreaming of frontier heroism and collecting
autographs of early pioneers. "There is a kind of moral sublimity
in the contemplation of their adventures and daring," he wrote.
"They tend to reinspire something of that simpliciyt of manners,
manly hardihood, and Spartan energy and force of character which
forms so conspicuous a part of the nature of the settlers of our western wilderness." [3]

He learned about Boone, "the Achilles of the West," through
Daniel's grandson, Albert Gallatin Boone. While inaccuracies dot
Flint's biography, Albert always maintained that it was the best
of the Boone accounts. Some vividness comes from Flint's romantic
conception of Boone as a walking embodiment of coonskin individualism, and America's unique contribution to history. In his
mind he saw Boone as he saw William Weldon in his own novel,
Shoshonee Valley: "disgusted with social and civilized life,
and anxious to purge his own soul by lonely treks into the interior."
To cleanse his own spirit, Flint traveled thousands of miles in the
west, suffering from fever and ague, always moving restlessly on.
His was indeed a life of quiet desperation, of endless wandering
and adoration. Only the strength of his own hero worship sustained
him.

Unlike the Parson, Flint did not hit upon any legend remotely
comparable to that of George Washington and the cherry tree. The
event of Boone's life which comes closest is the killing of a bear,
and the subsequent carving on a birch tree, "D. Boon kilt a bar."
How many trees have been subjected to real knifes, and how many
bears slain by imaginary Daniel Boones, historians dare not guess.

Flint pictures, without historical justification, his hero slipping
tartar emetic into the whiskey bottle of his Irish schoolmaster, and
this becomes the episode which ended Boone's brief schooling.
In his last chapter Daniel takes up the creed of the noble savage.
"Such were the truth, simplicity, and kindness of his character,

there can be but little doubt, had the gospel of the Son of God been proposed to him, in its sublime truth and reasonableness, that he would have added to all his virtues, the higher name of Christian."[4] When some objected to such fabrication on Flint's part, he replied with an unanswerable line that Parson Weems might have endorsed: "Like Pindar's razor, the book was made not for use but to sell."

And sell it did. Fourteen editions appeared between 1833 and 1868. Flint's stories were retold by others and his fanciful Boone dialogues plagiarized so blatantly, that even the typographical errors were copied without much correction. The Trailblazer most people read about today came first from the brain of Timothy Flint and has been public property ever since.

As with all heroes, Boone was idealized in literature as well as history. Even while he was still moving westward, he seemed to his contemporaries a fit subject for an American Odyssey or Aeneid. Daniel Bryan published in 1813 *The Mountain Muse, Comprising the Adventures of Daniel Boone; and The Power of Virtuous and Refined Beauty*. In this epic poem, the hero cavorted with the fates, His mission was superhuman:

> *"Of objects, which are link'd to the grand theme*
> *O'er all the mazy complicated chain*
> *That with sublime sensation swell the soul;*
> *Boone now in all its forceful influence felt."*[5]

Against the forces of evil the "sinewy sons of Enterprise" prevailed, pushing on into the "rude featured Wilderness". Finally reaching the Mississippi, they envisaged a time when "Freedom's Cities and Republics too" would prosper. As poetry it was a bit embarrassing; but it suggested a nice mythology.

The author who best moulded the fictional image of Boone was born in his father's village of Cooperstown, New York and raised near the eighteenth century frontier. James Fenimore Cooper's literary career began on a playful wager, but his novels soon established him a serious American writer. William Thackeray thought Cooper's Leatherstocking a better fictional figure than any invented by Scott, one to rank with Uncle Toby, Sir Roger de Coverly, and Falstaff. And Leatherstocking, like his fellow creations

Hawkeye, Natty Bumpo, and Deerslayer, was a thinly-disguised Boone.

Cooper specifically acknowledged his debt to the Boone stories and based part of *The Last of the Mohicans* on Daniel's rescue of his own daughter and the two other white girls from the Cherokees.[6] He said Boone went beyond the Mississippi "because he found a population of ten to the square mile inconvenient." While there is some question of the extent to which Cooper drew directly from Boone's life, it is certain that he used him as a model. Like Boone, Leatherstocking had a historic mission. Both appealed to an America intoxicated with the heady wine of Manifest Destiny, typifying moral stamina, courage, and will-power. Cooper's paragon looked and dressed like the real Boone: he was tall, leathery and solemn. His long rifle was as essential for a public appearance as his trousers. So was the coonskin hat, sitting casually on his noble head. The Old World could—and did—contemplate him in admiration.

The *Leatherstocking Tales* presented vividly and convincingly the struggle for empire in the forests, modeled actually on Boone's struggle for survival. Utterly simple and admirable, Leatherstocking demonstrated that it was not polish or costume that made for greatness. What a man was inside, not how he appeared, really mattered. In this way the country cousin, America, justified herself to that debonair rake, Europe.

During Boone's own lifetime he served as model for such books as James Hall's *Legends of the West* and Robert Montgomery Bird's *Nick of the Wood*. In the hands of a writer as skillful as William Gilmore Simms, clever variations of the theme appeared. Boone's reputation rose like smoke from a mountain cabin on a crisp, still December morning.

In the National Capitol, Horatio Greenough portrayed the contest between civilization and barbarism as a death struggle between Boone and an Indian brave. He set an artistic prototype. Many chose to use this figure, but only one artist painted Boone from real life. This was Chester Harding, who traveled to Missouri to see Boone in 1819. John J. Audubon, Thomas Sully, Alonzo Chappel, W. C. Allen, Reuben Macy, J. B. Langacre, and Y. W. Berry did portraits; but George C. Bingham best reflected Boone's symbolic importance in "The Emigration of Daniel Boone." This showed the old man leading a group of eager settlers into the new Eden. It epitomized American thinking on the subject and the leader.

Walt Whitman added considerably to the growing cult of the coonskin Moses. A Long Islander, Whitman fell in love with the western mirage, and then with the west, which he visited in 1848. His 1855 volume of poetry, *Leaves of Grass,* was a loud and indiscriminate yes. In it even a mouse was miracle enough to stagger sextillions of infidels. The stereotyped hero who roamed through its cacophonous pages was closely related to Boone:

> *"Come my tan-faced children,*
> *Follow well in order, get your weapons ready,*
> *Have you your pistols? have your sharp-edged axes?*
> *Pioneers! O pioneers!*
> *Have the elder races halted?*
> *Do they droop and end their lesson, wearied over there beyond*
>   *the seas?*
> *We take up the task eternal, and the burden and the lesson,*
> *Pioneers! O pioneers!"*

Thus Whitman glorified the kind of leader of which Boone was the original, praising the trailblazer's exploits in vigorous and explosive verse. He said well what many already believed: the true America was west.

Boone has long been a favorite with our historical novelists. Winston Churchill's protagonist in *The Crossing* (1903) meets Sevier, Boone, and Kenton in a fictional account of the Wilderness Campaign. Elizabeth Maddox Robert's *The Great Meadow* (1930) uses the spirit of Daniel Boone as a motivating factor. The family of Berk Jervis travels from Virginia to Harrod's Fort, where its members are separated by an Indian attack. The intervention of Boone brings about their final reunion. Stewart Edward White's' *The Long Rifle* (1932) has as its central figure Andy Burnett, who inherits a long rifle from his grandfather's friend, Daniel Boone. The list of novels also includes D. M. Henderson's *Boone of the Wilderness,* C. H. Forbes Lindsay's *Daniel Boone, Back-woodsman* Horatio Colony's *Free Forester,* A. B. Guthrie's *The Big Sky,* Caroline Gordon's *Green Centuries,* Katherine Clugston's *Wilderness Road,* and Felix Holt's *Dan'l Boone Kissed Me.*

More than all of these writers, however, it was dilatory Lyman C. Draper who brought Boone into historical prominence. Young Draper inbibed tales of frontier heroism from his father in nine-teeth-century western New York state, and read even more of them during his years at Graanville College in Ohio. He became Peter A. Remsen's protege, and collected material for the latter's histories and biographies. Eventually Draper moved to Wisconsin. There, as Secretary of the Wisconsin Historical Society, he set to work in 1854 to make its archives one of the most important in the nation.'

For half a century the meticulous Draper used his limited funds and support to assemble 478 bound volumes covering the years 1735-1815. No one is better represented in them Daniel Boone about whom 39 volumes center; five embody Draper's long-hand life of Boone up to 1778—still the most detailed and authoritative ever written. Sixteen contain information on Boone furnished by descendants, neighbors, and friends. Others deal with inscriptions, stories, and legends. They prove that Boone was the subject of apocryphal stories even in early manhood, and specify places that claim to be the one where "D. Boon Kilt a bar." There are "eye-witness accounts" of Indians being killed by Boone, in contrast to Boone's own statement that he killed only one Indian in all his life; letters from Boone's relations and associates; original documents and surveys; and notes and allusions pertaining to his life. While gathering these, Draper contacted all the direct and collateral descendants of Daniel Boone, and was authorized to do a biography. He collected a variety of documents unequalled for any frontier figure, and opened them up for historians and text-book writers. His material supplied valuable testimony about Boone's status among his contemporaries. Draper impressed a group of people who might not have been touched by Filson, Flint and Cooper. He made Boone a respectable subject of scholarly historical probing. Dusting off the coonskin hat, Draper found an exalted position for it in the academic hat-rack.

Draper's obsession with details eventually became a curse, and his procrastination an albatross. "I have wasted my life in puttering, but see no help for it, " he wrote. "I can write nothing so long as I fear there is a fact, no matter how small, as yet ungarnered." He was fascinated by the physical exploits of men he would have emulated, had not an undersized body and a desk job rendered such things impossible. Like Timothy Flint he found atonement in endless travel, copy work, and the dream world of vicarious adventure. How dark and somber it can be under the lengthening shadow of a great man!

In 1854 Draper and B. J. Lossing entered a contract for the joint authorship of a Boone biography. Draper's dallying prevented the partnership from maturing. It lasted, on paper, for fifteen years, during which Lossing published some Boone material on his own. Draper finally completed *King's Mountain and Its Heroes* in 1883. Exacting in scholarship but discursive in style, it embodied the romantic concept that frontiersmen, fresh from the farms, could defeat the disciplined regiments of the British tyrant. In 1889 Draper did a perceptive essay on the collection of autographs (a phase of the hero-building process in which he was a past master), but he never completed another book. No crumb from a hero's table was too small or insignificant for this little man. Like T. E. Eliot's memorable J. Alfred Prufrock, Draper wondered how he should begin, and how he should presume. Yet he did the archivistic job so well that, so far as the early frontier is concerned, no one need undertake it again.

*   *   *

Dan Boone's reputation got first aid from Dan Beard, whose Boy Scout organization became the most important youth movement in our history. Drawing consciously on the popular image, Beard turned millions of young Americans into trail-blazers and Indian fighters. Born in Cincinnati, Ohio, Beard studied art in New York and instructed there from 1893 to 1900. The outdoors called loud and clear. He went west and met such picturesque characters as Yellowstone Kelly, Buffalo Bill, John Burroughs, Bat Masterson, Buffalo Jones, and Charles Russell. But he admittedly modeled his boy's clubs on the figure Cooper had used for Deerslayer and Leatherstocking:

"I suggested a society of scouts to be identified with the greatest of all Scouts, Daniel Boone, and to be known as the Sons of Daniel Boone. Each 'member' would have to be a tenderfoot before he attained the rank of Scout. Eight members would form a stockade, four stockades a fort . . . I never realized that the Boy Scouts would sweep over much of the world and become my real life's work." [8]

The Boy Scout movement depended on stock Boone symbols: the rifle, the buckskin clothes, and the coonskin cap. Patent nativism and glorification of frontier days explain the movement's rapid growth. At the invitation of that perennial Boy Scout, Theodore Roosevelt, Beard visited the White House in 1907 to explain his plan and win official support for it. The conference ended with Roosevelt shouting "Bully!" and pounding on the table with his fist. It was Boone's greatest victory since Boonesborough.

Beard supervised the publication of the early editions of the *American Boys' Handbook*. This became the official Boy Scout manual which has been a best-seller ever since. His own *American Boy's Handbook* (1882) was the model on which all later editions were based. Beard claimed that more copies of this publication were distributed in the decade following World War I than any other volume except the Bible.

Boone worship reached its peak in the bicentennial year, 1934. Thousands of khaki-clad Scouts from all over America met in Covington, Kentucky, for a secular revival meeting. Parades and pageants were staged there, and all over America. The names of Dan Boone and Dan Beard, who had modeled his life, dress, and movement on the earlier Daniel's achievements, were linked together. This was entirely fitting. The two merged into the one lofty, anachronistic figure of the frontier fighter and hunter. Beard adapted the Boone story to suit an America hungry for symbols and scalps. A not unfitting reward came when an Alaskan peak was officially named Mount Beard by the Federal government.

During the Boone Bicentennial, the Daughters of the American Revolution, the American Order of Pioneers, and the Boone Family Association prodded politicians and officials into a frenzy of Boone adulation. S. M. Wilson tapped some of the prevailing clichés to describe Daniel Boone as "this Prince of the Pioneers, this Founder of Boonesborough, this foster-father of Kentucky, this favorite son of all America, this peerless pilot of the Republic, this instrument divinely ordained to settle the wilderness." What could a man add except "Amen"?

The General Assembly of Kentucky set up a commission to "promote and direct a fitting celebration of the two hundredth anniversary of Boone's birth." Shrines were established at Boonesborough, Boone's Station, Bryan's Station, and Big Licks Battlefield. Congress authorized the minting of 600,000 souvenir half dollars. Eulogies of Boone were heard everywhere. His position as pattern-maker for western American heroes was assured.

State pride has also contributed to the adulation. Pennsylvania, Virginia, North Carolina, Kentucky, Tennessee, and Missouri have all claimed Boone as their very own. Consider the contribution of a few local historians of the Old Dominion. The *Scott County History* of Robert Addington contains extravagant praise for Boone. Its author examines minutely every link in "the chain of cause and effect which connects us with Daniel Boone." William Pendleton's *Tazewell County History* calls Boone the greatest man who ever set foot there; only his presence enabled Virginians to push westward to Kentucky. Goodrich Wilson, author of *Smythe County History and Traditions,* credits Boone's vigorous defense of southwest Virginia with that area's emancipation from the Indians. Finally, Oren F. Morton, in his *Story of Daniel Boone,* proved that Pennsylvania-born Boone was a Virginian at heart.

Abingdon, a cultural center for western Virginia, is the locale of many Boone stories. The town site is said to have been his camping ground, and its creek is named after him. A local citizen still treasures a piece of bark on which is inscribed Boone's legendary trademark: "D. Boon kilt a bar." Although skeptical about this relic, James Taylor Adams, editor of the *Cumberland Empire,* admits Boone makes an admirable hero: "There are many legends of his bravery and daring adventures. He spent one winter and part of a summer in Russell County and his son was killed in Lee County. Scarcely a creek or hollow in this part of the country but a tree has been reported there bearing his name, initials, or the carved statement that 'D. Boon kilt a bar.' If all these inscriptions were true, Old Daniel must have put in the better part of his time carving on the bark of trees." [9]

Boone's has not been the type of fame to rival that of Washington, Jefferson, and Lincoln. Unlike these, he bears no relation with governmental or political symbols. Instead, he represents man's protest against the restraints of society and an ever-encroaching, self-righteous technology. Newsmen sensed this; for during World War II they wrote about Daniel Boone VI who, at his primitive forge in Burnsville, North Carolina, turned out hand-forged hollow-ground combat knives with deer-horn handles. Though aware of modern methods, the contemporary Daniel would have none of the electric hammers, welding torches, or pneumatic drills. "New ways are quicker," he was quoted as saying, "but old-fashioned ways are best." Thus a major American legend was brought up to date for our times.

William Carlos Williams has summarized Boone's appeal: "Possessing a body at once powerful, compact, and capable of tremendous activity and resistance when roused, a clear eye and a deadly aim, taciturn in his demeanor, symmetrical and instinctive in understanding, Boone stood for his race, the affirmation of that wild logic, which in times past had mastered another wilderness and now, renascent, would master this, to prove it potent." [10]

In this affirmation and this mastery, the reputation of the first major Western hero, the man whom others have closely followed, is preserved as a permanent part of the American heritage.

*   *   *

Among our major figures, Boone alone has a comic counterpart —Davy Crockett, that "yaller flower of the forest" whose career became a grotesque frontier joke. His saga is Boone's turned upside down.

In 1818 there lived near Shoal Creek, Tennessee, a frontier squatter who had, in his own colorful words, "suffered only four days of schooling." When his neighbors decided to set up a temporary government, they elected him justice of the peace. Davy Crockett's amazing career was thus launched. Throughout it all he relied on "natural born sense, and not on law learning; for I never read a page in a law-book in all my life." After a term in the state legislature, he accepted (apparently as a joke) the challenge to run for Congress. He won, and served satisfactorily.

The Whigs, stressing his eccentricities, humor, and lusty pioneer spirit, turned him into a vote-getting buffoon.

Party journalists wrote, but attributed to the almost illiterate Crockett, *Sketches and Eccentricities of Col. David Crockett* (1833), *An Account of Col. Crockett's Tour to the North and Down East* (1835), *A Narrative of the Life of D. Crockett, of the State of Tennessee* (1834), and *The Life of Martin Van Buren* (1835). Alexis de Tocqueville was intrigued by Crockett, referring to him as one who "has no education, can read with difficulty, has no property, no fixed residence, but passes his life hunting, selling his game to live, and dwelling continuously in the woods." The Whigs went so far as to let Davy sit on the platform with Daniel Webster. For a while Tennessee's greatest bear-hunter even expected to be nominated for the presidency. Instead, he failed to be re-elected to Congress. So he told his constituents they could all go to hell, and he would go to Texas.

Off he went. His death at the Alamo put just the right finishing touch to his own vigorous legend. Once the real Crockett was dead, the heroic buffoon and folk character took over, via the *Crockett Almanacs*, issued from 1835 to 1856. In them ghost writers attempted to fit humans and animals of Homer's proportions into the raw, gigantic, American landscape. Bumptious Davy mastered with ridiculous ease the cruel frontier world and the snarling beasts that dwelt in it. He made jokes of situations which too often were tragic; he mastered the impossible effortlessly. The backwoods became a fairyland.

In it the fairies played rough. Fed on Buffalo milk and weaned on whiskey, Davy sprouted so that his Aunt Keziah thought it was as good as a day's vittles to look at him. The animals finally stopped trying to defy him. "Is that you, Davy?" they would shout when he reached for his gun. "Yep," he would say. "All right, don't shoot. Can't you take a joke? I'm a-comin' down!"

Most Crockett tall tales were based on oral tradition going back to Daniel Boone. They are conscious inversions. Pranks, practical jokes, and boasts seemed beneath Boone. So a Davy Crockett who specialized in these very things was invented. His hero-makers were mostly Whig politicians, who saw that by using Crockett they might split the Jacksonians in the west.

People wanted to hear about that rascal Davy long after his political mission was forgotten. And they kept talking about him, until he got to be a hero. A paradox runs throughout his career: although he won fame because of his horse sense, he endured in folklore because of the nonsense written about him. Settling the frontier was grim business; Indians took real scalps. As often as not the people there laughed, as Mark Twain observed, so that they would not cry.

Hence there is almost a hysterical note to the accumulated gusto which gave us Davy Crockett. There is also poetic justice; for he is the necessary complement to the brooding Boone, rounding out the most genuinely American myth which our culture has yet created.

CHAPTER 6

The Lost Cause: Robert E. Lee

"A Prince once said of a Monarch slain,
'Taller he seems in Death.'"
—Ancient folk tale

When finally the smoke of battle cleared, this much was certain: the North had the victory, but the South had Robert E. Lee.

Almost a century after he took arms against the Union, Lee is today viewed as one of our greatest, if not our greatest, soldier, and a personification of the Lost Cause. His military defeats are considered inconsequential compared to his spiritual victories. Of all Americans, he comes closest to our conception of a true aristocrat.

Born in 1807 at Stratford Hall, Robert E. Lee led a life that was simple and unswerving—that of a soldier, a Christian, and a gentleman. After graduating from West Point in 1829, he served as army engineer, an officer in the Mexican war, and the superintendent of West Point. His Federal troops suppressed John Brown's raid on Harpers Ferry. When offered the field command of the Union army, he resigned his post to lead Virginia's troops in the Confederate army. Brilliant victories took him eventually to Gettysburg, from which he was forced to retreat. Thereafter he was on the defensive. In 1865, two months after being appointed commander-in-chief of all the Confederate forces, he surrendered his army at Appomattox. A civilian again, he became president of Washington College in Lexington, Virginia. In 1870, five years after assuming this academic post, he died. This is the brief history of the most admired Southerner in American history.

Lee legends have an unmatched mellowness and tenderness.

Consider these examples. One Sunday morning after the war, at an elegant Richmond Episcopal church, the Rector invited the congregation to come forward to the communion rail. A newly-liberated negro approached humbly and knelt at the altar. The people gasped. Bitter after the recent warfare, they held back from such an association. Looking up from his meditation, a white-haired figure saw this, walked quietly down the aisle, and took his place beside the former slave. The gentleman's name was Robert E. Lee.

As President of struggling Washington College, Lee urged a student to better his study habits, so he could stay on at the college. "We do not want you to fail," said the former warrior. "But General, you failed," blurted out the youth with a brashness characteristic of sophomores everywhere. "I hope you may be more fortunate than I," Lee replied quietly.

On his last visit to Northern Virginia, Lee was talking with friends who greeted him. A young mother brought her baby to him to be blessed. "What shall I teach him?" she asked. He took the infant in his arms, looked at it and the mother slowly, and said, "Teach him he must deny himself." This was the quality of the man.

While still commanding the Army of Northern Virginia, he was thought by his comrades to have almost superhuman ability and insight. As sober and independent a soldier as "Stonewall" Jackson said he would follow Lee into battle blindfolded. Even when he was retreating from the Northern onslaught, the Confederate Congress expressed its complete faith in Lee, and offered him dictatorial powers over the waning Confederacy. He craved no such power. At the Appomattox surrender John S. Wise said, "You are the country to these men. They have fought on for you without pay or clothes, or care of any sort; their devotion to you and faith in you have been the only things which have held this army together." It was the type of devotion Charlemagne, Arthur, and Napoleon had elicited. At the moment of darkest defeat Lee preserved his legendary aura. Grant's uniform was muddy and spotted; Lee's was immaculate.

Southerners admired his humility and earnestness in peace as much as his audacity and brilliance in war. The sacrosanct Lee was the solitary, noble figure in his twilight years, clad in a gray uniform from which all the Confederate buttons had been removed, making his way to a ravaged Virginia village to begin life anew. The impact of his death, a few years later, was felt by tens of thousands. At Lee's own college the editor of the *Southern Collegian* wrote: "We stop our paper from going to press in order to make the saddest announcement which our pen ever wrote. Our honored and loved president is no more. He died as he lived, calmly and quietly, in the full assurance of the Christian's faith."

The Lee Memorial Association, formed the day the General was buried, was composed largely of his ex-soldiers. The women would not be outdone in devotion; shortly afterwards feminine admirers met in a Richmond parlor and instituted the Ladies' Lee Monument Association. So successful was it that by 1887 they were able to lay the cornerstone of a sixty-foot statue of the General bedecked with sash and cavalry sword, mounted on Traveller. The twenty years between Lee's death and the statue mark the militaristic period of the hero-worship. Then Lee epitomized for Southerners their military command, their courageous defense, their honor salvaged from defeat.

The earliest Lee book appeared a few months after the surrender. Coming from the Richardson Press in New York, it was entitled *Southern Generals, Who They Are, and What They Have Done.* The publisher did not list the author, Captain Willian Parker Snow, C. S. A., until a second edition appeared a year later. Post-war anthologies, such as Emily Mason's *Southern Poems of the War.* also played up Lee of the battlefield. While Lee's own history of his campaigns was abandoned in 1866, three former associates, John W. Jones, Jubal Early, and Walter Taylor, wrote reminiscenses. Edward Lee Childe's biography appeared in France as early as 1874. Lee was carefully studied by the Prussian militarists in that decade. On a popular level, too, he proved an apt subject for Judith McGuire, Emily Mason, and James Lynch. The most readable early Lee novel was John Esten Cooke's *Mohun, or the Last Days of Lee and His Paladins.* (We have met Cooke before among the hero-makers of Pocahontas.) His book, begun just after Lee's death, gave a vivid contemporary account of Lee's career and leadership.

The first writer who moulded Lee's reputation sufficiently to deserve the title of hero-maker was an ex-Confederate private,

Talbott Sweeney. He sought a line of justification that would satisfy the skeptical Yankees. A native of Williamsburg, Sweeney studied at the College of William and Mary, and in 1849 entered the law school there. When the Civil War came he enlisted in the Williamsburg Guards. Later he served as head of the State Mental Asylum in Williamsburg, which was occupied by the Fifth Pennsylvania Cavalry in 1862. At sixty he set out to show that on Northern as well as Southern principles Lee's action in joining the Confederacy was justified, and to give him a national rather than a regional standing.

Sweeney's vindication was based on simple premises, though adorned with elaborate generalizations. If by following the dictates of a conscience Robert E. Lee was a traitor, then so were Oliver Cromwell, Patrick Henry, and George Washington. If Lee's interpretation of his loyalty to the Constitution was erroneous, then so were those of the patriots who wrote it and the legislators who adopted it. By reproducing excerpts from the Constitutional Convention in Massachusetts, Connecticut, New York, and Virginia, he made a strong case, and concluded with this tribute to the former Confederate chieftain:

"The shades of your patriotic and distinguished Revolutionary ancestors appeared to your vision and pointed out to you the only path which you could and should tread. . .But what shall be said of the reputation of Robert Edward Lee? Steeped in the red and black of Treason and Perjury, as his enemies declare? What monstrous and wicked absurdity and stupidity to think it" [1]

Sweeney was not the first writer to vindicate Lee; but he was one of the cleverest, and the first who got much of a hearing in the North. Influential Republicans wanted to make an example of Lee, the arch-traitor; but some of their colleagues, seeing that this would only create a martyr, opposed the idea. With the gradual emergence of a more tolerant point of view, and the healing of the open wounds of battle, Sweeney's Lee came forward. He was a man who had many other non-military claims to fame. Slowly the North came to view him not as a traitor but as a servant to his own high principles. In order to be shown as more than a mere soldier, Lee had to be championed by writers whose interest was not military, and extolled on different levels.

During the 1890's his story began to reach a larger American reading public through four new channels. Lee first appeared in an encyclopedia in 1890, when Nathan Burnham Webster did a sketch for *Chamber's Encyclopedia*. Appleton Company's "Great Commanders" series, was the first to be included in such a collection. Five years later William P. Trent's *Robert E. Lee* appeared in the "Beacon Biographies" series; during the same year George Marouby's *Robert Lee, Generalissime des Etats Confederes du Sud* was published in Paris in the Feron-Vrau "Les Contemporains" series.

Significant too were the juveniles. Whenever a hero reaches a position that necessitates his story being presented to children, he has arrived. G. A. Henty's *With Lee in Virginia* was well received and reissued twice in the next decade. Mary L. Williamson's *The Life of General Robert E. Lee, for Children, in Easy Words,* was widely read after 1895. In these and other accounts Southerners, while not belittling the achievement of Lee between 1861 and 1865, accentuated instead his greatness in the period 1865-1870. He had opposed removing Confederate bodies from Northern graves, on the grounds that this would increase antipathy. Whenever he had appeared in parades with officers of the adjoining Virginia Military Institute (where "Stonewall" Jackson had taught) he marched out of step, so as not to seem militaristic. He had even chastised a Washington College faculty member who scoffed at General Grant, and forbad him ever to do so again in his presence. Thus he won a spiritual victory.

The North, which after 1876 rejected the radical Republicans, sensed the importance of Lee's gestures and the extent of his magnanimity. Such a realization was expressed by a former Federal soldier who faced Lee's soldiers at Gettysburg, and represented the quintessence of New Englandism. He stands with the leading Lee hero-makers. Charles Francis Adams was a member of the only American family whose continuous leadership rivalled that of Lee's —a fact to be kept in mind here. Like Lee, he was trained to think and act in terms of family; like Lee, he was to know defeat more often than triumph in his life.

Son of the Union's Civil War Ambassador to Great Britain, Adams entered the U. S. Army as a first lieutenant. He was released to civilian life in 1865, a physical wreck, with the brevets of a brigadier general. No one would have expected him to call the country's attention to the genius of the leader of the Rebellion. Yet on October 13, 1901, Adams read to the American Antiquarian Society a paper called "The Confederacy and the Transvaal: A People's Obligation to Robert E. Lee." By prohibiting guerrilla warfare and preaching reconciliation, Lee had saved both North and South much misery, and avoided a possible repetition of Boer War tactics. The personality of Lee intrigued Adams, who during the next year prepared three papers which shocked Massachusetts; "Shall Cromwell Have a Statue?" "Lee at Appomattox," and "The Constitutional Ethics of Secession." If Fitzhugh Lee's acceptance of a major generalship in the United States Army during the Spanish American War helped bring together the South and the North, these studies by an Adams helped reconcile the North to the South.

Adams saw that the public attitude towards Lee was changing very rapidly, and said so in *Lee at Appomattox and Other Papers*. The criticism which his essays had drawn forth in his own section, Adams noted, "was in no case couched in the declamatory, patriotic strain, at once injured, indignant, and denunciatory or vituperative, which would no less assuredly than naturally have marked it thirty years ago."

George H. Denny, then president of Washington and Lee University, invited Adams to make the Lee Centennial address on January 19, 1907. A large crowd, including many who had studied under the General at Washington College, gathered to hear a former enemy of Lee praise him. "The situation," as Adams told his audience, "is thus to a degree dramatic."

In a carefuly phrased speech, a high point in Lee oratory, Adams placed him among the greatest Americans, not for his triumphs in the battlefield, but for those of his own mind. If Lee-the-soldier had been unable to save the Confederacy, Lee-the-citizen had helped preserve the United States. To overestimate this service would be difficult. The Yankee closed his speech with a quotation from another hero worshipper, Thomas Caryle: "Whom shall we consecrate and set apart as one of our sacred men? Whom do you wish to resemble? Him you set on a high column that all men looking at it may be continually appraised of the duty you expect from them." As he spoke, his audience gazed past him to the Lee monument.

Adams was Lee's most effective Northern apologist. Competition for such a distinction was keener in the South since most Confederates who could put pen to paper wrote something about the noble Lee. If one Southern hero-maker must be chosen, it should be Thomas Nelson Page. Born on a Virginia plantation in Hanover County, son of a Confederate officer and great-grandson of two state governors, Page grew up with praises of Lee ringing in his ears. He entered Washington College while Lee was still president there. To Page, the South was the recognized field of romance. Robert E. Lee, astride his white horse, led the field. He wrote his popular Lee biography "in obedience to a feeling that as the son of a Confederate soldier, as a Southerner, as an American, I owe it to my country." Never has a hero been more lovingly presented. "His monument," Page concluded, "is the adoration of the South: his shrine is in every Southern heart." At least in Page's heart, this statement was verified.

Between 1910 and 1930, Lee was metamorphosized from a figure idolized wherever the Stars and Bars had flown, to one admired everywhere. It is hard today to understand the stir caused in 1912 when the Massachusetts biographer, Gamaliel Bradford, published his *Lee, the American*. Bradford indicated Lee was no longer a mere military hero. No Southerner could have handled his subject with greater sympathy and warmth. Die-hard Yankees winced when they read it.

Lee's admirers considered him a man of infinite dignity and almost ascetic self-effacement. That Bradford, so different from Lee in training and experience, could grasp this was quite an accomplishment. Literary figures flocked to Lee's banner in the twentieth century, as historians had done in the nineteenth. Playwright John Drinkwater depicted Lee as a latter-day English country squire. Mary Johnston approached the General, who "exhibited sunny shreds of the Golden Age," with reverence. Lee was the impeccable hero of Ellen Glasgow's *The Battleground*, a soldier who held an army together with his personality. Most Southern magazines, and many Northern ones, published Lee poetry. Of all the literati who dealt with him, Stephen Vincent Benet has left the deepest mark.

Once again it was a Yankee who best stated Lee's case.

Native of Pennsylvania, Benet graduated from Yale in 1919. His first novel, *Young Adventure*, appeared in 1921. Seven years later he completed *John Brown's Body*. It won the Pulitzer Prize and revitalized interest in General Lee and the Civil War. For Benet, Lee was not a man of ice but of fire, who "gripped life like a wrestler with a bull, impetuously." At the end of a compelling description of Lee in Book Four, he writes:

> *"His heart was not a stone but trumpet-shaped*
> *And a long challenge blew an anger through it*
> *That was more dread for being musical*
> *First, last, and to the end. Again he said*
> *A curious thing to life.*
> *I'm always wanting something."*

Later Benet describes the last dreadful days before the Confederate surrender. One of the Southern soldiers says of General Lee:

> *"I never knew a man could look so still*
> *And yet look so alive in his repose.*
> *It doesn't seem as if a cause could lose*
> *When it's believed in by a man like that. . .*
> *But there is nothing ruined in his face,*
> *And, nothing beaten in those steady eyes.*
> *If he's grown old, it isn't like a man,*
> *It's more the way a river might grow old."*

The awe which Benet expressed for Lee has become more prevalent in recent years. Much has been made of Lee's religious qualities. The memorial window of Lexington's R. E. Lee Memorial Episcopal Church bears the inscription, "Numbered with Thy Saints in Glory Everlasting." The United Daughters of the Confederacy procured a memorial to General Lee in the National Cathedral in Washington, D. C. The inscription proves the rebel hero is now recognized as a national figure: "To General Robert E. Lee, a great Soldier to be placed in his proper rank among soldiers, a great Patriot to represent his native state and the Confederate States of America in their proper perspective in the nation's history, a great Churchman to have fitting recognition in his chosen church."

A Southern writer established himself among the chief Lee hero-makers, with a scholarly and weighty contribution. Years of work went into Douglas Southall Freeman's *R. E. Lee*. Seldom in the evolution of an American hero has the authority of a single biographer been so great. Born in Lynchburg, Virginia, in 1886, Freeman edited the Richmond *News Leader* for years, writing as an avocation on Lee and the Civil War. He opposed the historical vogue of debunking that prevailed during the early years of his career. In 1934 he dealt two blows at the specialists in smartness and light—his own dignified biography, and the Moore lectures at Dartmouth. In the foreword to *R. E. Lee* he wrote, "His quiet life, as engineer and educator, did not lend itself to the 'new' biography which is already becoming conventionalized. Neither was there any occasion to attempt an 'interpretation' of a man who was his own clear interpreter."

His Dartmouth lectures attacked the mediocre debunkers and their psychography. That the model he studied most assiduously was Boswell's life of Johnson helps explain his attitude towards the man whose career he traced so carefuly. Supplementing the four-volume biography were his *Calendar of Confederate Papers*, *Lee's Dispatches*, and three volumes on *Lee's Lieutenants, A Study in Command*.

Freeman employed two techniques which revealed the General in a new light. They highlighted effectively Lee's special genius. The first was the "fog of war technique." Military historians must relate only that which a given soldier knows at a given time. Since the man being discussed could not see on the other side of the hill, the writer must never judge him as if he could, or tell what actually occurred on the other side until he has completed the immediate picture. The second involved the conception of the problem of command. This is always a general's great problem. Those who command form a team which must work together. Coordinating this team is the commander-in-chief's primary function. Seen in this light, a general's apparent mistakes and retreats may fit into a much larger pattern in terms of which they can be justified or explained.

After these meticulous studies had been published, and Lee's life examined as carefuly as documents allowed, the South breathed more easily. Lee emerged in fact the pure and spotless character he had long been in tradition. No major blemish was discovered. Minor points had to be corrected; but Lee's right to a seat among great Americans was validated.

In tht middle of the Depression, devotees of Lee collected $250,000 to purchase Stratford Hall, the ancestral Lee home, and designate it a public shrine. When it was dedicated by the Robert E. Lee Memorial Foundation on October 12, 1935, Freeman gave the chief address. To many he was fittingly identified with the hero he had enshrined.

There are many legends about the birth and death of Lee. One maintains that Lee's mother was pronounced dead, actually interred, and later resuscitated, during her pregnancy. Even cautious historians have repeated and endorsed this. Other stories cluster around Lee's death. At the time there was no suitable coffin at Lexington. One floated mysteriously down the North River, sent by an unseen power. Actually two boys did find a coffin which was being shipped from Richmond to a local undertaker; it had been washed away from the packet landing by flood waters. On this basis tales of the mysterious coffin arose and still flourish.

The product of an agrarian civilization, Lee had a profound love of nature and the land. At the height of his military glory, he admitted he would have preferred to be on a small farm. His greatest joy in late life was to take long rides about the country on Traveller. His code was marked by its directness and simplicity. The God he venerated was the anthropomorphic deity of the Old Testament, and Lee was humble before Him all his life. He began and ended every day on his knees, believing literally in the Scriptures and God's participation in human affairs. Next to God came the family. To his wife and children Lee gave full devotion, and never tired of visiting and entertaining his many relatives. At parties he always preferred the company of women to men, and of daughters to mothers. Like Lord Chesterfield, he believed so much in the society around him that his acts not only followed but set the style.

Those concerned with family roots and continuity naturally

make much of Lee. His family record, stretching back even before Thomas Lee became the only native Virginian to be appointed Royal Governor, is impressive. Robert E. Lee IV graduated from Washington and Lee in 1949; the traditions still survive. Yet more than most American heroes, Robert E. Lee reached his pinnacle by accident. He would not have been idolized had not the Civil War occurred when it did. The war made that man, and not vice versa. Once we have studied the personality of Washington, Jefferson, or Lincoln, we can scarcely conceive of their not saving stamped their own character on their age. Certainly Lee would have lived a good life, and like so many Lees before him, won a niche in our history. But it was the military secession, and especially the South's inability to consummate it, that made him the dominant figure he now is.

Robert E. Lee was almost too good to make a universal hero. If only he had displayed more of the tragic flaws or emotional outbursts that make men sons of Adam! Even Dr. Freeman said that Washington was more interesting to study than Lee, simply because he seemed more human. We know what Lee did as a soldier and as a college administrator. Most of the rest, as with Hamlet, is silence. He did not write books or make speeches to justify himself. Never did he exploit his appeal or reputation; he refused to act consciously in the heroic manner. This was just as well. It is the inner, not the outer, man we admire.

Edwin Alderman, president of the University of Virginia, once said, "Some wonder why Virginia and the South give to General Lee a sort of intensity of love that they do not give even to Washington. Lee is a type and an embodiment of all the best of the state. Its triumphs, its defeats, its joys, its sufferings, its rebirths, its pride, its patience center to him. In that regnant figure of quiet strength may be discerned the complete drama of a great stock."[2]

Every major hero has local shrines, preserved and visited by his admirers. In the case of Lee, Arlington and Stratford Hall head the list. Also included are the Lee House in Richmond (present home of the Virginia Historical Society), various battlefields, bridges, and structures connected with Lee's military exploits, the Appomattox area, and the Lexington area. Lee Chapel, on the campus of Washington and Lee University, is his special sanctuary. In this

Victorian edifice, which Lee himself built, his body is interred, and his office and keepsakes are displayed. Valentine's recumbent statue of Lee was placed in the chapel in 1883. Wherever the visitor sits there, he gazes at the serene marble face of the General asleep on the field of battle. On either side stand venerated emblems of the Lost Cause, Confederate battle flags. Underneath the statue is the Lee family crypt. Whenever cadets from the adjoining Virginia Military Institute pass, they cease talking and salute the dead leader of the Army of Northern Virginia. Here lies an American saint.

The real sanctuary of Robert E. Lee is in the hearts and minds of people. For many he is the peerless soldier, the General on a white charger who defended the South. For the historian, he is a key figure of middle American history, whose decision to lead the Southern army, and later to surrender and urge reconciliation, shaped the national destiny. For the philosopher, he symbolizes an unmachined, agrarian way of life, which trusted in a simplicity abandoned in our age of technology. For the aristocrat, he is the model planter and the gentleman, an American embodiment of *noblesse oblige*. For the poet and novelist, he is the silent enigma, the romantic Cavalier who said little but did much. For the educator, he is the college president whose innovations revitalized Southern education. For the churchman, Lee is the undeviating Christian, whose trust in his God never faltered. For the genealogist, he is the flower of a great American family, the best proof that blood will tell. For the soldier, he is a military genius who said that duty is the sublimest word in the English language.

Every schoolboy knows the pronouncement of Light Horse Harry Lee about George Washington: "First in war, first in peace, first in the hearts of his countrymn." In the South the tribute no longer belongs to Washington who made the most of victory, but to the son of Light Horse Harry Lee, who made the most of defeat.

CHAPTER 7

Rugged Individualism: Billy the Kid

"Billy the Kid, he met a man
Who was a whole lot badder.
He didn't kid. Now Billy's dead
And we ain't none the sadder."
—Folk ballad

Billy the Kid is the "No" to the great American "Yes."

He was mean as hell, and killed 21 men before he was 21—not counting Indians and Mexicans.   A living legend in his teens, Billy was seldom seen by his pursuers. Those who did catch sight of him told of a gray horse, saddled and bridled, galloping along seemingly riderless except for a leg thrown across the saddle and an arm sticking out from beneath the horse's neck. At the end of the arm a gun barrel glinted in the sunlight.   And few who saw this ever came to tell of it.

This elusive phantom rider lived a full life before he was old enough to vote, and died just as he should have: with his boots on and his gun roaring.

The saga of Billy the Kid—his real name was William H. Bonney—is the most important desperado tale in our culture. The people of the Southwest sensed its importance even before Billy was caught up by immanent justice. When he took careful aim and shot Billy on July 14, 1881, Sheriff Pat Garrett knew he was performing the most important act of his life. His later descriptions showed awareness that he was serving posterity. The editor of the Santa Fe *Weekly Democrat* was equally enlightened, closing his account of Billy's death with these words:

"No sooner had the floor caught his descending form which had

85

a pistol in one hand and a knife in the other, than there was a strong odor of brimstone in the air, and a dark figure with wings of a dragon, claws of a tiger, eyes like balls of fire, and horns like a bison, hovered over the corpse for a moment, and with a fiendish laugh said, 'Ha, ha! This is my meat!' and then sailed off through the window. He did not leave his card, but he is a gentleman well known to us by reputation, and thereby hangs a 'tail'."

Yet Billy was not the type of person you'd look at twice on the street. He was slight, tipping the scales at 140 pounds and standing five feet eight. Like Joseph, Dhruva Karna, and Abe Lincoln, he was an "Unpromising Hero." Unassuming and quiet, he moved like a panther, peering out of gray eyes. His face was long, his hair light brown, his skin colorless, his hands and feet tiny. A good dancer and companion, he got along famously with the women, and assumed the airs of a dandy in town. The most conspicuous thing about him were his protruding front teeth, which led historian Dixon Wecter to classify him as an "adenoidal farm boy with a rifle," the type described by the cliché "dirty little killer." Frank Hall called him "the most desperate and bloody-minded civilized white man that ever cursed the border." Dr. Chesmore Eastlake, upon studying the one bona fide Bonney photograph, went to the length of diagnosing him as an "adenoidal moron and a coward." Nevertheless, he is the most admired bad man in our history.

It is impossible to say just what Billy was or did, because the legendary veneer has hidden the historical truth underneath. Even tabulating all the imposters who claimed to be Billy the Kid is difficult. A story that appeared in the *National Police Gazette* a month before Bonney's death, claimed the real Kid was actually a Colorado bandit named Billy LeRoy. (Burton Rascoe later proved a *Gazette* staff member named Richard K. Fox had dreamed up LeRoy.) In 1881 Thomas F. Daggett issued *The Life and Deeds of Billy LeRoy, Alias The Kid, King of American Highwaymen,* which was reprinted in 1883. The *National Police Gazette* for August 13, 1881 claimed the real Billy was a New York City fourth ward rough named Michael McCarthy, who specialized in butcher knife killings. This fostered a thriller called *The Life* of *Billy the Kid; A Juvenile Outlaw,* which reached the 100,000 circulation figure. Francis W. Doughty's *Old King Brady and Billy the Kid; Or The Great Detective's Chase* (1890) still had McCarthy as Billy.

Meanwhile, Billy had become enough of a figure to appear on the famous Beadle and Adams dime novel list. Europe discovered him too, via Le Baron de Mandat-Grancey's *La Breche aux Buffles* (Paris, 1889). In "The Cowboy's Christmas Ball," which appeared in Lawrence Chittenden's *Ranch Verses,* Billy became "Windy Billy;" so he remained in an anthology called *Cowboy Life.* In 1949 an oldtimer named Joe Chisholm said the real "Billy" was a Texas cowboy named Billy Claiborne, who was killed at Tombstone. These and many others have turned up with a "true" Billy the Kid; in 1950 an old man got in the news by re-stating the claim for himself and asking for a pardon from the Governor of New Mexico. "The Son of Billy the Kid" even showed Billy on the screen as a plump, balding banker; but in most celluloid appearences he is an Adonis dressed for the range.

Despite all these claimants and variations, there is no doubt of Bonney's authenticity and cussedness. The blood he spilled liberally in the Southwest was real blood. Underneath all the legend there was some reality.

William H. Bonney was born in New York City (of all places) on November 23, 1859, the son of William H. and Kathleen Bonney. During the Civil War the family moved to Coffeyville, Kansas, where the father died. The mother went to Colorado, and married a man named Antrim. By 1868 they turned up in Silver City, New Mexico. Here Billy reputedly killed his first man, a blacksmith who insulted his mother. Next Bonney and a partner supposedly killed three Indians for the furs they were carrying. Fleeing to the Pecos Valley, Billy was employed there by an early cattle baron, J. H. Tunstall.

Quickly sucked into the Lincoln County cattle war, he saw Tunstall killed by a posse of the Murphy faction, and Tunstall's partner shot, Bible in hand, before his burning house. Such sights were not designed to tame a man of Bonney's naturally sanguine temperament. He became a savage killer, putting his rare nimbleness to effective use. Tales spread of his incredible speed and accuracy with a gun. It was said that he practiced shooting by picking snowbirds off fenceposts at a gallop. Anyway, he definitely picked off Sheriff James A. Brady and a deputy, and refused to surrender when urged to do so by Governor Lew Wallace, who tried to bring peace to the territory.

When the shooting stopped, Billy concentrated on cattle stealing with such success that leading ranchers persuaded an Irishman named Pat Garrett to become sheriff and track down his gang. Garrett captured Billy and the desperado was condemned to death in 1881. But the Lincoln jail could not hold him; despite handcuffs and leg irons, he killed his guards and escaped. Two and a half months later he was trapped at Pete Maxwell's house in Fort Sumner, ambushed in a pitch black room by Garrett, and killed. Such is the outline of his career as it was written in ink, lead, and blood. Yet the story does not stop there. It goes on endlessly—in books, ballets, and movies, finding in the American imagination a fertile seed bed for enhancement.

Take, for example, his way with women. After his capture Billy was handcuffed and placed on the bare floor of an unheated adobe hut. Soon he was shaking from cold and exposure. An Indian girl named Deluvina pulled off her shawl and wrapped it around his shoulders. To her he gave the tintype that is perhaps his only authentic likeness in existence.

Not that Billy confined his activities to the lower end of the social scale. Miss Sally Chisum, chatelaine of her uncle's great mansion on the Pecos, and social arbiter of the county, found Billy as attractive as had the outcast Indian, Deluvina. Eugene Young reports euphemistically that "for many months she enjoyed the companionship of the killer." Sally herself has gone on record thus: "Billy had many admirable qualities. In all his personal relations with me he was the pink of politeness and as courteous a little gentleman as I ever met."

Another time Bonney (at least so the writer of a 1942 movie called *Law and Order* insisted) learned of an injustice done to a lady whose protector, an army lieutenant, had been shot. He took the place of the murdered man to save the fortune of blind Aunt Mary. After rounding up the lieutenant's slayers, he slipped away to become the hunted once more, his chivalric deed done. Females for miles around swooned with delight.

There are many stories about the lady Billy was visiting when Pat Garrett trapped and killed him. The kindest thing Billy's girl friend said to the sheriff was that he was too cowardly to meet Billy face to face; most of the other things are unprintable. Apparently pumping lead into his enemies was not Billy's only accomplishment. "In every placeta in New Mexico," attests Walter Noble Burns, "girls sing to their guitars songs of Billy the Kid. A halo has been clasped upon his scapegrace brow. The boy who never grew old has become a symbol of frontier knight-gallantry, a figure of eternal youth riding forever through a purple glamour of romance."

Billy was not so much contrived as endowed with traits of paragons of earlier cultures. In *The Hero: A Study in Tradition, Myth, and Drama* (New York, 1937), F. R. S. Raglan set up a dozen criteria for world folk heroes. Alfred Adler has been able to apply almost all of them to the heroic *Gestalt* of the Kid.[1] His birth, coming of age, initiation, consecration, inthronization, and mysterious death and burial all fit the age-old pattern. Yet the transformation of Bonney into Billy the Kid needed no intervening centuries. Two years before his death the wife of New Mexico's territorial governor referred to the Kid's boast that he had killed a man for every year of his life.[2] Bonney jumped from history into legend so rapidly that no one knows just what happened. Certainly four little-known Americans deserve more credit for the transition than Billy himself. This quartet was not of the literati. None of them had read Raglan's book or the folklore quarterlies. This doesn't seem to have hampered them. A fallen politician, a Texas cowpoke, a lawyer who preferred the outdoors to the court room, and an itinerant journalist helped give Billy his immortality. Ash Upson, Charlie Siringo, Emerson Hough, and Walter Noble Burns were their names. Hero making was their specialty.

Ash Upson is the major architect of the Kid's build-up. He recognized Billy's literary possibilities, sought out his slayer, and with him collaborated on an influential book. Marshall Ashmum Upson was born in Wolcott, Connecticut, in 1828. Like Ben

Franklin and Mark Twain, he got most of his education in a print shop. After a stint on James Gordon Bennett's New York *Herald*, he drifted westward to set up the Albuquerque *Press* and the Las Vegas *Mail*. For a while he dabbled in politics, serving as Adjutant-General of New Mexico. Unfavorable publicity, arising from his part in state speculation, drove him back to the printer's case. In 1881 he boarded with Pat Garrett, who that same year shot Billy the Kid. When Garrett decided to write a book about it, both to exonerate himself from charges that he had killed Bonney unfairly and to capitalize on the wide interest in the shooting, what was more natural than to turn to his literary housemate, Upson, for aid? Garrett himself was a man of action; words came hard. So, on his ranch near Roswell, he told the story to Upson who later confided:

"The book *Life of Billy the Kid* will be a success. Pat F. Garrett, sheriff of the county, who killed 'the Kid' and whose name appears as author of the work (though I wrote every word of it) as it would make it sell, insisted on taking it to Santa Fe, and was swindled in his contract. I live with Garrett, and have since last August. He seems *stuck* after me, and does not want to hear of my leaving." [3]

On March 12, 1882, the *Daily New Mexican* announced that the book was ready for sale, fifty cents a copy postpaid. Peremptorily titled *The Authentic Life of Billy the Kid, The Noted Desperado of the Southwest*, this slim volume of 137 pages is the fountainhead of most later Billy the Kid literature. It set the standard pattern of the Kid's career, from which few have deviated. What Bonney stories can be attributed to it? A dozen or more, even by a conservative count. We cannot analyze the book as we would a factual monograph; it is more literary than historical, doing for New Mexico what Mark Twain's *Roughing It* did for Nevada. Ash Upson considered himself a stylist. When he was trying to be grandiloquent he wrote such sentences as this: "The scintillating effervescence of genius hath succumbed to the practical life betwixt millstones of soup and pie, and once again I throw myself into the breach of common intercourse and condescend to mingle with the common herd." Fortunately for us, he spared *The Authentic Life* such diction.

Some of Billy's toughness got into the prose, as well as some
of Pat Garrett's plainness. Partiality is written on every page.
"All who ever knew Billy will testify that his polite, cordial, and
gentlemanly bearing invited confidence and promised protection—
the first of which he never betrayed, and the latter he was never
known to withhold." (Enter the notion that Billy was a chivalric
knight-errant, not a mere killer.) "If purity of conversation were
the test, hundreds of the prominent citizens of New Mexico would
be taken for desperadoes sooner than young Bonney." (Add a
dash of Sir Galahad.) "The aged, the poor, the sick, the unfortunate and helpless never appealed to Billy in vain for succor."
(Here comes Robin Hood.) "Billy was, when circumstances permitted, scrupulously neat and elegant in dress." (Put in a pinch
of Beau Brummel.) And so it goes, until a perfect and authentic
hero emerges.

Upson garnishes Billy's shady early years with glory. Among
the unverified activities and incidents that he expounds are these:
that the Kid was adept at cards when eight; that he knifed a loafer
who insulted his mother; that he killed three Apaches in Arizona;
that he killed a soldier blacksmith at Fort Bowie; that he took
up with a Mexican named Melquidez Segura, and raised hell
South of the Border; that he saved a wagon train, killing eight
Apaches with a prairie ax; that he rode eighty-one miles in six
hours to free Segura from jail; that with O'Keefe he fought off a
band of Apaches in the Guadalupe Mountains; that he killed Buck-
shot Robert; that he rescued Charlie Bowdre when the latter was
captured by his enemies; and that he murdered a rough character
named Bernstein. Few later accounts have bothered to authenti-
cate the tales.

Upson was pleased with his efforts. "I am now engaged in
getting together data for a full history of the county," he wrote in
1882, "the Indian Wars, the Harold War, several less important
vignettes and the great cattleman's war from 1876 to 1880. This
will be published by subscription." It never was. Professor
Maurice G. Fulton, Upson's biographer, thinks Ash left a trunk
full of papers and clippings which got lost. Upson's rapid decline
in his later years is alluded to in his obituary in the Roswell
Register for October 31, 1894. "He lived for forty years in viola-

tions of every law of health, and nothing but an incomparable vitality kept him alive for years. His many friends will regret to learn of his death, although it was not unexepected." Commented Maurice Fulton: "To put it more bluntly, Ash Upson drank himself to death."

*   *   *

Charles Siringo believed in finding out about Western life first hand. An old stove-up cow puncher, he gave his book *A Texas Cowboy* the colorful subtitle, "Fifteen Years on the Hurricane Deck of a Spanish Pony." Distributed by five different publishers for forty five years, it has sold over a million copies. To his many readers he brought word of the bloodthirstiest man that ever drew a revolver—Billy the Kid.

Siringo always played on the same three themes: his own experience as cowboy and detective, the role of bad men in the West, and the innate greatness of Billy the Kid. These sustained him and carried him from Texas to Hollywood, where he was technical adviser on western movies until his death in 1928. Real cowhands have vouched for the authenticity of Siringo's stories. *A Texas Cowboy* became the cowboy's Bible. "I camped one night at the old LX Ranch and they showed me an old forked tree where some bronc had bucked Charlie Siringo," Will Rogers wrote. "It was like looking at the Shrine of Shakespeare to some of those 'deep foreheads'." Written with glow and glee, it still sells in both cloth and paperback editions. Had this book been the only one to deal with the Kid, Bonney would still have been famous.

A high point is Siringo's meeting Billy on the LX range in the winter of 1878-79. The event kept growing in importance in Siringo's mind. *A Lonestar Cowboy* (1919) contained new details. Now he recalled giving the Kid his new ten-dollar meerschaum cigar holder, which Billy countered with "a finely bound novel which he had finished reading." (To see Billy as a collector of rare books requires inspired vision.) A year later Siringo wrote *The History of "Billy the Kid"* which added fuel to the legendary blaze. The Kid's romance with Dulcinea del Toboso, "the magnet that drew the Kid back to Fort Sumner when he should have hit the trail for Mexico after his escape from the Lincoln jail," was unfolded. The author remembered he had won Billy's Winchester rifle in a raffle at Stinking Springs, and revealed his admiration for his killer-hero with an account of his own campaign to place a lasting monument at the Kid's grave.

No one got the story of Billy over to so many people so well as Charlie Siringo. His significance as a hero-maker (especially in Hollywood) far surpassed his importance as a writer or historian. As J. Frank Dobie has pointed out, "He had almost nothing to say on life, but reported actions. He put down something valid on a class of lives, as remote now from the Atomic Age as Ramses II." [4] Far from annoying us, this remoteness attracts us. The fact that there can never be another Billy the Kid with a gray horse, with blazing six-shooters and the open range to cavort in, gives him a perspective of wild delight.

Emerson Hough, son of an Iowa farmer, spent most of his life looking west. Graduating from the Iowa State law school in 1880, he craved the excitement that Horace Greeley had promised those whose blood was sufficiently red. Teddy Roosevelt (who was one of Hough's idols) could not have conceived of a more desirable young chap. Aggressive, patriotic, hero-loving, Hough was a human Bull Moose.

The road west led him to White Oaks, New Mexico, where he put out his shingle in 1883. Nothing happened. On the rare occasions when potential clients stopped by, they learned he had gone out to collect folklore and stories in the turbulent back country. Or else he was heading out for Yellowstone Park on skis.

Neither legal acumen nor ski trips won for Hough a place in our story; but a horse and buggy jaunt around New Mexico with Pat Garrett did. As a direct result of that excursion he wrote "The True Story of A Western Bad Man," which came out in the September, 1901 *Everybody's Magazine.* It was one of the shortest pieces which ever worked a long-range shift in a hero's reputation.

The article, like many of Hough's books, dealt with Billy the Kid, "whose equal for sheer inborn savagery," he wrote, "has never lived." Hough saw the outlines of a pitchfork where others had only seen a six-shooter. To him Billy was a person of cosmic evil. "Providence alone knows through what miscarriage in the countless aeons of evolution the soul of some fierce and far-off carnivor got into the body of this little man, this boy, this fiend in tight boots and a broad hat."

The Story of the Outlaw, his next book, developed the notion of the struggle between good and evil further, and even gave Bonney's story an allegorical flavor. Pat Garrett became Justice as he tracked down this *Daemon Americanus* in the stark emptiness of New Mexico. To succeed he had to have almost superhuman ability, which Hough bestowed on him in anecdotal form. Once, the author writes, he saw Garrett put five bullets into a small post-card nailed on a distant tree, then say, "I'll be particular about the sixth and shoot the stamp off the corner." He did. At least it made a good story; one which helped damn Billy the Kid right into immortality.

Ranking with Upson, Siringo, and Hough is a fourth publicist who was the best writer of the lot. Born in Kentucky in 1872, Walter Noble Burns became a journalist while in his teens, and wandered westward to St. Louis, Denver, and San Francisco. There he boarded the brigantine *Alexander,* sailed off to the South Seas, and wrote his first popular book, *A Year with a Whaler.* He also had a go at the Spanish-American War, but struck his richest literary vein when he decided to write about the untamed west. *Tombstone, The One Way Ride,* and *The Robin Hood of El Dorado* all sold well; but it was his *Saga of Billy the Kid* (1926) that landed him among the myth-makers of American history.

Burns took up and developed the Bonney stories which Siringo had stopped working with after 1920, reviving and increasing the existing interest. His restatements were so clever that they started a chain reaction of Bonney pieces in the movies and magazines. To him Billy was as enticing and colorful a rogue as Robin Hood (on whom he modeled a good many Bonney escapades), Dick Turpin, and Fra Diavolo; he was convinced the Kid was destined to a mellow and genial immortality. Frozen egotism plus reck-lessness and minus mercy, Billy had worked out the necessary formula, and "painted his name in flaming colors with a six-shooter across the sky of the Southwest."

With the "debonair courage of a cavalier" Billy possessed "the afflatus that made him the finished master." Onto the nineteenth century American scene, fate had placed the fragile and fiery figure of a lad "born to battle and vendetta, to hatred and murder, to tragic victory and ultimate defeat." It was a drama of Death and the Boy. Billy had something inside him that enabled him to defy destiny, "to wave Death a jaunty good-bye and ride off to new slaughter." The readers shuddered—and read on.

At last Billy had a backer whose technique was up to his heroic task. Burns could turn a mean metaphor, and coin an apt phrase; Billy's story genuinely interested and challenged this life-long journalist and handler of words. His mission was to turn various unrelated stories into a saga. Considering the impact his work had, he succeeded.

While the quartet was working out the grand strategy, publishers like Beadle and Adams were turning out gory pulps which took Billy right to the people. In *Silver-Mask, the Man of Mystery,* Billy held up the stage, kidnapped the heroine, shot up the town, and behaved like a first-rate hellion who took proper pride in his work. Street and Smith even co-featured him with Buffalo Bill, which was quite a compliment. *Buffalo Bill and Billy the Kid: or, The Desperadoes of Apache Land* (1906) saw the two of them dispose of two hundred Indians without getting a smudge on their beautiful blouses.

Billy's appeal has been felt on other levels as well. The distinguished musician Aaron Copland composed in 1938 a *Ballet Suite from Billy the Kid,* which was acclaimed in the highest music circles. *Notes* written for the first performance showed that Copland had got the feeling of the man he was dealing with: "Billy in prison is, of course, followed by one of his legendary escapes. Tired and worn in the desert, Billy rests with his girl. Starting from a deep sleep, he senses movement in the shadows. The posse has finally caught up with him. It is the end." But the end, as with all heroes, is merely the beginning.

Anyone who doubts this should study James C. Dykes' *Billy the Kid Bibliography* (1953), which documents fully the rising spiral of interest. Billy has permeated the American scene until his blackness has found a permanent place in our heroic spectrum. His passport to fame has been infamy.

So far we have dealt solely with written accounts of Billy. But the troubadour touch is more significant in the long run than the printer's. Oral legends, passed down from one generation to another, form a Homeric succession that goes on independently of the written word. Inexhaustible are the stories of Billy's cool courage and dramatic death. They are the stuff of which reputations are ultimately made. "As each narrative adds a bit of drama here and a picturesque detail there," notes folklorist B. A. Botkin, "one wonders what form these legends will assume in time, and in what heroic proportions Billy the Kid will appear in fireside fairy tales a hundred years or so from now." [5]

Just as much of Billy's fame is oral and not written, so also is much of it commercial and not historical. The mere term "Billy the Kid country" is a lure for tourists. As a source of revenue, Billy rivals the Grand Canyon or the Carlsbad Caverns, and is being advertised, merchandized, and exploited accordingly.

Meanwhile the situation Omar Barker portrays in *Billy the Kid Rides Again*, in which Billy is pursued across the sky by his numerous victims, is validated by recurring stories of boys playing Billy in jest and in earnest, for little stakes and big. Two Easterners imitating Billy recently held up a Southern Pacific train; another was inspired to kill a man, and paid for his re-enactment with his life. In *Pinon Country*, Haniel Long suggests that the New Mexican state museum establish a file under the heading "Results of Hero-Worshipping William Bonney." It would be a revealing one.

Yet Americans never forget that he got what was coming to him. The knowledge of this inexorable justice provides the catharsis lacking in lesser sagas. Billy's tale is the creation of the Protestant ethos. His contemporaries were not only Protestants, but Victorians, inherently sure that right was right and wrong wrong, with the twain never meeting. If they cried at his early death, they applauded whatever force demanded it.

William H. Bonney symbolized the pastoral epoch doomed by the railroad, the tractor, and the homesteader. He went down grimly with both guns roaring defiance and death. His particular crimes are dated, but his appeal is not. Twentieth-century readers like their heroes raw, with good red blood on them. Having read

the tough novels of Hemingway, Caldwell, and Faulkner, and seen
such iron-jawed movie idols as Bogart, Cagney, and Raft, they are
attracted to this juvenile killer. He went through all the scrapes
the movies have later contrived, without a fall guy or double. Even
with mirrors, the fictionists haven't been able to improve on
this fact.

Billy played his part superbly. The Las Vegas judge who sentenced him to be hanged wanted to make sure his dire pronouncement sank in. "You are sentenced to be hanged by the neck until
you are dead, dead, dead!" intoned the judge. "And you can go
to hell, hell, hell!" Billy retorted.

After he had been shot, the townspeople dragged Billy's body
across the street to a carpenters shop, where they stretched it out
on a bench. Candles were placed nearby, casting flickering shadows on the face of the hardened killer. The next day he was buried
in a borrowed white shirt too large for his slim form and placed in
a plain wooden coffin. Admirers scraped together $208 for a
simple gravestone, later splintered and carried away by relic
hunters. He had been on this earth exactly twenty-one years, seven
months and twenty-one days. That was long enough to create an
American legend.

"The Kid,' wrote Ash Upton, "had a lurking devil in him; it
was a good-humored, jovial imp, or a cruel and bloodthirsty fiend,
as circumstances prompted. Circumstances favored the worser
angel, and the Kid fell.' His damnable life ended with a deserved
death. Since God condemned, Americans have forgiven. May
God have mercy on his soul.

CHAPTER 8

Prince of the Plains: Buffalo Bill

"Caesar and Cicero shall bow
And ancient warriors famous
Before the myrtle-wreathed brow
Of Buffalo Williamus"
—Anonymous ballad

In no American do myth and reality clash more sharply than in Buffalo Bill Cody. He lived in two worlds at once and he tamed the Wild West sufficiently to bring it indoors. Glass balls supplanted eyeballs as scout's targets. The Western mirage found a permanent home in that verdant part of the imagination where buffaloes will always roam.

Long before a toupee was fitted to his balding leonine head, Cody was the Prince of the Plains. Could anyone imagine a more adventurous or satisfying life than his? Wherever he went, he made history. When he entered the arena on his white charger and said, "Ladies and gentlemen, permit me to introduce to you a Congress of Rough Riders of the World," spectators tingled. Children idolized him. Presidents, czars, kings, and potentates (according to his well-oiled legend) befriended him. Even Queen Victoria was entranced, and saluted the American flag at his show. Everywhere the name of Buffalo Bill was magic, for he personified the American dream.

But triumph turned to ashes in his handsome mouth. For years he dwelt in the shadows just outside the floodlights of sham hero worship. He knew what it was to be alone on the bone-haunted plains; in a creaking railroad car clicking off endless miles; in foreign lands. Women doted on him, but his own wife sought a

98

divorce. Men promised to devote their lives to him, but stayed only long enough to fleece him. Sick children improved at his touch. His only son died in his arms.

Galloping forward on his white horse, Cody looked as free as the air. Actually he was putty in the hands of shrewder men. Despite his large income and success, he finally petitioned the Federal government for the $10 monthly Congressional medal-holders' dole. Toward the end he had to perform daily to avoid bankruptcy, going through every show with the persistent fear of death in the arena. Here was poverty in opulence, despair in hollow triumph: the fulfillment of the American nightmare.

Born in Scott County, Iowa, in 1846, William Frederick Cody was the son of a farmer. When his father died of pneumonia in 1857, the young lad became the head of the family and went to work as an office boy on horseback for Russell and Majors. During the Civil War he was a jay-hawker who stole horses from slave owners, and a private in the Seventh Kansas Cavalry.[1] After marrying Louisa Frederici in 1866, he was employed by the Goddard Brothers to hunt buffaloes for construction crews of the Kansas Pacific Railroad. After eight months at this Cody claimed he had bagged 4,280 buffaloes. The legend of "Buffalo Bill" began to grow.

Vivacious and popular, Cody was greeted as he rode through camp by such ditties as:

> *"Buffalo Bill, Buffalo Bill,*
> *Never missed and never will;*
> *Always aims and shoots to kill,*
> *And the company pays his buffalo bill."*

Whether Cody surpassed other buffalo hunters is something else again. Charles Jesse Jones ("Buffalo Jones"), for example, outshone and outshot him without half trying. This Plains adventurer found our buffalo hunting so tame that he went after musk-oxen in the Arctic. There he hunted in temperatures of 50° below zero, was attacked by wolves, encountered hydrophobia among his animals, and beat off carnivorous insects. Yet who has ever heard of "Buffalo Jones"? No one but the buffaloes.

When construction work stopped, the buffalo market collapsed and Cody was out of work. He turned to civilian scouting for the Army and saw service under Generals Sheridan and Carr. By 1873 there was no further need of his specialty. The full-time plains career of America's best-known plainsman came to an abrupt end when he was in his early twenties.

Bill Cody reversed Horace Greeley's famous dictum. Eastward he went, taking the buffalo legend with him, searching for a job as coachman or fire engine driver. By the turn of the century he had become the hero of the plains by courtesy of Eastern huzzahs.

Nature had superbly fitted Cody for the heroic role. No one could have looked his role better than he. He towered over ordinary mortals, as had Washington and Lincoln; was fond of white horses, as were Alexander and Napoleon; and had a massive Olympian head, like Lee and Jefferson. Best of all, he had no inhibitions about believing Cody stories or about carrying them into his daily life. His was a world of naive wonder. He never learned to differentiate between what had happened in his life and what had been invented. To him myths were reality.

Cody's principal hero-makers were Ned Buntline, Prentiss Ingraham, and John Burke. Also helpful were Nate Salesbury, Texas Jack Omohundro, Dexter Fellows, Courtney Ryley Cooper, and Johnnie Baker. To them belongs credit for making Buffalo Bill the most highly publicized figure in Western history. What they did was not easy; no one should underestimate their endeavors. More spectacular men had to be outdistanced. Mountains had to be made out of molehills.

But let us not do Bill Cody an injustice. He had, after all, demonstrated that he was a virile fellow before he turned from the outdoor bison to the indoor Elks. For good and sufficient reasons Phil Sheridan, Wild Bill Hickok, and Frank North considered him one of their kind. The Wild West he domesticated for show purposes was basically authentic. The ballyhoo came up out of the East.

Mistaking Cody's later veneer for his true character, some have scoffed at him unfairly. Herbert Blake maintained that "Cody was not a great scout, not a great shot, and not an Injun fighter. He never killed an Injun in his entire career." In Irving Berlin's musical, *Annie Get Your Gun*, Buffalo Bill acted like a harmless blowhard. What the debunkers overlook is that what Cody was, not what he did, made him famous. His sense of timing was superb. He knew just when a grand gesture was fit and proper.

During an 1876 Baltimore performance, he received a telegram from General Sheridan saying the Sioux were on the war path. Would Cody return immediately to service as a scout with the United States Army? To put the question was to answer it. Without waiting for his cue, Cody dashed on stage, read the message, and announced he was through playing at war. The crowd roared as he dramatically departed for the station. When he arrived in Cheyenne, Wyoming, he was still wearing his theatrical black velvet suit with gold lace and silver buttons; and it was thus he joined the Fifth U. S. Cavalry.

Buffalo Bill "took the first scalp for Custer" and avenged his slaughter—or so the American public came to believe. Did Cody actually kill Chief Tall Bull or (as some intimate) was the tall bull in Cody's story? Conflicting versions make interesting but confusing reading. The *New York World* credited a Lieutenant Hayes with the Chief's death. In Cody's autobiography he claimed to have fired the fatal shot at 400 yards. Subsequent accounts had the Scout sneaking ever closer. By the time *True Tales* was published, the distance was down to 30 yards. When Cody decided to re-enact "with historical accuracy" the killing in his show, he disposed of Tall Bull with a knife.

Meanwhile his fellow campaigner Lute North swore under oath that his brother Frank North had killed the Indian. "I asked Frank why he didn't correct Cody, but he just laughed and said he wasn't in show business," Lute explained. Cody never tired of citing a newspaper account of the Tall Bull adventure which ended "Among those killed was the noted chief Tall Bull, killed by Cody, Chief of Scouts." The first nine words had actually appeared in the *New York Herald*, but not the last six.

Whether or not Buffalo Bill really did scalp Custer's slayer, he undoubtedly carried a scalp around with him for years afterwards. An exasperated army officer offered him $50 to get rid of the grisly trophy. Never a man to treat money lightly, Cody agreed, and mailed it off to his wife. Her tart reply indicated little appre-

ciation of the historical value in the upper portion of what might
have been Tall Bull, or of the claims of her husband.

"Will Cody, don't you ever send me another Indian scalp as
long as you live," she said.

"I'll do better than that," he replied. "I'll never scalp another
Injun!" He never did—except, of course, in dime novels and the
imagination of the world.

Cody didn't need new scalps to win friends and influence audiences; showmanship sufficed. Everything about him impressed
and delighted his contemporaries. Reputedly a man's man, he
cultivated a rich line of rhythmical profanity. Maledictions
rolled from his lips like liquor from a jug—and the jug itself
was not an object from which Bill was estranged. He was so
drunk when he enlisted for the Civil War that he evidently didn't
know what he was doing. The Western habit of taking a snort of
whiskey before breakfast he found "more refreshing than brush-
ing the teeth." Yet no amount of liquor could keep him from
stirring the heart of Indian squaw or European lady alike. They
loved him drunk or sober.

As the amount consumed during shows increased, his manager
made Bill sign a contract restricting himself to ten glasses of
whiskey a day. Clutching his dry throat, and noting that the contract said nothing about the glasses' size, he bought ten huge beer
seidels. The next audience, in Denver, guessed as much. Cody
swung his lasso with such telling effect that he had to his credit
that afternoon three calves, seven Indians, a lemonade vendor,
and the Mayor's wife.

No ceremony was so solemn as to take Bill's mind off the bottle.
Called upon to perform a marriage ceremony, he *ad libbed* briefly
before reaching the climactic line: "Whom God and Buffalo Bill
have joined let no man put asunder. Let's have a drink."

Men more subtle and sober than Bill made him a paragon.
Richard Walsh's well-documented biography tells the story of
Cody's rise.[2] The men most responsible for it, Buntline, Ingraham,
and Burke, form the greatest pressbox infield in the major league
of American reputations. No account of Clio's hero-makers can
ignore them.

Ned Buntline was, in an age of screwballs, an amazing character. Author of at least four hundred novels during his hectic lifetime (once he wrote a 60,000-word thriller in a week), he never invented a fictional character who lived a more incredible life than his own.[3] Born in Harpersfield, New York, in 1821, Buntline's real name was Edward Zane Judson. His father was an author and hero-maker in his own right. In addition to biographies of George Washington and Patrick Henry, the elder Judson wrote *Sages and Heroes of the American Revolution*.

Appointed a midshipman by Van Buren in 1838, young Edward soon showed what kind of chap he was. In a single day he challenged thirteen midshipmen to duels, fought seven, marked four opponents for life, and emerged unscratched. Next he participated in a Seminole Indian war, from which he returned telling how he had killed a large jaguar with his hands. Back in Paducah, Kentucky, he began a magazine called *Ned Buntline's Own*, employing the pen name he used thereafter.

In Eddyville, Kentucky, he captured two murderers single-handed and unarmed. Afterwards he himself killed William Porterfield, who had been rash enough to accuse Buntline of committing adultery with his wife. The citizens of Nashville thereupon lynched Ned and strung him to a tree. The rope broke. The Sheriff took Buntline back to jail, presumably to die. Ned had other plans. "I hasten to tell you I am worth ten men yet," he wrote a friend. "I expect to leave here for New York in three or four days." He had not yet begun to fight.

In the East he enjoyed double nuptial bliss, keeping one wife, Kate, in Westchester County, and another, Lovanche, in New York City. While commuting between homes he wrote *Ned Buntline's Own*. A leader in the 1849 Astor Place riot, in which 21 persons were killed, he was confined for a year on Blackwell's Island. This provided the opportunity to write a new series of novels. When released he was brought home on admirers' shoulders and honored with a torchlight parade. A prime mover in the Know-Nothing Party, Ned got so involved in political intrigue that he had to flee to the Adirondacks in 1856. Accepting his setback stoically, he proceeded to acquire a new home and wife there.

Soon the drums of civil war were beating. Buntline could never resist drums. As a member of the First New York Mounted Rifles, he was enlisted, promoted to sergeant, and dismissed from the service after a furlough which entailed, among other things, attempted marriage.   During his subsequent month's confinement at Fort Hamilton he turned out two novels, then headed west looking for new adventure and fresh copy.   At Fort McPherson he encountered a handsome young scout whom he decided to re-name "Buffalo Bill" and to feature in dime thrillers.   A new American hero was the result.

Cody's autobiography tells how Buntline looked that first day: "He was stoutly built, and wore a blue military coat.   On the left breast were pinned about twenty gold medals and badges of secret societies.   I told Major Brown he looked like a soldier—but what a good mark to shoot at on the left breast!"   Of all the decorations, the one the Scout coveted most had George Washington's head on a gold shield with two American flags crossed above it.   Cody invited Ned to ride his fiery horse, Powder Face.   Seeing how well he rode, Bill proposed that he help scout for Indians.   "I was to deliver a temperance lecture tonight," Buntline said, taking a drink; "but no lecture for me when there is a prospect of a fight!"

Buntline did not invent the nickname he gave his new friend. Even if he did not know of Cody's prowess as a buffalo killer (and it is hard to imagine that Cody kept it a dark secret), he probably chose it as one already popular on the frontier.   The *New York Weekly* announced in December, 1869, that Buntline had completed a novel on *Buffalo Bill: The King of the Border Men.*

Its hero was a literary descendant of that first historic Western hero, Daniel Boone.   That is to say, he was modelled on the Leatherstocking whom James Fenimore Cooper popularized. With Leatherstocking's garb and skills, Buffalo Bill was better fitted for Kentucky than Kansas.   Buntline was more concerned with what his readers wanted than with what plainsmen actually did.   He went to Cooper rather than to nature for details.

Buntline's hero was not hampered by facts.   Cody admitted he had arrived at Summit Springs, where Tall Bull met his death, four hours after the fighting.   The German woman whom the Indians had captured, Mrs. Weichel, was safe long before then. Not so in the dime novel.   There, Buffalo Bill arrived just as the Indian Chief was bringing down the tomahawk for the death blow.

Coming on at a full gallop, he grabbed the reins with one hand, drew his pistol and shot Tall Bull between the eyes with the other, and raised his star-spangled sombrero in a gentlemanly flourish to the rescued lady—presumably with a third hand.

This magnificent description was merely the beginning of Buntline's service to Cody. So impressed was he with his protege that he persuaded him to enter the theater. Buntline would write the play, and Cody would be the star. "Texas Jack" Omohundro (who hailed from Virginia) and Bill came east in December, 1876. Buntline had neglected to hire a cast, rent a theater, or write a play. While Cody and Omohundro rounded up extras on the Chicago streets, Ned procured a theater and started writing a suitable piece. Four hours later *The Scouts of the Plains* was completed and hotel bellhops were copying parts. Reporting on the play, and the conditions under which it was written, one vitriolic reviewer asked why it had taken so long to write; but most of them liked it anyway.

The man for whom buffaloes held no fear trembled when confronted with the footlights. Not so Buntline, who was so confident he could carry off his own part that he didn't bother to write out his lines. The Indians were to capture Cody and prepare for a meal of roast Buffalo Bill. "Texas Jack" and Buntline would save him from the burning stake and shout, "Now come on, you Redskins!" The trio would then avenge themselves on the newly-hired extras until all had died an excruciating death, and the audience was choking with smoke and emotion. They choked all right. From the moment Buntline rescued the utterly speechless Cody by asking, "Where have you been lately, Bill?" until the last Indian died, spectators cheered and applauded the West-brought-indoors. Buntline later wrote such sequels as *Buffalo Bill, Buffalo Bill's Best Shot*, and *Buffalo Bill's Last Victory*. With a man like this to dream up adventures, what chance had Cody to remain a mere mortal?

Buntline not only modelled Cody after the earlier pattern of the woodsman hunter; he also gave heroic continuity to the idea of Manifest Destiny. In appreciation, Cody wanted to name his son after Ned, but let himself be convinced that he was historically obligated to favor Kit Carson. In 1873 the restless Buntline tired

of the Prince of the Plains and moved on to other ventures. But
he had created an American legend, and made it flourish.

Before going, he introduced Cody to the man who continued this
work—"Arizona John" Burke (who came from the District of
Columbia).   Burke's early life was spent on the road, as stock-
company actor, acrobatic troupe manager, and free-lance journalist.   Meeting Cody changed his life: "I have met a god."   He
was to repeat this throughout the years spent visiting newspaper
offices, turning out stories and interviews, defending Cody against
slander, and inventing new myths to supplement those that succumbed to reality.   Toward the last, many dropped the aging
and decrepit Cody.   Burke stood by to the end.   It was for
"Arizona John" that Buffalo Bill called on his deathbed.

Burke, who knew just what he wanted his hero to become and
why, put aside his Prince Albert and his cultivated whiskers (worn
flying buttress style), and went "Western."   Gentleman Johnny
became Arizona John.   When Buntline and Cody separated, Burke
inherited the already thriving legend, and expanded both its basis
and its appeal.   Henry Nash Smith summed up his accomplishments in *Virgin Land*: "To Burke belongs the credit for carrying
through the major revision of the character of Buffalo Bill as Buntline had originally conceived it . . . He was to become an epic hero
laden with the enormous weight of universal history; to be placed
beside Boone and Fremont and Carson in the roster of American
heroes."

Burke so wedded fact and fancy that no completely reliable
biography of Cody has yet been, or ever will be written.   As
troupe manager, press agent, and personal advisor, he pedalled a
thesis about Cody.   "Buffalo Bill stands unchallenged as the
Chevalier Bayard of American bordermen; he was the guide to
the New World of the mighty West, and his name ranks with those
few immortals who were not born to die."   Untenable, rhetorical,
even ridiculous?   Cody's generation did not think so.   At this
distance, our forebears may appear gullible.   But since we are
at this distance, how can we say, never having seen Buffalo Bill
on his proud prancing white horse?

Burke found a female counterpart to the Plainsman and brought
her into prominence.   Little Annie Oakley, girl sharpshooter who

ranks with Calamity Jane as one of our two chief Western heroines, grew out of John Burke's press-agentry. "Little Missy" brought a feminine touch to the Cody show. Annie was as impressed with the Boss as were all the others. "Our outfit was more like a clan than a show business," she wrote. "We remained just one big family, with Buffalo Bill at its head—" and with Arizona John as its brain.

Burke's task required special talents. Everybody liked rotund "Arizona John." All doors were open to him; people were impressed as he eulogized the Scout of the Plains. Newspaper, railway, and theatrical offices welcomed him. Even when editors doubted his tales, they printed them. Burke could secure railroad cars when none were to be had, rent theaters when they were already under contract, strike a chord so delicately balanced between sentimentality and savagery that even skeptics found themselves standing at the box office clamoring for tickets. When scandal plagued Cody, Burke found some plausible explanation to divert attention. He had a way with Indians, especially when firewater jeopardized the whole company. A man who could talk with kings and yet not lose the common touch, Burke had the power and enthusiasm that come from unquestioning devotion. He believed in Cody as much as Cody believed in himself. In serving he found fulfillment.

Arizona John adjusted his propaganda to the town being visited. In Boston, Cody was nine-tenths Irish, descended from an ancient line of Celtic kings; in New Haven, a spiritual brother of Garibaldi and Italian patriots in the Risorgimento. When the troupe played a Germanic town in Wisconsin or Minnesota, Burke said that the original spelling of the Scout's name was "Koditz." Even those who realized he was merely making Cody all things to all men acquiesced. This is what the English poet Coleridge called the willing suspension of disbelief.

When finally the Prince faced bankruptcy, Burke stayed on, sacrificing his career, his salary, almost his livelihood. As Cody's credit declined Burke's stature grew. The glib promoter became an admirable man in those last nightmare years. Courtney Ryler Cooper left this account of aging Arizona John:

"One wintry morning in Denver, I watched him, whiskers flying, threadbare coat pulled tight around his rotund form, set forth to what I knew by experience would be a meager breakfast. But in ten minutes he was back at the circus offices, a copy of the *New York Times* tucked under his arm. 'You didn't take long for breakfast, Major,' I said. He grew red-faced.

" 'Well, I — I just decided I didn't want any,' came at last. 'I noticed this *New York Times,* and I just thought I'd see whether it had anything to say about the Colonel. He's in New York now, you know.'

"I bought the Major's breakfast that day. The ten cents with which he had started for his coffee and rolls had gone upon the altar of his adoration." [4]

That a person so different from John Burke in background, temperament, and interest as Prentiss Ingraham could take over the Cody cult shows the range of Buffalo Bill's appeal. "The only request I have to make, Ingraham," the Scout said to the most prolific pulp writer in American history, "is that you will not depict me with an axe in one hand and a war club in the other, knocking out brains." If Ingraham honored the request, it was the only acknowledged method of killing Indians his dime novel hero eschewed. His superhuman Buffalo Bill performed such feats that even Cody finally exclaimed, "Gosh, the things they write!"

Mississippian Prentiss Ingraham was a Confederate officer at 18, fighting with Withers' Mississippi Regiment of light artillery. In 1864 he was Commander of Scouts—a title he later applied frequently to Cody. After the Confederacy surrendered, this young firebrand moved to Mexico and marched with Juarez against the French. As a soldier of fortune he fought in South America, Austria, Crete, and Egypt. In Cuba he was both an army colonel and naval captain. Captured by the Spanish and condemned to die, he escaped to the United States, where he took a job writing for Beadle and Adams. That publishing house, from 1856 to 1898, sold thousands of dime novels and penny dreadfuls to the American public.[5] The Southern colonel with the slouch hat and walrus mustache became their most successful and prolific writer. Composing in longhand, Ingraham completed an incredible number of novels—one thousand!

Buffalo Bill, whom he met on a trip west, figured in 200 volumes signed or ghost-written by Ingraham. Here was a Cody library turned out by one man in two decades—a feat no one has duplicated. Sample titles reveal the romantic pattern Ingraham employed: *Buffalo Bill and His Merry Men or The Robin Hood Rivals, Buffalo Bill's Grip or Oath-Bound to Custer, Buffalo Bill's Boys in Blue or The Brimstone Band's Blot-Out.* A typical Ingraham characterization appeared in *Buffalo Bill, from Boyhood to Manhood.* One who loved nature, the Scout was "more at ease in the trackless wilds than in the turbulent cities." (A similar and equally questionable legend existed about Boone.) Cody stood "as a barrier between civilization and savagery, risking his own life to save the lives of others." His place in history was exalted and obvious.

Ingraham anticipated the rise of the plainsman as a hero when he wrote the first cowboy novel in 1887. *The Cowboy Clan or The Tigress of Texas* glorified Buck Taylor, the King of the Cowboys in Cody's Wild West Show. Buck's feats became the showman-cowboy's standbys: throwing a steer by the horns and tying him single-handed, busting bronchos, and leaning from the saddle at a gallop to pick up a neckerchief from the ground. Buffalo Bill and the imaginative Ingraham saw both the possibilities of the type in general and of Taylor in particular.

Ingraham bedecked Cody with finery which made Joseph in his multi-colored robe look pale, and surrounded him with spectral apparitions and beautiful slightly-tarnished maidens. He soon encountered the annoying tribute of countless imitators. By 1900 the weekly Buffalo Bill Stories carried this warning: "Beware of Wild West imitations of the *Buffalo Bill Stories.* They are about fictitious characters. The Buffalo Bill weekly is the only weekly containing the adventures of Buffalo Bill (Col. W. F. Cody), who is known all over the world as King of Scouts."

The adventures became ever more weird and far-fetched, involving Apache dwarfs, red buzzards, headless horsemen, rope wizards, the Klan of Kan, and the Horde of Hermosa. Finally, Buffalo Bill himself tried a Cody novel, urging the publishers to take out a few killings if necessary. Ingraham's plots moved from the unlikely to the incredible. Cody admitted this, and poked fun at his sister for perpetuating falsehoods in *Last of the Great*

Scouts.[6] Cody's wife, who brought suit for divorce against him
on charges of adultery, discredited many of the stories. "My
grandfather had met Buffalo Bill, Kit Carson, and Jim Bridger,"
wrote James Stevens. "He said that Buffalo Bill was the biggest
liar he had ever met and that Jim Bridger could tell the biggest
stories. There was a difference grandpa said." In *The Truth
About Buffalo Bill* (1929) Herbert Cody Blake labeled Bill a
fraud that had been foisted off on the public.

Although Cody was not all the things he or his publicists claimed,
he was not a fraud. His true caliber was shown by his final
determination to pay off bad debts and to maintain his self-respect.
There was a good reason why his Wild West Show succeeded: it
fulfilled every boy's dream.

This also helps explain Cody's European vogue. In England he
was the darling of Queen Victoria's Jubilee. The Queen herself
watched as the kings of Denmark, Saxony, Greece, and Belgium
rode in Buffalo Bill's Deadwood stage coach. Cody's troupe went
to France, Spain, Italy, the Lowlands, Austria-Hungary, and Scan-
dinavia, spreading the legend of the American West, paving the
way for the cowboy movie of the twentieth century, depicting an
uncouth yet romantic life which Europeans liked to think of as
uniquely American.

Stories of Cody's challenging Bismarck to a duel, racing English
thoroughbreds, breaking in the wild horses of the Prince of Ser-
monetta, greeting Pope Leo XII in the Square before St. Peters,
dancing on Mount Vesuvius, and camping in the Roman Coliseum,
made all the papers. European artists and writers used Cody and
his troupe as subject matter for paintings and stories. Charles
Henckel's portfolio of Buffalo Bill drawings appeared in Munich,
helping Germans visualize Cody on a "Buffeljagd" (buffalo-
chase) or "Im Galopp schiessend" (shooting while galloping).
Henry Llewellyn Williams' *Buffalo Bill* was an English best-seller.
With a smugness that befitted his times, and pleased his readers,
Williams concluded: "Is more needed when H. M. the Queen and
the Prince and Princess of Wales have been to see Cody's show?
They have admired the lady-rifle shots, the ponies, the equestrians,
and spoken to the terrible war-chiefs with whom Mr. Gladstone has
confabulated." [7]

In 1888 Cody's publication under his own name of *The Story of the Wild West and Camp-Fire Chats* showed how infatuated he was with men's valor. Such tributes as this filled the book: "Had Crockett been at Troy, at the historic siege, Homer would have immortalized him in his heroic verse." But beneath the clichés was a sound theory. "Only upon occasions of greatest peril do heroes have their birth. The evolution of brave men in the wilds of the Atlantic slope was as natural as a metamorphosis in the insect world, but their valorous deeds excite our admiration none the less." This evolutionary notion was central in Frederick Jackson Turner's thesis of the West, which Cody's passage antedates by five years. There is more to the book than glittering metaphors.

In desperate situations, Cody observed, heroic remedies must be employed. He cited those devised by Boone, Crockett, and Carson. Boone was a "curiously quiet man, little given to speech, and less inclined to speak of the incidents of his strangely eventful life." Crockett's autobiography contained "not a few unsubstantial tales that, despite their frequent exposure, still cling tenaciously to nearly all the biographies, but which I have eliminated, or repeated only to deny." (Suppose Cody's biographers had taken the same point of view!) Kit Carson, after whom he named his only son, he found overly modest. This "served to obscure important incidents in the life of a justly historical personage." Cody's book reveals a grasp of history which his critics have seldom acknowledged. Under different circumstances Cody might have been as good a press agent as Buntline, Burke, or Ingraham.

Buffalo Bill figured in the development of the Western movie, that celluloid common denominator of American life. He was not only the prototype of a hero who has since ridden through hundreds of "oaters" and "hayburners," but also the first actual hero of the genre. In 1910 Sam Goldenberg released a slide series showing Buffalo Bill and his associates busy making the West safe for Americans. The same year Harry Powers made the first moving picture of the Wild West Show, "three hundred thrills in three hundred reels." So successful was this pioneer attempt that the Essanay Company began releasing weekly one-reel "Broncho Billy" stories. Billy went from tribe to tribe, maid to maid, broncho to broncho. He may have changed his love every Saturday, but his purity and integrity continued firm throughout 375 movies.

In 1913 newspapers carried a story about a young girl named Dorothy who desperately resisted a necessary operation until her mother said, "Remember Buffalo Bill. You know he is brave and never breaks his word." Little Dorothy underwent her trial bravely; knives held no fear when the mind could be filled with such visions. The Saturday afternoon miracle play was working its subtle alchemy on the American mind.

In order to film the "true story" of the last Indian fighting, Cody and two Denver backers joined with the Essanay Film Company to form the W. F. Cody Historical Pictures Company. From the Secretary of War, Cody got permission to use regular army cavalry in the films, and from the Secretary of the Interior, agency Indians. With the help of six army generals, scores of cavalry, and hundreds of redskins, he made several films. The intricacies and problems of the new art form were too much for him. His movies were not a financial success.

Cody lived to see William S. Hart, Harry Carey, and Tom Mix flourish as the star system invaded the movies. Their careers demonstrated something his had already proved—working on the Western range isn't nearly as profitable as bringing the range indoors for Eastern audiences. Movie cowboys began to turn to swimming pools and garages instead of corrals. America changed not only in body but in spirit during his lifetime.

Cody never let his personal difficulties alter the mask which the hero-makers had made for him. Desperately he wrote to a close friend: "Won't someone who knows the law come to my rescue? God bless you. I am old and tired." A touching story of the elder Cody is told by his ward and secretary, Dan Muller. When they had returned from the last European tour, the white-haired trouper asked, "Did you have a good time in Europe, Dan?"

"I sure did, Colonel," Muller replied.

"That's the first time you ever called me Colonel, Dan. How come?"

"I guess it just slipped out, Uncle Bill. Everyone else calls

you Colonel. When I'm talking to them about you, I call you
Colonel too. I kinda like it."

Cody beamed at the young man. "Damn if I don't myself,
Dan!" [8]

Here was conceit so guileless that no one could condemn it.
Here was a man so American in history, manner, and personality
that we may be excused for forgetting the actual facts about
William Frederick Cody. To those who knew him well, he was
half-mountebank. But to the thousands who saw him only in the
ring, he was the West: he represented history. The final salute
with which he closed his show was a benediction. He epitomized
a whole phase of the Western movement and victory on the hazard-
ous plains. Even those who realized that it was a contrived thing
admired Cody's manly conduct when creditors instead of redskins closed in upon him. To his own code and his own image
he was faithful.

According to the quatrain already quoted, he always aimed
and shot to kill, and the company paid his buffalo bill. A half
century later we see it was not the company, but the country, that
paid Cody's bill. So far as heroes go, the nation got a bargain.

CHAPTER 9

The Sign of the T: Henry Ford

"The Case of Little Reuben occurred only twenty-three years after Our Ford's first T-Model was put on the market." (Here the Director made a sign of the T on his stomach and all the students reverently followed suit.)—Aldous Huxley, *Brave New World*

History is bunk. All the art in the world isn't worth five cents. Reading books musses up your mind. Literature is all right, but it doesn't mean much. The jagged crystals of sugar damage your stomach. Cows, horses, and creeds will disappear from the earth. Don't ruin a son by sending him to college. Anyone who smokes or drinks shouldn't be employed. The theory of evolution is part of the Jewish plot against the Gentile world. So was the assassination of Abraham Lincoln.

These statements and dozens like them were all made publicly by an American hero. He was no backwoods bigot or mere theorizer, but one of the most respected and practical men of our time; the last of the billionaires. People who never heard of Washington, Lincoln, or the Declaration of Independence knew his name well. It bounced over the world's highways daily. The name was Henry Ford; its bearer drove a tin lizzie up Olympus.

Ford had, as much as any man of his times, a sense of mission. "Machinery is the new Messiah," he claimed. If this be true, Henry Ford is a saint and his blueprints are Holy Writ. That our offspring will make the sign of the T and measure time A.F. (After Ford), as Aldous Huxley mischievously suggests, is unlikely, but they may well revere him as a miracle maker who assembled a brave new mechanical world. Outside his factory, he

114

lacked heroic dimensions, but he achieved immortality as the Great Mechanic, the Know-How King.

Ford had no sympathy for intellectuals and dreamers. Nor had he any reason to think that as a diplomat, historian, or sociologist he had succeeded, despite his strenuous efforts in these callings. He loved his factory, gloried in its productivity, and exulted in being a mechanic. For forty years he depended on his own tools for a living. After that he employed a mechanical army without peer or precedent. His life was a progression from watches to horseless carriages to Model T to Model A to V-8 to B-24.

At Ford's the mechanic was Superman. Because "Cast Iron Charlie" Sorenson made machines and assembly lines fill incredible quotas, he was the most admired employee Ford ever had. After awarding him a six-figure salary he reportedly added, "If that isn't enough, Charlie, take some more." Even world wars raised problems that for Ford called for mechanical solutions. "It is my earnest hope to create machinery to which those who so desire can turn to inquire what can be done to establish peace," he told the press when his peace ship sailed.

My Philosophy of Industry, which appeared a decade later, showed Henry Ford to be still a mechanic dabbling in sociology. "Just as accurate gauges and methods produce a smooth-working, efficient machine, so clear thinking, clean living, square dealing make an industrial or domestic life successful and smooth-running." The Master Mechanic made human rehabilitation sound simple. We should be able to renew our human bodies as we mend a defect in a boiler. "Machinery," he wrote, "is accomplishing in the world what man has failed to do by preaching, propaganda, or the written word. Political opinions don't really make much difference." To him morality was "merely doing the sound thing in the best way." Ford's followers in Aldous Huxley's *Brave New World* quite appropriately made the sign of the T on their stomachs, not on their heads or hearts.

Of Scotch-Irish lineage, Henry Ford was born in rural Michigan in 1863. Hating farm chores, he spent his spare hours fixing farm machinery and watches. At sixteen he overrode his family's wishes and went to Detroit. To appease his parents he made a second short try at farming, after which he married and returned to Detroit. As an Edison Company employee he rose from night fireman to chief engineer. Then he quit to spend all his time marketing the gasoline quadricycle he perfected in 1896. He moved effortlessly into the infant automobile industry and, in 1903, he set up the Ford Motor Company with a capital investment of $28,000. Five years later the first Model T came from his factory; five years after that his assembly line was a reality. In 1914 he established a minimum wage of $5 a day in his plant and was skyrocketed out of obscurity. His rugged Model T became America's leading car and the subject of a unique folklore. Before the Great Depression he had sold 15,000,000 tin lizzies and become a billionaire.

Ford's later career was anti-climactical. The Model A and V-8 cars did not maintain the Model T's supremacy. Labor and plant difficulties multiplied; the son who had held the title but not the powers of president of the company died in 1943. Henry remained in control of the empire he had created until senility and death overtook him in 1947. Over 100,000 Americans from all walks of life filed by his casket for a last look at the mechanic almost no one called Henry to his face. The man was gone, but his name and his cars rolled on into history.

Ford's workaday and respectable rise lacks the color and drama that went with Phineas Barnum, Diamond Jim Brady, and Jubilee Jim Fiske. He reflected the strength of the rural America which sustained his legend, but this was insufficient grounds for his status. We must go deeper to find his unique strength. Whimsical and retiring, he was at his worst in public appearances. Few admired him, and even fewer could claim to have been his friends. Most workmen thought of him as a spy and slavedriver; his legend did not spring, like the Lizzies, from the assembly line. The Mechanical Wizard was more esteemed by those who drove Fords than by those who made them. "To get along with him," an employee reminisced, "you had to have a little mean streak in your system."

During New Deal days Ford's reputation went down; when his pro-Nazi tendencies became known, it hit rock bottom. After his death Ford's fame underwent the hysteria of depreciation that frequently follows a hero's death. In 1953, during a highly publi-

cized fiftieth anniversary of the Ford Motor firm, this trend
was reversed. His heirs dramatically opened Ford's private
papers to the public; for although he had said history was bunk,
he had collected enough personalia to cover 5,000 feet of shelves
in the new Ford Library.

Life magazine suggested that we take "A New Look at Ford,"
and devoted fourteen pages to improving his national standing.[1]
Other magazines followed suit. Company advertisements took
advantage of the technological growth that followed World War
II; Henry Ford II worked hard to improve public relations.

Perhaps the time is ripe to note objectively just what the living
Henry Ford's attitudes were, insofar as we can piece them together
from existing documents and memories.

Throughout his long life Ford suspected social innovation,
criticism, and expert opinion. A dissenting voice infuriated him.
He fired so many people that a special name was finally coined
for the unfortunates—the Ford Alumni Association. Once he
decided to replace all physicians at the Henry Ford Hospital with
chiropractors; another time he cut off milk deliveries at Greenfield Village because medical men would not say that his son
Edsel had contracted undulant fever. "Never trust ear-piddlers
or lawyers," he said. His personal world was as superstitious as
his factory world was scientific. Fear of Jews, John Barleycorn,
the du Ponts, and international bankers would not let him rest.
Black cats, broken mirrors, omens, and coincidences terrified him.
Never would he change a sock that had been put on inside out.
Not impressed with church theology, he nonetheless believed in
reincarnation. This is how he reasoned about it: "When the automobile was new and one of them came down the road, a chicken
would run straight for home, and usually get killed. But today
when a car comes along, a chicken will run for the nearest side of
the road. That chicken has been hit in the ass in a previous life."[2]

The mind of the Automobile King roared down the highway
of night without headlights. So affluent that when he crashed
through the barricades no one chastised him, he listened so seldom that he learned little from other drivers. On he rolled,
a hit and run driver whose victim might be the Jewish race,
the Catholic religion, labor unions, leisure, the New Deal, or

Wall Street. Ford's prejudices were those of rural mid-western America. William Jennings Bryan, that crusading enemy of city slickers and religious modernists, supplied him with his political credo. Like Bryan, whom he befriended, Ford was a pacifist and isolationist. When newspapermen came to the docks to cover the departure of the Ford peace ship for Europe, it was Bryan who posed with Ford on deck.

"Any customer can have a car of any color he wants, provided it's black," he told his advertising staff. Only after a public rebellion reduced sales would he admit that he was not the final arbiter on how an automobile should look. As his dogmatism increased with his assets, so did his bitter opposition to unions. The Ford Motor Company was run like a feudal dukedom, and governed, said *Fortune* magazine in 1941, by a mutually distrustful group of executives, "most of them without titles, with no clear lines of authority or responsibility anywhere delineated." If he trusted few men, he idolized one who encouraged him to build automobiles. This was the tinkering Thomas A. Edison, whose relics Ford collected in a special museum, and whose front yard Ford caused to be dug up and carried reverently to Dearborn. He even kept Edison's dying breath in a bottle.

Both Ford and Edison were cut from the same extraordinary bolt of cloth. Considering how highly we prize the gadgets and artifacts with which their two lives were obsessed, it is small wonder indeed that America has lionized them. They were the Rover Boys on the Trail of New Trinkets.

An episode from Ford's early career accents his Edison idolatry. In 1914 he hired a special train to make the Detroit-Port Huron run on which Edison had worked as a boy. He purchased a vendor's box, and had Edison sell once more his nickel treats. Then, at the end of the run, Ford arranged to have his guest send a telegram from the station where he had served his apprenticeship. The aging Edison ticked out a halting message to his son in New Jersey. Delayed by Ford's historical pageantry, a distant operator broke in with, "Tell that kid to get off the line." He was right. There was a kid on the line, and another kid had arranged for his being there. Ford remained, in all but mechanical matters,

a child. Like his own model T's he was a triumph of functional-
ism, made to go but not to ponder.

Once he got going, Ford was hard to stop. Under him burned
the fires of John Calvin's hell; because of him the Reformation
conquered the River Rouge. His strict Scotch-Irish rearing left
a deep mark on him, which wealth and leisure could never conceal.
Engraved over his fireplace was Franklin's line, "Chop your own
wood and it will warm you twice." Laziness was at the bottom of
America's troubles. The Bible verses he memorized dealt with
hard work, frugality, and justification by works. Rich Henry is,
among American heroes, merely a mechanized version of Poor
Richard.

If God gave John D. Rockefeller his dimes, he must also have
given Ford his dies. If men would only listen to him and do his
bidding, thought the Motorman, he would run them as effectively
as he did his factories. "When I think about the thousands of
families dependent upon my enterprise," he said, "there seems
to me to be something sacred about the Ford Motor Company."
Recent critics have found so much wrong with Ford's methods and
policies that they have overlooked the lofty ends. The money he
made neither spoiled nor satisfied him. In the best Calvinistic
tradition, he considered himself his brother's keeper—whether his
brother liked it or not. Not to remove the stain from his workmen's fingers, but from their souls, did he outlaw smoking in his
plants. When he announced he would pay a minimum wage of $5
a day, he took it for granted that only moral people deserved such
a rate. He assumed that he could manage men as he could manipulate machines. That he never fully understood the social effects
of his actions should not make us forget that he never lost his
concern about them. Aware that his innovations changed millions
of lives, he was determined to deal with the human consequences.
Even at his worst he was only trying to graft a new branch onto
the tree of rural American life. No other industrialist of his era
made so extensive, or so unsuccessful an effort.

*   *   *

Though America's leading industrial figure, Ford was unlike
any of the other heroes we have examined. His personality was

not pleasing, and his utopian dream was unsuccessful. Yet he became, while still alive, a popular folk hero. This cannot be explained by saying the people were wrong about the real Henry; instead, they invented a legendary Henry who had a Model T brain. As with that contrived folk hero, Paul Bunyan, there is really a Henry A and a Henry B, quite different in history and character. Such a division has been the people's prerogative for centuries, and figures differing as widely as Ulysses, Roland, Robin Hood, Billy the Kid, and Eva Perón demonstrate it. Both Henrys are oversimplifications of capitalism. In fact and fancy Henry was a farm boy, of humble parentage; a tinkering dreamer who didn't mind putting his visions to the test; a person whose natural ability carried him forward in a highly competitive field; a mechanical genius in a mechanized age. A major need of his day was cheap transportation. He provided the answer, on a scale no man before him had even visualized. Here the two Henrys split, Henry A becoming a tyrannical motorman, and Henry B the guiding spirit in a culture which has used its productivity as a chief means of survival. Henry B is as fortunate as Henry A is pathetic. Legend makers have succeeded in dramatizing early Ford stories, such as his first successful run in a gasoline buggy during his early manhood. They have made as much of the last hours of preparation as of the hours when Lindbergh was defying the lonely Atlantic, or Lincoln was awaiting word of the chance meeting of the Northern and Southern armies at Gettysburg. Ford worked around the clock until, at two in the morning, he was ready for the final test. Rain drenched the muddy Detroit streets, but he didn't even notice it. Would the contraption run? Mrs. Ford put a cloak over her shoulders and went ahead of him with a lantern. For a terrible moment nothing happened. Then Ford found that a screw had come off; he replaced it. The thing ran. The automobile age had begun. Here was drama that the man on the street could understand.

Even when Henry Ford became a billionaire his hands stayed clean, for no man had been robbed. Where no business had existed he had created one. By 1940 one out of every seven Americans was employed in the motor car or allied businesses. Ford remade transport and put the Horatio Alger myth on wheels. Clerks and farmers entrusted him with the $100 so lovingly tucked away in the mattress; Henry was on their side. Hadn't all the giant corporations called him crazy, and hadn't the *Wall Street Journal* attacked him? He'd made Detroit in 1914 what California had been in 1849: the end of the rainbow.

The Ford five dollar minimum day came with a number of strings attached. Only workmen who were morally fit qualified. Married men had to be living with and supporting their family; single men over 22 had to be living "wholesomely" and displaying "proud thrifty habits;" men under 22 and all women had to be the sole support of their next of kin. Henry was as anxious to keep vice down as he was to keep production up. Rural America, fearing the sins of the city, thought it a fine idea. The just would be rewarded, and the unjust cast out. That the reward, at least monetarily, averaged less than $1,000 a year per worker in 1930 didn't destroy the illusion.

Eventually the Motor King became a touchstone for testing proposed changes and laws. Ford's was the American system, and anything that hurt him hurt America. In a culture which had made the dollar an almighty thing, Ford collected a billion. Yet, said the legend, he was as simple and sturdy as when he plowed his corn fields or tinkered in his tiny garage. This popular conception of Ford collided with certain historical facts, but overran them and rolled on.[3] It was hard to explain how a humanitarian could allow cold water to be turned on shivering unemployed workmen, or have police spies to watch all employees. People outside Detroit knew little of these things. It was hard to reconcile Ford's alleged simplicity with his 100,000 acre Georgia plantation, fashionable London home, private railroad car, and million dollar Dearborn estate complete with $30,000 pipe organ, $37,000 boathouse, and $69,000 garage. Ford's legend-makers answered with a counter-offensive. Didn't Henry love the old-time square dances and country hikes? Wasn't he still a dirt farmer at heart? Hadn't he borrowed 2 cents to buy the first Edison commemorative stamp, being out of change at the time? Hadn't he foiled the Wall Street bankers who tried to destroy him? These touches reassured the public. The tin lizzies served not only to transport Americans, but to foster tales, slogans, and jokes about the man who was responsible for their being there.

Lizzie-lore is a key to understanding Ford's reputation. Early Model T's, objects of awe and delight, symbolized what Ford could do and what America would become. Ugly but useful, Lizzie came just in time to create a suitable basis for a new machine age folklore. No mechanical object has ever been the butt of so many jokes, or source of so many wisecracks as the Model T, alias Leaping Lizzie, Little Bo-Creep, Rolls Rough, Wanderer of the Waistland, the Answer to a Walking Maiden's Prayer, Bouncing Betty, Graf Zep's Uncle, Lizzie of the Valley, Passion Pot, and variations beyond number. Folklorist B. A. Botkin collected over a thousand Lizzie nicknames for a piece in *American Speech*. Some, such as Flapper, No Charleston, and Wanted—A Bootlegger to Share Our Home, were dated by the 1920's. Some, like Henrietta Elizabeth Van Flivver or September Morn, affected the grand style; others moved over into Freudian realms. Consider, for example, the label, "I'm a second son of a last year's Lizzie," accompanied by a pair of coconuts hung from the differential.

The labels stressed Lizzie's all-round cussedness, and capitalized on America's fondness for slogans and wisecracks. They were mechanical adaptations of the mule and burro stories of European folklore, redone in the American idiom. When you saw a car bumping along labeled, I'm from Texas, You Can't Steer Me; Columbus Took a Chance—Why Can't You; or Sugar, Here's Your Daddy, you knew what country you were in. And you knew frontier optimism wasn't really dead when others read, We Ain't Climbed Pike's Peak Yet, or Lazy Loping Lizzie on her Last Lengthy Leap. Lizzie's maker also figured in all the buffoonery. His staff called him Mr. Ford, but his customers preferred Henry. Flivvers were inscribed with lines like, Turn over, Sis, Henry's Here, or Don't Worry, Lizzie, Henry Will Fix You Up. Behind all the razzing was pride in Ford's achievements. "When better Buicks are built, Fords will pass them," went a popular slogan. Even Lizzie's obvious failings, such as a tendency to drop vitals en route, came in handy. Follow Me for Ford Parts was a favorite.

Ford jokes flourished like Ford labels, both orally and in printed joke books. The usual theme was confidence in the man and cars which were transforming America. They stressed inventiveness, productivity, or some ingenious triumph at the Ford plant. After-dinner speakers told about the old lady who sent her tomato cans, or the farmer his tin roof, to Detroit, and got a Ford car back by return mail. Rural humorists poked fun at the rich Eastern banker who paid $15,000 for a fancy French limousine but kept a Model T in the trunk to pull it out of mud holes. They told the sad tale of the Ford worker who dropped his wrench on the assembly line and was twenty cars behind when he bent over and got it. Few of the jokesters knew it, but their tales were cast in the mould that had served for centuries. The Ford joke was the drug-store chronicle of the new gasoline age. Neither Jove nor Charlemagne nor Beowulf had done anything more remarkable than Henry Ford, who turned bits of tin into automobiles.

Had you heard that next year's Lizzies were going to be yellow so they could be sold in bunches like bananas? That Ford planned to paper the sky with flivver planes? That Model T's were being shipped in asbestos crates, since they came off the assembly line so fast they were still hot and smoking? That a man got rich fol-lowing Ford cars and picking up the parts that fell on the road? That Uncle Jeb got shaken up in Lizzie until the fillings came out of his teeth? That the next Ford would come with a can opener, so you could put doors anywhere you wanted them? That Henry would pay $100 for any flivver joke which made him laugh?

Though not as frequent as they once were, Ford stories still thrive on the American scene. In May, 1953 Art Thomas, owner of a 1908 Model T, was fined for speeding. His court room comment was in keeping with the Lizzie tradition: "It was only hitting on three. If it had been hitting on all four I doubt if they would have caught me." On and on the jokes go, enhancing the reputation of a man few Americans saw or heard. They keep Ford in the realm of heroic immortality.

Lizzie brought golden days to Ford. Introduced at the 1907 Chicago Auto Show, the Model T went immediately into produc-tion. Henry offered a stripped car. Everything was standard and interchangeable, which made for simplicity of operation and re-pair. The end product was the first workable solution to the problem of putting a democracy on wheels. As the 1920's rolled along on sturdy Ford axles, politicians even began to talk of two cars in every garage. Henry never endorsed such extravagant notions; one would do, if it were a Ford. In two decades he produced 15,456,868 Model T cars in thirty assembly plants, selling them for as little as $265 apiece. When he started making Model T's his surplus balance was $2,000,000. Before he changed to a new engine it was $673,000,000. Although by 1923 he had not spent a penny on advertising for five years, he was making 7,000 cars a day and still not filling all orders. Ford seemed to have answered the criticism about capitalistic production methods, and the vitality of laissez faire. Instead of condemning what Ford did, the Russians tried desperately to imitate it. Europeans poked fun at Ford's methods and products, but envied Americans their Ford cars. A British writer predicted that Americans would eventually give up their homes to live, wed, and die in their Lizzies.

By 1925, however, Ford sales were declining. The public rebelled against Lizzie's absence of comfort, beauty, and style. Chevrolets, Reos, Overlands, Dodges, and Buicks improved until they matched Lizzie in performance, and surpassed her in style and comfort. Ford refused to change. Reluctantly he agreed to an elaborate advertising campaign to win back Lizzie's buyers. Falling sales continued, showing that even in Lizzies there was a saturation point. Finally the Ford plant was converted to another standardized engine, the Model A, which lasted from 1927 to 1931. Again the public balked. A disillusioned Ford finally acquiesced to a yearly model and to the trimmings he so detested. Stories continued about Henry. Many of them can be attributed to the clever and able men whom Ford hired to promulgate the Ford image. His assembly line chief, his public spokesman, and his personal factotum — Charles Sorenson, William Cameron, and Harry Bennett by name — were instrumental in making him a major culture hero. The post-war success of his grandson, Henry Ford II, has rejuvenated that reputation in the 1950's.

*　　　*　　　*

"Cast Iron Charlie" Sorenson made Ford a hero by making Ford cars. Supplementing Ford's own mechanical talents, he perfected mass production. Fourteen years younger than his boss,

Sorenson advanced where the Old Man faltered. Henry was past forty when he produced his first car, and seventy by the time Franklin Roosevelt came into power; he needed a production lieutenant who could grasp his often poorly-articulated vision and turn it into metal. In Charlie, who joined the Ford staff in 1906 to help put the third car together, he found such a man. Sorenson pulled a Model T chassis 250 feet through tentative assembling in 1913 to test out a new conveyor belt principle. Up to then it took 14 hours to put a Ford together; that one was completed in one hour and a half. King Christian of Denmark made Sorenson a Commander of the Danneborg Order, and with good reason. The rugged Dane was in fact what the folk hero John Henry was in legend: a steel driving man. Instead of driving railroad spikes, Sorenson drove men. Foremen who couldn't meet his quotas were discarded like defective engine blocks. In the factory his decision was law. Like Ford, he was outside the factory an Anteus lifted off the ground. Sorenson never looked beyond the end of the Ford production line. His motto was, "Unless you can see a thing you can't simplify it; unless you can simplify it, it's a good sign you can't make it." Here was a mentality with which Ford could do business.

Sorenson got the production kinks out of the Model T, Model A, and V-8 engines. Ford gave him the privilege of placing the stamp on the fifteen millionth Model T car. When in 1941 Ford made his famous boast about turning out a thousand planes a day, Sorenson saved face by building and overseeing the Willow Run bomber plant. His unchallenged supremacy as a production boss won him a certain heroic reputation in his own right. Here was a man who had sat up all night in a California hotel room, to emerge the next morning with the finished sketch of the world's largest bomber plant in his pocket; who could get from paper to plane while others merely worried about how to set up the project. A War Department official requested that Sorenson send his organization chart to Washington. "We don't operate that way," Sorenson replied. This ring-tailed roarer left bureaucracy to others. Like Daniel Boone and Andy Jackson before him, he craved elbow-room.

Most people gave Henry Ford the credit due to Sorenson. They saw the name Ford on the finished product—not that of the man who had made it possible. This fact made Sorenson indispensible in fostering the popular image. He was to Ford what Kit Carson had been to Fremont, or Stonewall Jackson to Lee. He got things done, using methods more becoming to a militarist than to a diplomat. He kicked stools from under men who sat too long, and axed desks whose occupants were no longer needed. He thought of Ford cars, and not of men who had problems off the assembly line.

Nothing showed better how a senile Ford had lost his grasp than his firing Sorenson in 1944. News of the dismissal almost set off a panic in the Rouge plant. Charlie had cursed and driven his men. Still he was the cement that had held Henry Ford's system together. The one man who had figured in every Ford production triumph was superseded at last. The Ford system, as old Henry had devised it and Sorenson had run it, was now a thing of the past. Only the Ford reputation and the assembly line kept going.

Henry Ford was at best half-articulate and contradictory; to make him appear a hero, someone had to stand between him and the American public. That man was William J. Cameron, who spoke so frequently and so skillfully for Ford that the two became one so far as the public was concerned.

Cameron became prominent when, as a staff member of the Detroit *News,* he wrote an editorial called "Don't Die on Third." Drawing an analogy from the baseball player who never scored a run, Cameron pointed out that any unfinished job is equally unavailing. This variation on the Hubbard "Message to Garcia" showed that the young journalist was clever with platitudes. In later years, Cameron described himself at 19 as "a half-baked iconoclast who drank in Robert Ingersoll and William Jennings Bryan, and was caught up in the liberal ferment of the time." Whatever liberal ferment Ingersoll and Bryan brewed never turned into wine after Cameron joined the Ford Motor Company. He succeeded E. G. Pipp, who resigned in protest against Ford's racialism, as editor of Ford's newspaper. A Detroit columnist had called that sheet "the best goddamned paper ever published in a tractor factory." Under Cameron it became a powerful medium for building up what Cameron called the "Ford image." He had a clear picture of how he thought Ford should appear to the world, and what he should represent. He sold the notion to Ford and set about promulgating it. His Ford image was a composite of the virtues of early America, now marvelously combined in a single man who never died on third. The Ford Motor Company, Cameron maintained, was merely the lengthened shadow of that one man; other men "dwindled in size when Henry Ford walked into the room."

His press version of the image was influential; but the radio was Cameron's most successful outlet. He convinced the Old Man to sponsor an hour's musical program at a time when most Americans would be home to hear it. The result was the Ford Sunday Evening Hour. For four years Cameron sandwiched Ford in between Friml and Romberg, reserving six minutes a broadcast for the job. Over 300,000 carefully chosen Cameron words got into Ford Sunday Evening Hours, with an accumulated effectiveness which only Roosevelt's Fireside Chats surpassed.

Cameron assured the public he had no theories or causes to promote, but was merely trying to make a "modest contribution to straight thinking and common sense." Ford's six-minute man was by no means unprejudiced. He was, for example, a founder of the anti-Semitic Anglo-Saxon Federation, and its first president. He violently opposed labor unions, federal aid, and the New Deal, acting as the articulate alter-ego of the befuddled and semi-literate Henry Ford. For a generation Cameron engineered the whole Ford public relations program. He became, in effect, his Master's Voice.

In elaborating on the Ford fundamentals he made ample use of clichés. From the Bible he drew references. Laissez-faire capitalism became "a pillar of cloud by day and fire by night that our people have followed from the beginning." He spoke of progress in a prayerful voice. Roosevelt's braintrusters were "busy young men who have been making picture puzzles of the American way of life;" unemployment insurance seemed to him "a sure way of insuring that there will always be unemployment." But the flames of his fiery indignation failed to heat the thin soup of the shivering breadlines of the 1930's. Most of Cameron's thinking, like Ford's, was outdated. Yet his words did not go unheeded. Many Ameri-

cans wanted to hear the old saws and quips. They wanted a com-
prehensive philosophy of industry, and William Cameron provided
it in terms they could understand.

To defend Ford he championed the machine as a device, and
mass-production as a method. He endorsed uncritically the doctrine of progress and the utilitarian slogan of the greatest good
for the greatest number. "Hand-tied knots were good, but buckles
were better," he said. "Buttons were simpler than buckles and
zippers were best of all." Here was a justification of progress that
every man who wore pants could appreciate.

Cameron said civilization was not produced by the machine, but
the machine by civilization. That some intellectuals questioned
the mass mediocrity created by technology infuriated the Ford
image-maker. "Why do bookmen find the machine repugnant?"
he asked. "It prints their books. It makes possible their science
and refinement." The more he examined the thoughts of a group
that "drew its bread from the system it scores," the more certain
he was that they were pathological.

Cameron insisted that Ford's greatness lay not only in what he
did with machines but also what he did for men. Aware that Eli
Whitney had used interchangeable parts, and the meat packing
industry the assembly line, long before Ford appeared on the
scene, he maintained that for his boss the central question was,
"How can we produce enough units for all, with the minimum
human toil in pleasant factories, paying wages high enough to
allow workers to buy their products?" This put an altruistic and
democratic stamp on Ford's system. Cameron understood this
better than Ford. Hero-makers are often more perceptive than
the idols they help create.

Ford was opposed to unions. Yet Cameron pictured him as
lovable "Henry," the workingman's friend, moving about his plant
in shirtsleeves, figuring out ways to make life better via higher
production. He built on the favorable foundation laid by Ford in
proclaiming a $5 minimum day in 1914. Although Cameron was
so close to Ford that he must have entertained doubts about the
wisdom and far-sightedness of his employer, he never aired these
doubts on Sunday evenings. He made of the Ford story a success-

ful and convincing thing, and kept it shining bright before the American people.

Henry Ford believed in personal devils, so it was natural that one of his associates should be his exorciser. Harry Bennett did not manage the plant like Sorenson or the Ford image like Cameron. He catered to Ford's personal wishes and plans, carried out scores of his schemes, and became the only real crony the Motorman ever had. Ford explained in a few words why he kept him at his side. "Harry gets things done in a hurry." Savoring of blue shirts, secret tunnels, and the third degree, ex-boxer Bennett seemed more apt to bring melodrama than direction to Ford's complex industrial empire.

Few took seriously this strong-arm Harry, who avoided four-in-hand ties because they gave tough customers a handy means to steady a man before punching him, until he was made head of Ford Service, the plant spying force. Observers then noticed that many of Ford's decisions were being announced, even made, by Bennett. When Ford made him director of personnel, with power to hire and fire practically at will, it was plain that Bennett was a major power at court. In his dotage Ford even put the Little Man in the Basement, as newspapermen called Bennett, on his Board of Directors, and phoned him every morning upon rising from bed. He knew Bennett, of all his associates, would carry out his orders without question, never letting dubious means dampen his enthusiasm for desirable ends.

The Little Fellow was touchy about his small stature and poor education. This sensitivity cost many able Ford executives their jobs. "I'd always wished I were a big man, and all my life I took on jobs meant for men bigger than I," he wrote. By pursuing every erratic whim of Ford's mind, he acquired power. Whenever the voice of the Old Man came through, Bennett would look around for the Burning Bush. Because Ford loved to play cops and robbers, Bennett became a master at it, adding an authentic touch by cultivating friends in the underworld. Ex-convicts were put on the Ford payroll under a policy of rehabilitation.

Indeed, Bennett himself was one of the first persons Ford hired with rehabilitation in mind. In 1916 an ex-Navy boxer named Bennett, but nicknamed "Sailor Reece," walked 160 miles across

Africa to board a tramp steamer returning to the United States. Only five feet seven inches tall, he was pugnacious, and did much of his thinking with his right arm. At the Battery Park customs house he slugged a guard, and would have been detained had not Arthur Brisbane, a witness of the bout, taken him in charge. Brisbane was looking for a toughie to recommend to Henry Ford as policeman at the River Rouge plant. Knowing that 75,000 war workers would soon descend upon his factories, Ford had come to New York to hand-pick assistants. Ford impressed the ex-sailor immediately. "I won't work for the company, but I'll work for you," Bennett said. And so he did, surrounding himself with helpers who were, in Bennett's own words, "a lot of tough bastards, but every goddam one of them a gentleman." Had he been better grounded in semantics, he might have chosen the word desperado instead of gentleman.

If his vocabulary was limited, his devotion to the Master was not. No Captain of the Guard ever hovered more lovingly at the palace gates. When Ford was hospitalized in 1932 Bennett roped off half a floor for him. Ford to him was a billion-dollar charge, and he handled him accordingly. Even when Henry was in the wilds of Michigan on vacation, Bennett saw that he got his favorite oil of black walnuts with the morning doughnut. As a senile old man confined to his room, Ford tried daily to get through the morning call to his uncritical shadow.

For a generation Bennett served as informer, chief of police, mouthpiece, labor czar, and carrier of tales. So as to be prepared in case of gunplay, Bennett became an expert marksman, and kept an air-gun in his office. With it he shot the tips off employees' pencils and butts off the cigars of visitors who violated the no smoking rule. His desk was the plot board for the strong-arm crew, and the bottleneck for all visitors.

Bennett developed a theory about his attachment to heroic figures. "There was always something in my make-up that attracted me to the great," he wrote. "As well as I could put it, I was attracted to the man who could do what I couldn't. . . . The world quickly forgets its admiration for its past hero. When I saw a big man knocked down, I had a strong impulse to help him." [4] This statement explains not only why Bennett worshipped

Ford, but why he was at his best in the years when Ford's reputation and ability were in a decline. To stick by his crumbling idol appealed to Bennett. Sometimes he even thought the tail was wagging the dog. In *We Never Called Him Henry*, he claims he "taught Mr. Ford not to fool me," and that "I alone convinced Mr. Ford of his mistake."

For his devotion Bennett was rewarded with five homes, one of which had a forty-foot secret tunnel between the house and the garage, which was reached when the shower wall swung open. His Grosse Ile residence had a secret device which opened a private bar and revealed stairs descending to an all-steel yacht. Both Edsel Ford and Henry Ford II disliked the ex-boxer. When the latter became president he disposed of the Little Czar who had done so much to shape and bolster up his grandfather's views. Old Ford had developed through Bennett a thorough-going spy system. Service men watched workers, undercover men watched service men, special agents watched undercover men, Bennett watched everybody, and Ford himself worked Bennett like a puppet. Setting up such a system intrigued Ford. When finally it all worked to perfection, he made one of the most revealing remarks of his whole career. Looking over his domain, he said, "It isn't fun any more." But Harry Bennett, with his gold-plated revolver and his dream of being like Wild Bill Hickock, found it fun to the very end.

A detailed study of Ford's early years, by Pulitzer-prize historian Allan Nevins, appeared in 1954, and put up a case for including a fourth Ford associate in the ranks of the hero-makers.[5] Because of his skillful administration and brilliant organizing ability, the book implies, James Couzens made the Ford Motor Company a reality. An early partner, Couzens left the mechanical problems to Ford, and concentrated on business methods and policy. His contribution, though silent and unspectacular, was an essential one.

Yet Couzens does not seem to have had the insight, the flair, of the real hero-maker. His contribution was neither as long-standing nor as telling as that of Sorenson, Cameron, or even Bennett. Commenting on the Couzens references in his review of the book, J. K. Galbraith wrote (in the February 28, 1954 *New York*

Times), "It is certain that, while the Ford Motor Company might not have survived without him, Couzens would never have brought the company into being. It was Ford who had the priceless quality of imagination."

A stronger contender than Couzens, if one must look for a fourth hero-maker, is Henry Ford II. Rich men's heirs are usually the foils for their forebears, the poor lads who work their way up the ladder. But in the Ford story, the rich heir has done so well that in his thirties he already ranks as one of grandfather's hero-makers. He may even become an industrial hero in his own right. This is the man who signs memos "HF II." Ever since he fired Bennett, young Henry has shown that he intends to be boss, and to restore the Ford car to its former primacy in the automotive field. Much of the profit made during his first years of control went into new plants and modernization. In 1953 he announced that $500 million would be spent in two years to increase the company's car-making capacity of 2,378,000 a year by 30%.[6] Like his grandfather, Henry Ford the Second has dramatic sense, and has already shown that he intends to keep the Ford name on Olympus. Recent advertisements indicate that, in addition to selling cars, the new management is out to canonize Henry the First and Last.

*   *   *

In his later years Ford became an antiquarian, spending thousands of dollars to preserve artifacts and documents of the way of life his mechanical improvements had helped destroy. This pious turning to the past fascinated Americans. Rumors about his projects swelled the Ford folklore. Had you heard that Ford wanted to ship the Florida Everglades to his museum? That he was going to buy Plymouth Rock, the French Navy, the Russian crown jewels? Did you know he wanted to move the Great Wall of China? Would Henry give a Ford car to any girl who didn't bob her hair, or to any woman who never sat in, or on, knickers? Such questions pointed up a Ford trait that endeared him to America. When Henry decided to make a public gesture or statement, he generally ended by falling flat on his face. His social theories wouldn't work, his prejudices were untenable, his

political hunches were unfounded. The Ford blunders, many of
which made the headlines, showed just how fallible this disciple
of industrial infallibility really was. When the public decides
a man is a snob (as it did about Hamilton, Van Buren and Dewey)
it will never give him its heart. Whatever else Henry was, he was
not a snob.

That Henry Ford was quite as apt to be wrong as the next fellow
was best illustrated by the chartering of the ill-fated 1917 peace
ship which was to "get the boys out of the trenches by Christmas."
Convinced by a Hungarian named Rosika Schwimmer that a
floating Chautauqua would bring Europe to its senses, Ford char-
tered the "Oscar II" for the job. Commenting on Ford's decision,
John Dos Passos says (in *The Big Money*): "Any intelligent
American mechanic could see that if the Europeans hadn't been a
lot of ignorant underpaid foreigners who drank, smoked, were
loose about women and wasteful in the methods of production,
the war could never have happened." So the Great Mechanic
embarked, having authorized the sending of a cablegram to Pope
Benedict VII who, alas, had died in 983 A.D. The American press
gave the event as much space as to Woodrow Wilson. Reporters
had a field day, describing at length the reformers, utopians, and
crackpots who went over for the trip. All State Governors were
invited, but only the Governor of North Dakota sailed. Ford's
old friend William Jennings Bryan went. A picture of him holding a squirrel cage on deck, arranged by a clever photographer,
made the rounds of American newspapers. The climax came when
the bizarre Mr. Zero, flophouse reformer, jumped into the North
River and swam after the peace ship, which had sailed off before
he arrived.

Henry Ford was not long in perceiving that his efforts weren't
going to empty many trenches by Christmas. Claiming to be sick,
he returned as quickly as possible. Reporters met him to ask
gleefully whether he had made any important discoveries about
Europe. Henry, who never let a social blunder get in the way of
his business eye, said yes. While in Europe he'd discovered there
was a seller's market for tractors in Russia. Later on, Soviet
orders helped sustain Ford during the Depression.

That Ford could claim history was bunk and still set up historical

museums created a newsworthy paradox.   When in 1919 he sued
the *Chicago Tribune* for a million dollars on a libel charge, the
defense used the occasion to expose Ford's ignorance of history
before the world.   Ford was made to admit he didn't know there
had been an American revolution in 1776, and that he thought
Benedict Arnold was a writer.   Rather than read aloud in court,
he admitted he preferred to leave the impression that he could
not read at all.   Ford was awarded 6 cents in damages.   The public
got a million dollars in chuckles.   In 1934 Ford announced
that he had purchased the authentic Pittsburgh birthplace of
Stephen Foster.   When competent historians showed he had been
the victim of a hoax, he merely bought "sworn statements" to support his claim.   He thought the plans to reconstruct Williamsburg,
Virginia, were silly and so stated publicly.   Later the Rockefeller family turned the early capital into an important tourist
center.   Ancient history was Ford's weakest suit.   He maintained that cars and airplanes had existed before written records
were kept.   All in all, he was as out of place in a history discussion
as a prairie schooner would have been on the Ford assembly line.

Some Ford blunders were quite harmless; others were not.   At
various times he launched crusades against tobacco, liquor, unions,
Jews, Catholics, international bankers, and anti-Nazi statesmen.
Articles on "The International Jew" ran in the *Dearborn Independent* for twenty weeks.   In each issue was printed the claim
that, "The statements offered in this series are never made without
the strictest and fullest proof."   Four volumes of anti-Jewish writings were issued by his Dearborn Publishing Company in lots of
200,000.   Copies were particularly prized in Nazi Germany.
When sales sagged, Ford recanted on his Jewish stand; his claim
that he never knew the articles were being published was nonsense.

Deeply isolationist and anti-British, Ford flaunted his pro-Hitler
sentiments for years.   In 1938 he accepted the Award of the
Grand Cross of the German Eagle from the Third Reich, and was
photographed with the Cross pinned on a specially made dress
suit.   "I don't know Hitler personally," he told the *Detroit Press*
in 1939, "but at least Germany keeps its people at work."   Fritz
Kuhn, leader of the German-American bund, was on Ford's pay-

roll; William Pelley, Silver Shirt leader, and Gerald K. Smith, professional bigot, also received Ford aid.

But the people forgot how confused Henry had been in politics when he promised to turn out a thousand planes a day to lick the Axis. He never did so, although Charles Sorenson eventually produced many B-24 bombers in the Willow Run factory. What Henry the mechanic could do always offset what Henry the blunderer tried and couldn't do. His crotchety integrity and wry petulance delighted rural America. His short, crabby answers matched those of Cal Coolidge. Indeed, the lank figure of Henry Ford could easily pass for Uncle Sam. There was no frustration or regret mirrored on his lean face. Public figures came and went; but Ford kept producing cheap cars.

Although it had its comic moments, Ford's career when viewed as a whole was a tragic one. Endings of heroes' stories are almost always tragic. There is so much sorrow in Everyman's life that he looks for and expects it in the lives of the great; from this he gets a major comfort. In what sense was Billionaire Ford tragic? He put cars and filling stations on every road, but kept thinking in horse and buggy terms. He devoted his life to perfecting a technology for the future, but spent his last years among exploded delusions of the past. His life was associated with machines, but he longed to dance at the village maypole or sun himself on the porch of the Wayside Inn.

Realizing that he had created problems for the twentieth century, Ford tried desperately to solve them—always in terms of the nineteenth or eighteenth. He never perceived what he had actually created. Charles Chaplin's masterful burlesque of the assembly line in the movie *Modern Times* could not have amused Ford, who intended to free men's minds by the very devices Chaplin ridiculed. At River Rouge, just as on Brook Farm, Ford expected the workman to begin his real day after his routine work was over. His error came in confusing means with ends. The River Rouge plant proved, as Chaplin's movie implied, that a world in which production becomes an end in itself is as inhuman as the machines themselves.

The men on the assembly line could have told the Mechanical Wizard that he had perfected the cycle of production but not the lives of those who produced. Sameness and tedium ate into their souls. Night-foremen would tell of men who worked efficiently though sound asleep, muscles moving but brains dormant. A Ford worker was not allowed to speak to a pal, or break the monotonous rhythm of the line. If a machine stopped, a bell rang automatically and a foreman came running. The joke about the workman who dropped his wrench and got twenty cars behind wasn't so funny when you knew that as a result he was fired. An employee couldn't even go to the toilet if a substitute were not available to fill in. No wonder men cursed Henry Ford in sixteen different languages. If all their pent-up hatred had burst forth at once, it might have wiped the River Rouge plant off the map.

The one man at the plant who couldn't perceive this was Ford himself. His mechanical obsession turned finally into a monomania. He came to love the sight of driving pistons and the sound of whirring wheels. He was a mechanical Captain Ahab, adrift on a steely sea, pursuing not the white whale Moby Dick but some black phantom Lizzie. Like Ahab, he could neither turn back nor ever hope to succeed in his weird quest. Ahab could tell the species of a whale by the way it spouted; Ford, the make of a machine by the way it purred. But neither special talent was of ultimate avail. At the climactic moment, Lizzie destroyed Ford with the same impersonal and evil ease with which Moby Dick sent Ahab and the *Pequod* down into the silent sea.

Henry Ford's life stretched from Gettysburg to Hiroshima. As much as any other American, he brought the two historical landmarks within one lifetime. To say this does not mean that he entered the atomic age in triumph. When he died at 83 he was an embittered old man. Though he worked on it for a lifetime, he failed to produce a mechanical key to happiness. As a final irony, this genius of technique died by candle-light, the electric power having failed.

No life-long friends were at his death bed. He had never learned that men were not machines to be tested, exploited, and junked. He had driven away his most loyal associates—even, in the end, Sorenson, Cameron, and Bennett.

Ford's boast that "his" men would never vote for a Ford union had backfired when they did so by a huge majority. His social ineptitude may well have contributed to his only son's early death. It may have been instrumental in his oldest grandson's majoring in sociology at Yale. Intricate machines purred at his bidding, but his own human thought process defied him. Never once was he humble enough to admit it to himself or his friends. The closest he came to it was when, after seeing order all about him, he remarked, "It isn't fun any more." The statement stands as the final assessment of Henry Ford's mentality. One of his last projects was to rebuild the school house of Mary and her lamb. There was obvious irony in this, for from the little red school house the mind of Ford had never graduated.

Still Ford was a world figure, especially admired in Russia and Germany. Soviet technocrats envied his achievements. Germans lined up all night to buy securities when he built a plant in the Reich. Books about Ford in a dozen languages show how great was his influence outside America. What Ford's philosophy might come to mean to the Orient, no one can say. Japan and India have added such terms as "Fordize" and "Fordism" to their vocabularies. Who knows where this might lead millions of machine-starved Asiatics?

Henry Ford has passed into the realm of legend. To different groups he represents different things. To the psychologist he is a mechanical Peter Pan, whose human understanding never increased. To the economist he is our Sorcerer's Apprentice, who discovered how to make the broom carry water, but not how to stop the broom. Philosophers think of him as our Frankenstein, inventor of a robot which became the master and the nemesis of its maker. For the citizen who dotes on mass-produced objects, Ford looms up as a Prometheus who brought the secret of a new mechanized fire from heaven. To Europeans he symbolizes our industrial, mass-produced civilization, the full showcase and the empty mind. More than any man of his age he embodied our technological triumphs and human failures, and the still potent dream of a democratic society of economic equality, to be achieved through mass-produced abundance. The contrast between the beauty of the Ford factories and ugliness of their workers' lot poses a crucial problem for our time: how can the human being maintain his individual dignity and freedom in an industrial society?

Ford's epitaph should read: "He put us on wheels." Already we are skeptical about where those mindless wheels may take us. We recall Will Rogers' remark that America is the only country on earth where a man can ride to the poor house in a Ford car. Ours is a great spiritual poverty existing in material opulence. Daily we ride back and forth to earn our meager bread. When we get a few weeks of vacation from our routines, we sit back and watch the Fords go by or get behind the wheel of our own Ford. The intuitive mechanical genius of Henry Ford has made this possible. He also brought us a message: machinery was the new Messiah. Will Henry the Mechanic prove to have been a latter-day John the Baptist?

PART III

Stereotypes

and Prototypes

CHAPTER 10

Onward and Upward: The Self-Made Man

"Strive and Succeed, the world's temptations flee
Be Brave and Bold, and Strong and Steady be
Go Slow and Sure, and prosper then you must
With Fame and Fortune, while you Try and Trust."
                                              —Horatio Alger

I am a sturdy lad. I know I can climb the golden ladder with only my talent and talons to sustain me. Nothing can stop me, because I have both pluck and luck. True enough, my father has been killed, and my dear mother takes in washing. As an honorable son I sell papers. Neighborhood bullies pick on me, but there's always a cheery gleam (not fostered by beer, you may be sure) in my blackened eyes when mother washes them. I know there is always room on top.

I could seek better prospects; but being a sturdy lad, I cannot desert my ailing mother. Then the tide turns. One day I find a wallet which a Rich Man has dropped. Shall I keep the money, and buy mother much-needed medicine? No. Innate honesty makes me take it to the Rich Man's house. The door is opened by his lovely blue-eyed daughter, an imperial young lady. My clean but ragged clothes bring a sneer to her thoroughbred lips; but I know she is Good Beneath, and does not understand me. Hence I love her from that moment forward — though she is Far Above me.

As I back away from the house (she must not see the patch on the seat of my pants) her father comes in. His face lights with joy as he sees the wallet. The grin broadens as he counts the money and finds it all there. "You will be rewarded, young

man," he says. Come by my office and you shall have a job."
Young Venus thaws a bit at this. With reluctance but determination I reply, nobly, "You are kind, Sir, but Ma's alone, sick, and
she needs me."

But she does not need me for long. Her gallant heart gives out
over the scrubbing board, and she goes to her reward, knowing
I have been tried and true. With her last gasp she tells me to
take Rich Man's job. I do. As his office boy I carry papers,
trim pencils, and yearn for the alabaster daughter. I move
quickly up the ladder. My chief competitor is a flabby, mustached
young man of Social Position. He wants not only the junior
partnership; he wants the white goddess. So I watch him closely
and discover (by pluck and luck) that he's a secret swindler. At
the climax of the affair he resists, but in vain. (I live clean and
he smokes.) I get the promotion and the girl. She is something
of a prig and a bore, but then I am as priggish as she. Our
children are *really* brought by the stork. I inherit the Rich Man's
job. We live Happily Ever After.

This, briefly, is the slightly burlesqued saga of one of the most
persistent American heroes, the self-made man. His hold on the
American mind has been amazing. Time has transformed but
not destroyed his rugged image. Detractors have ridiculed him
in vain. He still shouts "Invictus," clutches his Horatio Alger
novel to his breast, and plunges into the open market place. He is,
and has long been, the nation's *beau ideal*. No hero has a more
realistic grip on glory. It can be checked by a certified public
accountant.

The heroic self-made man is not exclusively American. His
roots go back beyond commercial, scientific, and religious revolutions which shattered the medieval synthesis. "Success," wrote
Aeschylus, "is man's god." Englishmen like Adam Smith,
"Diamond" Pitt, and Samuel Smiles figure in our hero's family
tree. His godfathers strode the streets of London, Manchester,
and Paris long before Betsy Ross allegedly sewed together the
first Stars and Stripes, or Pocahontas reputedly saved John Smith's
neck on the block. Yet the riser has strutted so long and so
effectively on the American scene that most Americans consider
him as indigenous as maize, tobacco, and juke boxes.

The history and evolution of the self-made hero in America is a complex thing, involving our belief in progress, the rise of capitalism, the migration of Calvinism and Darwinism, the role of the frontier, the notion of "calling," and the effect of the man-land ratio on a new culture. The rise of cities, industry, individualism, and the middle class come in too. No one man is the prototype. Thousands of Americans have varied the pattern according to their own needs and opportunities.

Nor is the self-made man's viewpoint static. Before the Revolution he was mainly religious, as Cotton Mather showed. With the rise of deism and militant democracy the orientation became political; witness Benjamin Franklin and Andrew Jackson. Middle America and post-Civil War America rallied behind the sign of the dollar, and economics became the area in which the self-made man excelled. In that golden day, many admirers publicized him, notably Horatio Alger and William McGuffey. In the contemporary Age of Anxiety, when Freudian symbols and character analyzing flourish, the self-made man must be a master of psychology. He must know how to state questions so that all answers end up being yes. Once he depended on driving power, but now he insinuates himself into authority.

The first settlers of America had hardly disembarked before they were being told that God favored the diligent and frugal. There were no positive assurances that such traits belonged to the elect; but there were powerful hints. While material prosperity did not necessarily assure God's favor, it looked powerfully like just that to the mortal eye. If the workers weren't worthy of salvation, who was? Pick up thine ax and swing.

Because he embodied the quintessence of orthodox Puritanism in America, Cotton Mather spoke effectively about the self-made man. Precocious, ambitious, and pontifical, Mather (1663-1728) tended to associate the will of God with the monthly balance sheet. "'Tis not honest, nor Christian, that a Christian should have no Business to do," he observed. His eyes glowed with satisfaction when they fell upon Proverbs 22:29: "Seest thou a man diligent in his business? He shall stand before kings." The implication was plain enough. Thou shalt find a fitting work,

and in this work thou shalt succeed.   Religion and activism
were equated.

Mather's most imposing book was *Magnalia Christi Americana*.
For pious hero-worship it is unexcelled in American biography.
The longest character sketch has to do with Sir William Phips,
a self-made man.   He took the road Alger heroes later travelled,
from rags to riches and fame.   Never mind if he erred slightly
and indulged in a little piracy.   Boys will be boys.   At the end
Phips succeeded, "defying pale Envy to fly-blow the Hero."   For
the New Englander seeking a moral sanction for money-making,
here was a book to ponder.

Other works demonstrate even more clearly how Mather wedded
Puritanism to ambition in early America.   His *Two Brief Discourses* quite bluntly asserted that man must serve Christ, and
achieve success in a personal calling. *The Essays To Do Good* held
it was every man's privilege and duty to help the Lord, but wealthy
people could do the most.   They were stewards, whose special
ability gave them special opportunities.   "Honor the Lord with
thy substance; so shall thy barns be filled with plenty."   One
even detects the suggestion that charity itself can be a profitable
business venture.

Benjamin Franklin is the best colonial example of the self-made
man in America.   There is a direct relationship between the
thoughts of Mather and Franklin.[1]   The Philadelphia sage adopted
rather than imitated Mather's outlook, writing like a Puritan and
living like a pragmatist.   Franklin's own *Autobiography* and *Poor
Richard's Almanack* (issued from 1733 to 1758, and subsequently
as *Poor Richard Improved*) had a great impact on America.   His
homely maxims influenced the colonies more than all the formal
philosophies of the time combined.   The debt in both instances to
Protestant mores and particularly to Cotton Mather is plain.
Mather's *Essays To Do Good*, Franklin admits in the *Autobiography*, "had an influence on some of the principal future events
of my life."   Yet Mather's God is unlike Franklin's God-without-
thunder.   The thunderbolt which was the stern voice of Jehovah
to Mather, trickled harmlessly off a kite string, into Ben's
Leyden jar.

Franklin knew better than to turn openly against the American

Puritanical household morality. Instead, he substituted a political and economic base for the religious one of Mather. Writing from the commercial capital of the New World, as a diplomat who had distinguished himself at Versailles, he emphasized about the self-made man things that belonged to his age and temperament. Never immodest, he listed his own achievements in a best-seller autobiography because he thought his life "fit to be imitated." He extolled the "incontestable virtues of frugality, industry, cleanliness, resolution, and chastity." "Lose no time. Be always employed in something useful; cut off all unnecessary actions." Even more familiar are the aphorisms popularized in almanacs which (like the Bible) were read everywhere in America. God helps them that help themselves. He that would catch Fish, must venture his Bait. Idleness is the Dead Sea, that swallows all Virtues. Be active in Business, that Temptation may miss her Aim. The Bird that sits is easily shot. Here was ample preparation for the Great Barbecue ahead for the America that was to turn inexorably to urbanism and industrialization.

Politicians capitalized on the self-made man theme. Nineteenth century candidates for office talked fast to explain why they had not risen from a log cabin, if such advantage had been denied them. They seized upon Franklin as a ready-made symbol linking eighteenth and nineteenth century ideology. A series of Franklin Lectures was instituted at Boston in 1830 "to encourage young men to make the most of their opportunities." Presently Franklin monuments appeared in city squares, and his likeness on stamps, coins, and medallions. His had been a fully satisfying American success story; he was worthy of imitation.

The same man who aided Washington up Olympus helped Franklin. Parson Weems, who could spot a potential hero on a cloudy day without his glasses, turned his hierophancy on Poor Richard's creator in 1796. He asked Jefferson for Franklin stories "to be cooked up into a savoury dish for Juvenile palates," and dashed off a life of Franklin. It went through eleven editions. Still Franklin was overshadowed by that rip-roaring coonskin hatter from the West, the first poor boy to make the White House, Andrew Jackson.

Jackson can best be understood against the background of an

America in which the value of manufacturing increased more than tenfold between 1810 and 1860. Coal, land, oil, power, metals were plentiful. Come and get it! When Phineas Barnum said that having more land than people in America meant that anyone could make money, he was stating a truism. Old Hickory saw that with the new economic prosperity, democracy would become militant. So he picked up his sword and franchise, got in front of a group of voters, and said, "Follow me!" They did—right to the White House lawn. On Jackson's inauguration day, hell-raising was advanced to a new level. A rough-and-tumble self-made man had become chief executive of our nation. The political pattern for the next century had been set.

The swaggering, self-conscious mood of the Jacksonian period was reflected in art, literature, and education as well as in politics. Democracy was made into a secularized religion, with the self-made man as its high priest. A poor Virginia orphan named Henry Clay, who became a Republican candidate for president, first used the term "self-made man" in a Congressional debate on February 2, 1832. Under different guises, and in other connections, it had already long been understood throughout America. Such men as Clay and Jackson rose not by revolution but resolution. To a Creole aristocrat who saw Jackson for the first time he looked like "an ugly old Kaintuck flat-boatman." To most Americans he seemed just like one of themselves magnified a few times. Under him the perfumed gentry trembled, the national bank collapsed, and the ambiguous phrase "equal opportunity for all" meant something. Old Hickory said that if the job was too hard for the man, you ought to get rid of the job. A fellow could vote for an executive like that, and whoop at the privilege.

This new democracy was built squarely on the old morality and on the self-made man cult. It scorned the bones of a buried ancestry, and determined to remove the political obstacles that got in the hero's way. Success was the end point. Individual success justified not only the man but the institutions under which he served. If will power be a true criterion of the hero (as it is for the self-made man) Jackson ranks high among America's great. A story which Franklin Roosevelt told in his third "Fireside Chat" illustrates the point. Once a small boy was asked whether or not

Andy Jackson would go to heaven. His reply was as final as it was spontaneous. "He will if he wants to," said the boy. Horatio Alger couldn't have improved on that line.

A few years after Jackson's death a neurotic and pallid young American, who reflected little of Jackson's optimism, left San Francisco and moved to a village at the foot of the Rocky Mountains. In a small hut he rested and brooded, asking himself a question he dared not answer: "Am I, dear God, a failure?"

The man was Horatio Alger, Jr. (1832-1899). His own story is more intriguing than most of his heroes' and reveals more about American life. Born of old Yankee stock in Massachusetts, Horatio was the first son of a stern Unitarian minister who was a walking blue law. He damned human activities leading to enjoyment and prescribed as remedies generous portions of piety. His son became known at Gates Academy and Harvard College as "Holy Horatio." Indignantly Horatio changed his Harvard lodgings when his landlady appeared in her negligee. "I might have seen her bare, but I did not look," he wrote.

Confused and unhappy, he persuaded his parents to let him journey to Paris, where he learned things which the Unitarians had never stressed. He looked. His Paris diary contains two lines more worthy of immortality than any others in the Alger canon: "I was a fool to have waited so long. It is not nearly so vile as I had thought."

Back home he reformed and became a Unitarian minister. It was an impossible situation. In 1866 he moved to New York to launch his literary career, writing juveniles for William Adams ("Oliver Optic"). His pose was plainly Byronic; since there were no Alps close at hand, he took refuge in the stormy metropolis instead. Political biographies being in demand, he turned out three with titles-of-the-times: *Webster: From Farm Boy to Senator*, *Lincoln: The Backwoods Boy*, and *Garfield: From Canal Boy to President*. He finished the last of the three in thirteen days, to get it to the publisher before Garfield died. But biography was not his medium; he needed the freedom of fiction. Alger turned out 135 novels which sold at least 20,000,000 copies. The books were not carefully constructed or written. Yet they became dicta for two generations of rising Americans. Alger made no apologies. He knew they were pot boilers. "I should have let go," he confessed. "How many times I wanted to! Writing in the same vein becomes a habit, like sleeping on the right side. Try to sleep on the left side and the main purpose is defeated — one stays awake." [2] While other writers did single volumes, Alger turned out whole series — the *Ragged Dick, Tattered Tom, Brave and Bold, Luck and Pluck, New World, Way to Success, Campaign, Atlantic,* and *Pacific.*

Because he customarily wrote two books simultaneously, he sometimes got his characters mixed. Hence Grant Thornton disappears mysteriously from *Helping Himself* (chapter IX) only to pop up and thrash a bully in *Hector's Inheritance* (chapter XIII). Did Alger's readers mind? Not in the least. To them an Alger novel was as much a part of the scheme of things as state fairs, Sunday, and the Declaration of Independence. He never let them down. Even as the novel was being written, some real-life American of Alger's day would be living the legend he heralded. James B. Duke was peddling his first tobacco; Henry Ford was moving up from his job of polishing steam engines; Thomas Edison was graduating from his newspaper hawking; and John D. Rockefeller, after a period of unemployment, was lining up a job. Their rises reaffirmed the nation's faith in laissez faire capitalism and in Alger. The times not only made the novels; they also justified them.

None of the peaches and cream of his books spilled over into Alger's life. There is pathos of his tipping the Astor House desk clerk to point out celebrities, or pounding the drum in newsboys' parades. A violent affair with a married woman, the antagonism of his family, and his failure to rid himself of despair, lined the face of the plump balding author, and caused him to seek refuge in the Newsboys' Lodging House in New York City. To the end he wrote steadily, desperately, parodying his own earlier style, writing for boys because he couldn't write for men. Finally even the Sunday School teachers found it hard to read his little sagas with a straight face. The gilt had long since worn off his style. At the century's end he died quietly in a drab dormitory room. Sometime before he had written, half in jest, his own epitaph. No one could have written a better one:

"Six feet underground reposes Horatio Alger, Helping Himself to a part of the earth, not Digging for Gold or In Search of Treasure, but Struggling Upward and Bound to Rise at last In a New World—where it shall be said he is Risen from the Ranks."

*   *   *

No Alger hero got a more romantic start than that which legend accords to William McGuffey (1800-1873).   In 1818 Thomas Hughes, builder of the Old Stone Academy on the Pennsylvania frontier, was riding through Trumbull County, Ohio.   He passed a rude log cabin near the road, and overheard a woman praying devoutly in the yard—beseeching God to help devise a way to educate her poor children.   So moved was Hughes that he arranged to have her oldest son enrolled in his Academy.   The boy was William McGuffey.

The story illustrates what Americans want to think about the man whose schoolbooks became an American byword.   Of Scotch-Irish stock, McGuffey was born on a pioneer homestead, where he spent the sixteen years.   Graduating from Washington College in 1826, he became professor of languages at Miami University in Ohio.   His later career at Cincinnati College, Ohio University, and the University of Virginia was distinguished, but his importance for us stems from his textbook writing and moralizing.

McGuffey wrote his First and Second Readers in 1836.   By 1850 over 7,000,000 copies had been sold, and by 1870, 40,000,000; more than 122,000,000 appeared by 1920, justifying Mark Sullivan's contention that half the school children of America began their reading with them.   And the story of their distribution did not end there.   Henry Ford, a self-made man and a devotee of McGuffey, had the entire series re-issued and widely distributed in 1925.   If ever a man moulded the mind of America's youth, and entrenched the gospel of the self-made man, it was William McGuffey.

His Readers were a skillful synthesis of bourgeois virtues and capitalistic maxims.   They were carefully prepared "to exert a decided and healthful moral influence" over the reader, dealing with self-reliance, the advantages of industry, and the importance of well-spent youth.   McGuffey's Second Reader included Parson

Weems' invention about George Washington and the cherry tree; here one hero-maker helped another. McGuffey's admiration for great men was not confined to America. The Third Reader contained these well-known lines about Napoleon's initiative and daring when confronted with the Alps:

"Is the route practicable?" said Bonaparte.

"It is barely possible to pass," replied the engineer.

"Let us set forward, then," said Napoleon.

A source from which McGuffey borrowed continuously was Poor Richard. Franklin's apt and catchy proverbs were ideal. "Lazy Ned" and "Idle Jane" were the fall guys in McGuffey-land. Terrible was their demise once they thumbed their nose at push, pluck, and principle. Testimonies of the effectiveness of McGuffey's readers have come from McKinley, Harding, Taft, Mark Twain, Lew Wallace, and many of the Gilded Age's Robber Barons. McGuffey and Alger were the two bees who carried the pollen of success most industriously through America.

Had Elbert Hubbard written nothing but "A Message to Garcia," which appeared in *Philistine* in 1889, he would still be important in self-help literature. Drawing from an episode in the Spanish-American War, the essay stressed the virtues of reliability, performance, and trust. Its vogue our more sophisticated age finds hard to comprehend. One man, George Daniels of the New York Central Railroad, distributed over 1,500,000 copies. Translated into Russian, French, and German, the story with the self-help moral was soon a globe-trotter. Hubbard was not the kind of man to let so good a thing pass by. He moved forward by taking *Little Journeys to the Homes of Great Business Men*. In saccharine, stilted phrases he praised the hands that held the purse-strings. Of Jim Hill he wrote, "Clio will eventually write his name on her roster as a great modern prophet, a creator, a builder. Pericles built a city, but this man made an empire." Business to Hubbard was a divine calling, the best means of redeeming the world. The ark of his covenant was stored in the bank vault, and he wanted merely to stand with the high priests who hovered around it.

Alger's closest rival as a writer of juveniles was a New England minister, William Thayer. Thayer's biographies of Lincoln,

Grant, and Garfield flooded nineteenth century homes; that of
Lincoln went through 36 editions. The Thayer formula for success was simple. Be born poor. Adopt good principles. Keep
fighting until you reach the top. That was all there was to it, but
it was enough to get him elected to the state legislature and to
provide him with a sizable income for life. *Tact, Push, and Principle* (1881) was Thayer's most influential book. As a Christian
minister he took the viewpoint that religion not only condoned,
but demanded success. The Gospel of Wealth joined the gospels
of Matthew, Mark, Luke, and John for Thayer.

They did so too for a Baptist minister named Russell Conwell,
who came to Philadelphia in 1851 and, in the basement of his
church, founded Temple University. So far as self-made heroes
are concerned, Conwell's major contribution was a speech called
"Acres of Diamonds." He delivered it over 6,000 times. Work
your own back yard, where diamonds may well be, and don't go
drifting off after greener pastures, was his main point. "Tens of
thousands of men and women get rich honestly. But they are often
accused by an envious, lazy crowd of unsuccessful persons of being dishonest and oppressive. I say, 'Get rich, get rich, get rich!' "
This was the pulpit diet on which our grandfathers' souls were
nourished.

The leading editor of the self-help cult was Orison S. Marden.
His highly popular magazine *Success* explained to thousands of
readers how they could "make mental mazdas of their minds."
Among its features were character building charts and "personal
experience letters." Marden also turned out volumes like *Pushing
to the Front* (1894), which went through 250 editions. In Japan
it was referred to as the "new Japanese Bible," and in Guatemala
the president distributed it as a prize to public school children.
President McKinley thought there was "nothing more worthy to
be placed in the hands of American youth," and John D. Wana-
maker said he would have given up "at least one meal a day to
buy one of the Marden books." Hubbard, Thayer, Conwell, and
Marden reflected in their writing and thinking the shift of power
from the great circus at Washington to the great casino at Wall
Street. Finance began to attract the best brains, leaving the
mediocre ones for government. Men like Gould, Fiske, Vander-

bilt, and Hill wielded tremendous power. Hundreds still dreamed of occupying the White House, but thousands dedicated themselves to making money.

In the twentieth century, which has rejected so many of the economic principles of the nineteenth, the self-made man literature has splintered and degenerated. Mark Twain foresaw this; he wrote a biting satire of Horatio Alger's world in *The Adventures of Huckleberry Finn*. On the surface it is a child's story; underneath it is a novel of complexity, bitterness, and compassion.

A violent and positive reaction against Alger's happy stuffy world came from the naturalist writers of the early twentieth century, especially Theodore Dreiser. This group tended to view man as a superior animal rather than a sacred creature; and concentrated upon his more elemental events and motives. The central actor in three of Dreiser's novels, Frank Cowperwood, got ahead, not by returning the Rich Man's wallet, but by keeping it. Life to him was nasty, brutish, and short. His formula for survival was consecrated egotism.

As a young boy Frank Cowperwood stood in front of a store window tank and watched as a lobster caught and devoured a squid. This was the whole lesson of the world around him. The lobster ate the squid by supreme natural right. He'd be the lobster, society the squid. Dreiser's heroes liked their Darwinism raw, and did not mind a little blood on it.

Equally tough and amoral were the dozens of detective heroes modeled on Dashiell Hammett's Sam Spade. His was a world of erotica and violence, and in book after book the detective went through the same harrowing business: "On the average he makes love to three or four sexually magnetic women, consumes four or five quarts of hard liquor, smokes cartons of cigarettes, is knocked on the head, shot, and bruised in fist fights from seven to ten times—while groping his way through a dense fog as far as breaking the case is concerned . . . It is like the enmity between animals; there is nothing personal in it." [3]

Another literary reaction to the Alger lad is the Ernest Hemingway hero, who *will not* get ahead and doesn't care. So to hell with you. A handsome fellow, a hunter, a lover, he is usually a newspaperman, always on the move; he writes novels by day and

collects girls and material by night.   Bullfights intrigue him.
Bourgeois values disgust him, and he is constantly drawn to primitive areas, particularly Africa.   Because he knows the world is
a shoddy place, he takes his fun in the company of the "initiated."
He is quietly desperate, cheerfully dissipated, and highly entertaining.   Two generations of American college students and writers
have grown up trying to be like him.

In the winter of 1953 Hemingway had a chance to act out the
fictional role he had created.   While giving his fourth wife, "Miss
Mary," a "Christmas present" flight across darkest Africa, he
suffered two plane crashes and was reported lost to the crocodiles.
Miraculously he survived, emerging from the jungle clutching a
bunch of bananas in one hand and a bottle of gin in the other.

Not until the following May did Hemingway, inventor of so
many tight-lipped heroes, admit what physical damage had been
done: "I jammed my spine, ruptured my right kidney and liver,
collapsed my intestine, suffered a concussion which seriously
affected my eyesight, and was burned seriously on the scalp when
the second plane caught fire."   And where was Hemingway when
he made this recitation?   In Madrid, which he was visiting "for
the peak of the bullfighting season!"   "Pappy" Hemingway not
only invented a heroic stereotype, he also illustrated it.

But the toughest of the tough—indeed, the *reductio ad absurdum*
of the whole type — came after World War II with the sadistic
monsters of Mickey Spillane.   Here distortion passed beyond the
realm of terror, and back to humor.   The only thing to do, were
one to take him seriously, would be to call the S.P.C.A.   There is
a point of brutality and sensuality beyond which heroes stop being
men.   This will never do.

The defense of the pure-and-simple self-made man fell into the
adolescent but skillful hands of Tom Swift and Tarzan.   Tom,
the hero of a long series of boys' books by Victor Appleton, based
his success on the perfectibility of machines.   By using all the
latest gadgets, Tom managed (from the turn of the century to
mid-Depression) to preserve justice, white supremacy, and the
American home.   To his millions of young readers, he promised
Better Things for Better Living through Science.   He was Horatio
Alger's Sturdy Lad with rockets on.   Of course he Got Ahead

supersonically. Urbanism and technology presented no problems to Tom. He operated in a technological fairyland.

Edgar Rice Burroughs' Tarzan, almost literally a self-made man, grew up among the wild animals of Africa. Instead of facing the problems of capitalism, he dealt with the primordial jungle. Suckled by a female gorilla, he befriended Tantor the elephant and feuded with Numa the lion. Leopard-women, ant-men, white renegades, and even men from Mars tried in vain to outwit him: for he was really the son of Lord Greystoke, an English nobleman. He was a triumph of human brawn and instinct—to say nothing of behaviorist psychology.

Like the Alger heroes, Tarzan had pluck and luck. White men appeared from time to time, bent on stealing gold, ivory, or Tarzan's favorite ape. In such instances duels were inevitable. Tarzan let his opponent empty a revolver into him before swinging off on a liana vine—thus showing that he bore the evil world no hard feelings. He fits into the niche created by Rousseau genera- tions ago for the Noble Savage.

The earlier types have not gone completely. "Just call me *sui generis*," said Huey Long, one of the century's fastest-rising American politicos. During World War II, Henry J. Kaiser dem- onstrated that the day of tycoons was not completely past. But ever since the I.C.C., the anti-trust laws, and the income tax came, the tycoon has been fighting a losing battle for estate and esteem. Field after field has been removed from the realm of Alger and McGuffey's free enterpriser. Technology has so complicated in- dustries that only those with tremendous resources can seize them. Think, for example, of how much it takes to produce a new model automobile, put out a metropolitan daily, or start a new airline. The individualistic tooth-and-claw self-made hero is disappearing from economic fields because the laissez faire economics to which he was wedded is fading.

A generation ago such writers as Drieser, Garland, Norris, and Crane introduced with naturalism the notion that the dice were loaded against ambitious young Americans in a monopolistic and nepotistic society. Depression literature was full of despair and cynicism. A new psychology of self-help was born.

"The next time we are tempted to give somebody 'hail Columbia' let's pull a $5 bill out of our pocket, look at Lincoln's picture on the bill, and ask, 'How would Lincoln handle this problem if he had it?' " This line from Dale Carnegie's *How to Win Friends and Influence People* is enough concerned with the self-made Abe Lincoln to establish the continuity with the past, and enough concerned with servility to epitomize the Depression trend. In October, 1929, Aladdin's magic lamp blacked out. Onto the scene rushed an ogre who mauled the financial structure, at a cost of more than fifty billion dollars and untold human suffering. A long-proud, Algerized nation was forced to create a whole new set of symbols: the frantic look, the slammed door, the endless walk, the shoes lined with newspapers, the straggling breadline, the soupbowl with the lonely potato, the grimy hands warmed over sputtering fires in hobo jungles.

Even while the mighty were still falling on the Wall Street front, torn to shreds by the tickertape, the attitude towards success and business heroes was altering. Psychology became the new key. Before that winter was over Walter B. Pitkin had published *The Psychology of Achievement*, and J. J. B. Morgan (with E. T. Webb) *The Strategy of Handling People*. In 1931 Professor Charles R. Gow of the Massachusetts Institute of Technology came forward with an approach known as "Humanics," duly detailed in *Foundations for Human Engineering*. With 1932 came August Myers' *Human Engineering* and Stuart Chase's *The Nemesis of American Business*, reflecting the fear of the times. And in the fall of 1933, *Time* reprinted a Cincinnati newspaper ad which indicated that an epoch of hero worship was closing: "Have complete course on 'How to Become a Success,' will swap for room rent." Subsequently *Life Begins at Forty* was written to console the middle-age failures and *You Must Relax* was published to justify the enforced idleness of millions of unemployed. The technicolor dream of the heroic businessman had become a nightmare. The new advice was not to put on your armor, but to take off your hat.[4]

Among the purveyors of the new approach to success, the most influential was certainly Dale Carnegie. He was born on a farm near Maryville, Missouri, in 1888, where his father fought a losing battle with the perennial floods of the One Hundred and Two

River.   Between his farm chores, Dale sandwiched in an education at the State Teachers College at Warrensburg, Missouri, riding to and from school on horseback, studying by lamplight after midnight, and feeding the pigs at 3 a.m. so as to free him for the morning dash for culture.   After graduating he sold correspondence courses, lard, and Armour Star bacon.

His thoughts turned to the big city; he went to New York and enrolled in the American Academy of Arts.   Among the things that impressed him there was Carnegie Hall. He changed his name from the Missouri spelling of Carnegey to Carnegie.   Jobless and despondent, he contemplated suicide, just as had Horatio Alger. To the manager of the 125th Street Y.M.C.A., who let him teach public speaking there, must go special credit for his surviving. By 1916 he was able to hire a hall — Carnegie Hall — for his speeches.   With a Times Square office, assistants, such unusual honorary degrees as B.Pd. and B.C.S., and a ghost writer to do research on famous men, he gained momentum.

Carnegie believed Americans respected historic successes and Niagara Falls for similar reasons; cubic tons of water and cubic tons of wealth are overwhelming.   His *How to Win Friends and Influence People* (1937) went through 17 printings in five months. Newspapers, advertisements, radio programs, and free demonstrations popularized his method.   Carnegie moved from business to domestic problems, dispensing marital advice with a sincerity not evident when he declared himself a bachelor so as to avoid explaining his divorce.

Sinclair Lewis defined Carnegism as "yessing the boss and making Big Business right with God."   Two key rules in *How to Win Friends and Influence People* are: "Never tell a man he is wrong," and "Get the other person saying 'yes, yes' immediately." Yes your enemy into complacency and your friend into acquiescence.   Among the reviewers of the book who were not impressed was James Thurber.   "The disingenuities in his set of rules and in his case histories stand out like ghosts at a banquet," he commented.   Thurber added a rule of his own for Carnegie to ponder: "Exclamation points, even three in a row, do not successfully convey depth of sincerity or intensity of feeling." [5]   But in 1937 730,000 Americans bought Carnegie's volume despite Thurber.

In 1940 Carnegie turned up as a supernumerary in the New York City Center performance of the ballet "Sheherazade," to the delight of the *New Yorker*, which sent a reporter around to cover the event.   Among the comments garnered there was one by an assistant manager named Michael Mindlin.   "It's like a big Freudian deal," said Mindlin.   "The man makes a specialty of being everybody's pal, then gets rid of inhibitions by pretending to chop ladies' heads off in a ballet."   He had touched on a vital point.   The new names for the rungs in the ladder of success are ego, super-ego, and id.

Under his different guises, the self-made hero is always the Cinderella of our bourgeois society, the personification of the equalitarianism at the basis of our political structure.   From the very first we were opposed to the pomp and circumstance of kings and to all prerogatives of aristocracy.   Performance, not birth, we have held as the true measure.

Only in certain fields, such as business and politics, has equalitarianism prevailed; and here the self-made hero has been most at home.   In art, philosophy, music, and science we honor great men, but we do not assert that anyone who tries hard can do just as well.   The admiration we feel for Winslow Homer, George Gershwin, and Albert Einstein is different from the homage we pay Thomas Jefferson, Andrew Jackson, and Abraham Lincoln. The maxim for the first group is "Geniuses are born, not made;" for the second group, "Every boy can be president."   It is the heredity versus environment argument, with the self-made men on the environment side.   In America, whatever the achievements of the two groups, the latter has given us the most popular and beloved heroes.

Viewed in this light, it seems unfair that the self-made man should have been the target of violent attacks in the 1920's and '30's.   He may have been naive, but he was not a boob.   His sense of values may have seemed crude, but it was a part of the pattern of his times, his education, and his experience.   Whatever his failings, he made distinct—and notable—contributions to America.   He may have been more earthy than ethereal and a stranger to the golden rule, but he helped fulfill the material promises of the Promised Land.

CHAPTER 11

The Giant and the Jackass:
Paul Bunyan and Joe Magarac

*"Maybe the scholars have been following a false lead;
maybe popular literature isn't a folk art at all."*
—Bernard DeVoto

In the U.S.A., land of the Big Build-Up, much that passes for folklore is really fakelore. Scholars have found that Paul Bunyan, Joe Magarac, Pecos Bill and other "ancient characters" are (like Mercutio's wound) not so deep as a well, nor so wide as a church door. But what we have done with them (again like the wound) is enough; 'twill serve.

Only a purist, convinced that "the folk" are holier than specific contrivers, resents what has happened. A hero is a hero, no matter who creates him, or why. Too many folklorists think they are scientific when actually they are sentimental. They deplore efforts of corporations or political groups to invent new symbols and characters, without realizing that in our society these are the natural agencies to do such things. Like everything else, folklore and mythology are shaped by the culture in which they flourish.

A lumber company was the prime mover behind our modern Beowulf, Paul Bunyan—but that doesn't make him any less vigorous than old Beowulf, or Aeneas, or Samson.

Take that fellow Samson. Chances are, as one tough-minded folklorist recently pointed out, that he was nothing more than "an overgrown Asia Minor country boy who made his first unpremeditated bid for fame when he leaned against a shaky pole in the tent of some other desert-dwelling character and—in his awkwardness—caused the shelter to collapse. Relatives and friends trans-

158

formed the tent into a pillar and Samson's reputation was made." [1]

Delilah? Probably just a pretty hill-billy gal who didn't get a wolf-call from the Babylon bucks until neighbors started to spread tales about her. Then the boys looked her up; but they hardly thought students would be doing it in twentieth century encyclopedias.

The whole thing makes one wonder if in a few generations folklorists will be rushing around getting old timers to tell what they remember about Lydia E. Pinkham, Al Capone, Bing Crosby, Babe Ruth, and Mae West. By then, the Babe will have become as sturdy a figure as Samson, and Mae will have Delilah beaten on several points.

Fake and folklore are delightfully intertwined in Paul Bunyan. *Fortune* magazine chose him, a few years ago, as "the one fictional character fit to stand with the nation's historical heroes." For, said the editors, Paul is "a genuine American folk character, created by the people themselves, in the bunkhouse and ordinary logging camp." Such a claim has been made many times, before and since. Paul is said to have grown out of the American environment by some folksy process, a pure product of mass creativity. In his preface to a Bunyan collection by Harold Felton, Carl Sandburg asks who made Paul Bunyan and then answers: "The people, the bookless people, they made Paul and had him alive long before he got into the books for those who read. Paul is as old as the hills, young as the alphabet."

The giant lumberjack described by *Fortune* and Felton was not born in a bunkhouse, but in an advertising office. He was considerably younger than the hills—no older than a promotion scheme of the Red River Lumber Company; not as old as Sandburg's *Chicago Poems*.

This is not to say Paul never was a lumber hero. Certain old loggers talked about him before the office crews wrote about him. Their oral yarns didn't concern the universal roustabout but a vocational in-group hero whose talk and feats could appeal only to those on the inside of a highly specialized business. These jargon-filled tales, mainly concerned with exaggerated adversities and tender tyros, were funny only to the initiated. When times and methods changed, and the need for brute strength and endurance passed, the oral Bunyan tradition began to die out too.

The few authentic Bunyan camp stories recorded before World War I were supplied by men who were even then old. How little general appeal these stories would have may be judged from the following example, written down by a lumberjack in 1916 at the request of Professor Homer A. Watt:

"Paul B. Driving a large Bunch of logs Down the Wisconsin River When the logs Suddenly Jamed in the Dells. The logs were piled Two Hundred feet high at the head . . . When Paul Arrived at the Head with the ox he told them to Stand Back. He put the Ox in the old Wisc (River) in front of the Jam. And then standing on the Bank Shot the Ox with a 303 Savage Rifle."

The Bunyan known to most Americans—he might be called Paul Bunyan II, to distinguish him from Paul Bunyan I, the lumberjacks' bona fide hero—is a giant of a considerably different order. He has a literary, not a folk origin. He speaks a "printed page" English and not vernacular English, and never gets technical or profane. He utilizes parachutes, steam-driven concrete mixers, pipe lines, and other devices unknown before the turn of the century; and he ranges far afield to work in mines, airfields, and ranches, but never as one group's hero. His exploits are not passed on in ballad or song. Nor do workmen improvise on the old themes at their leisure, or invent new situations. Most lumberjacks do not read the literary accounts where the real improvisation takes place. Today Paul Bunyan serves a multitude of functions and ends that the creators of Paul I never dreamed of. For Paul II is no mere comic hero. On the contrary, he is an exponent of American "know-how," industrialism, and the "American way of life." Dan G. Hoffman, a leading Bunyan Scholar, has pointed out that "as a symbol of American size, strength, and ingenuity, he threatens to replace the less lively figure of Uncle Sam."

With a nod of deference, then, to the declining Paul Bunyan I, who might in different circumstances have grown to be a regular ringtailed roarer, perhaps even the hero of an American epic, we turn to Paul Bunyan II, who has usurped his forerunner's role and supporters and disguised himself as a folk hero in popular and learned accounts.

The first poem about the literary Paul was published in *The American Lumberman* in 1914. The author was Douglas Malloch:

"Those were the days in Michigan
The good old days, when any man
Could cut and skid and log and haul,
And there was pine enough for all . . .
Paul Bunyan (you have heard of Paul?
He was the kingpin of 'em all,
The greatest logger in the land.
Paul Bunyan bossed that famous crew:
A bunch of shoutin' bruisers, too . . .)"

As the reader might suspect, these verses caused no literary sensation. But the Bunyan boom was on its way. That same year William B. Laughead, who more than any other man deserves the title of creator of Paul II, began his work. It was not as a poet, however, but as an advertising layout man trying to sell lumber. His Paul Bunyan was conceived, in a manner of speaking, on a commission basis.

Details of Laughead's early efforts are fortunately preserved in an interview which appeared in the *Minneapolis Sunday Tribune* on September 7, 1947. When the Red River Lumber Company decided to move from the well-worked timberlands of Minnesota to California, the secretary of the company, Archie D. Walker, was instructed to devise an advertising program to publicize the move and acquire new customers. Walker passed the problem on to his cousin, a young free-lance advertising man named William Laughead. Thus Walker may be thought of as Paul's literary grandfather, or the *homo economicus* in Paul's family tree; though he does not pretend that his achievement was a great event in the history of American folklore. "All I wanted to do," he has said, "was to sell lumber."

The man Walker called upon to help him with this task was a happy choice. Laughead had worked for eight years in Minnesota logging camps, moving up from choreboy to assistant bull cook and on to timber cruiser, surveyor, and construction engineer. When he went into the advertising business he hoped to put his logging lore to good use; this assignment was almost too good to be true. Right away he remembered some funny stories about an imaginary lumberman which might make good copy if they were put into a palatable form. The name usually given this character, Laughead recalled, was Paul—Paul Bunyan.

Laughead says he first heard of his hero-to-be from some old loggers in Minnesota. He sensed that Paul would make a good trademark for a lumber company. His antics were distinctly color-ful; except for Malloch's poem he had not appeared in print; and, for all practical purposes, he was totally unknown to his fellow Americans. Of course, the jargon-filled and frequently profane Bunyan stories the old-timers had told were unsuited for a general reading public, but Laughead saw distinct possibilities.

After a few months he produced a booklet of 32 pages called "Introducing Mr. Paul Bunyan of Westwood, California." It was divided equally between Bunyan material and straight adver-tising. A "warning" on page one indicated that Laughead intended to pass Paul off as a widely-known folk hero and a paragon worthy of taking care of Red River Lumber Company problems:

"Everything we tell you about Red River lumber and its manu-facture is the Gospel Truth. Everything we tell you about Paul Bunyan is lumberjack mythology. Paul is the legendary hero whose exploits have been related to generations of tenderfeet from time immemorial. We have gathered some of them up, and pass them on to you with a few trimmings of our own."

It would be very interesting to know just what those "few trim-mings" were; today Laughead is not sure where recollection ended and contrivance began. For inventing such Bunyanesque characters as Babe the Blue Ox, Brimstone Bill, and Big Joe the Cook, he takes full credit. No one disputes his claim that he first vested Bunyan with a commercial mission. He was personally responsible for devising the first pictorial representation of Paul Bunyan (his Paul has a round face, black hair, and a cat's-whis-kers moustache), which was copyrighted as the Red River Lumber Company trademark. Accompanying the original portrayal is a reminder that "he stands for the quality and service you have the right to expect from Paul Bunyan." Under the picture is the warning that the picture is "registered." It is as clear a case of *ars gratia pecuniae* as one will find in the annals of American heroes.

After a slow start the Bunyan booklets picked up speed, and gained wide circulation in a few years. In 1922, when Laughead was made a regular employee of the Red River Company, he pre-pared a larger pamphlet which was mailed not only to potential customers but also to newspaper editors, historians, and the general public. All found the Bunyan stories to their liking. For the editors they made good copy; for the historians, grounds for endless speculation and quibbling; and, for the general public, items that inflated the national and regional egos. The lumber states knew a good thing when they saw it. They decided that Bunyan was a latter-day epic hero who had been roaming around in their forests since they were planted. Minnesota became belligerent over Bunyan, and possessive about all stories or legends that surrounded him. Neighboring states like Michigan and Wisconsin fought to center Bunyan lore within their boundaries. Paul and his Blue Ox bedecked the walls of the new Student Union Building at the University of Wisconsin, while Michigan supporters proclaimed that the "Saginaw Paul Bunyan" was the real thing. Far Western states entered the competition with enthusiasm; in the last decade Oregon has become one of the leading promoters of Bunyania.

Soon scholars joined copywriters employed by tourist centers, chambers of commerce, state agencies, and booster clubs in the campaign to win national recognition for Paul. Many devised methods to prove that he was indeed a folk hero, a kind of Beowulf west of Boston; others explained why the lumberjacks had decided that Babe the Blue Ox was precisely 42 axe handles and a plug of Star tobacco between the eyes. A somewhat hardbitten scholarly segment, finding more of the hoax than the historical in Paul, squared off for wordy battles with the faithful.

America was ready for Paul Bunyan. High-powered advertising and journalism needed copy. Historical and literary scholars —and, more particularly, the rising school of folklorists—needed subjects to investigate. Painters and poets were searching for new native themes. Chauvinism gave a nudge and Paul Bunyan filled a cultural vacuum.

Bunyan promulgators did a good job. Their candidate is now generally regarded as the leading American folk hero. So far as organizational backing is concerned, the Red River Lumber Company remains Paul's best friend; it has distributed 100,000 Bunyan pamphlets and, incidentally, a good deal of wood. Finally, the firm sold all its lumber, and the same Archie D. Walker who put Laughead to work creating Bunyan in 1914 helped to

liquidate the company's holdings in 1945.   There is something
characteristically American about this.   In the lifetime of a single
man much of the timber of two heavily-wooded areas had been cut
with little thought of the morrow.   The stories fabricated to sell
this lumber were reaching their greatest popularity just as all the
Red River Lumber had been marketed.   Whether that gentler and
in many ways more appealing folk hero, Johnny Appleseed, will
be able to keep up with Bunyan is a question folklorists have not
been able to answer.   For some reason the hero who planted trees
has not fared so well as the one who cut them down.

Meanwhile other writers had not waited for the liquidation of
the Red River Lumber Company to make use of its symbol, "registered" or not.   In the 1920's, newspapers in both Seattle and
Portland featured tall tales about Paul Bunyan supplied by their
readers. Another lumber-company publicist—James Stevens—has
become nearly as important as Laughead in popularizing the
legend.   In 1925 he produced the first group of Bunyan stories to
be published by a New York press.   This volume he later supple-
mented by several articles in popular magazines, a second edition
of the book, and a willingness to do battle with anyone who dared
to challenge the folk authenticity of Paul Bunyan II.

Whatever Stevens' merits as a historian or folklorist, he is a
gifted writer and devout worshiper at the axe-hewn Bunyan altar
he has so diligently helped to build.   Originally his interest in
Paul was purely professional.   He was director of public relations for the West Coast Lumberman's Association when he first
learned of Laughead's success.

Bunyan booster Stevens gave the giant a new elegance. His Paul
was "powerful as Hercules, indomitable as Spartacus, bellowing
like a furious Titan, raging among the Queen's troops like Samson
among the Philistines."   The lumbermen who raided the forests
were "toiling demigods and sweating heroes" of the dark woods,
workaday poets who created "the marvelous mythical logging
camp, with its cookhouse of mountainous size and history of
Olympian feats."   Though Stevens demonstrates to his own satisfaction that the historical Bunyan was a Frenchman and though he
constantly utilizes the framework of the classical hero in his own
stories, he is sure that "Paul Bunyan, as he stands today, is abso-
lutely American from head to foot;" that thousands of lumber-

jacks "contributed their mites to the classical picture of Bunyan," who "will live as long as there is a forest for his refuge, as long as there are shadows and whispers of trees."

Though Stevens' book was a popular success, it had its detractors. J. Frank Dobie, Texas scholar and folklorist, noted in a review that Stevens "assumes the liberties of a judicial novelist, frequently putting his own dull ideas into the mouths of his characters, even of the great Paul himself." Dobie found some sections "utterly foreign to the bunkhouse yarn."

A more thorough-going attack on Paul II was launched by Carleton C. Ames in his article "Paul Bunyan—Myth or Hoax?" in *Minnesota History*, March 1940. While others merely speculated about whether the old lumbermen really knew about Paul, Ames took to the field to find out. Touring northern Minnesota and the drainage basins of the Marinette, Wisconsin, Chippewa, and St. Croix rivers, he interviewed hundreds of lumbermen, with startling results. Not one of them had ever heard of Paul Bunyan. "It seems incredible," concluded Ames, "that if the Paul Bunyan yarns had any kind of circulation during the heyday of the loggers, they should not have come to the attention of at least some of these individuals."

Cries of defamer and debunker were showered on the young investigator from all sides. Newspaper editors peppered their editorial pages with anti-Ames tirades; there was even a suggestion that the state legislature should investigate the University of Minnesota. But other scholars came to Ames's defense. Mrs. Grace S. McClure, State Librarian of Michigan and a native of the Saginaw region which was supposed to be a Bunyan stronghold, said that in hundreds of talks with lumbermen she had never found a single one who knew about Paul Bunyan, and that she didn't even know of the literary accounts in Michigan until around 1930.

Stevens had a chance to reply when he wrote an introduction for a second edition of his Bunyan collection in 1948. In it he castigated the professors who had "sweated their pale blood to prove the legend a hoax, only to expose themselves as futile dabblers in nonsense." He also revealed that for three years he and his wife "gave time and income to the pursuit of clues and the study of wearisome old lumber-trade publications" in the hope of finding some bit of documentary evidence to prove that Bunyan was older than the pale-blooded scholars intimated. Nothing was found. The Paul Bunyan that Mr. and Mrs. Stevens were defending and the disappearing oral hero of the lumberjacks were different creatures, with different origins and histories, brought into being for different purposes.

Yet the "genuine folk hero" had caught on. He was prominent at both the New York and California World Fairs in 1939. He has made his appearance in ballet, opera, painting, and poetry; artists as different as Robert Frost, Carl Sandburg, W. H. Auden, and Benjamin Britten have celebrated his exploits in various ways. Books about him continue to appear. Dell McCormick prefaced one with the assurance that "the spirit of Paul Bunyan lives on in America, and no task becomes too great or difficult when we think of the hardships Paul endured and the mighty exploits he performed." In a wartime volume, Thomas Binford hurried Paul off to fight the Nazis and Japanese. Among other feats, Paul assembled 500-ton airplanes by the thousand, built a 15,000-ton steel ship in five days, and bombed Germany with redwood logs. Walter Blair has gone so far as to suggest that "when World War II started, Paul invented high income taxes, corporation taxes and such, and stopped worrying."

Bunyan benefits from that adaptable American hero pattern from which Mike Fink, Kit Carson, Davy Crockett, and Daniel Boone are cut. Paul is an oversized Boone, sharing Carson's mobility and Fink's colorful vocabulary, and improving on Crockett's extraordinary feats. Of course, Paul has more "know-how" than any of his nineteenth century predecessors. With the shift from an agrarian to an industrial society, one might predict that there would be a shift from heroes who use their hands to heroes who use machines. So it is with Paul II. Robust, uncouth, destructive, resourceful, friendly, when he moves into the forest he gets things organized and he get results; he can't be very much concerned with who or what suffers in the process. Where others think in terms of tens or hundreds, he thinks in terms of thousands. He believes in the survival of the fittest.

W. H. Auden suggests that in essence Bunyan is a bumptious, swaggering, optimistic nineteenth-century Victorian, " a projection of the collective state of mind of a people whose tasks were primarily the physical mastery of nature." Paul II of the advertisements does not subdue nature (as Boone and Crockett did) with his physical strength alone. He depends on the latest technology and machines, and enjoys nothing more than a flowing pipe line. He is obsessed with the problem of saving time. He devises methods of doing things faster and with less effort. In short, Paul Bunyan has brought the assembly line to American folklore. He stands for efficiency plus.

In an age which has enjoyed unprecedented business expansion and prosperity, Paul Bunyan has become ever more prominent. As new industries and factories are opened, advertising agencies have put him to work and sent him to fight. Back in 1941 Bunyan went to war with the greatest ease. It was a war of production and procurement, and in these matters Paul was a past master. Hadn't he had boys skate around his skillet with bacon on their feet to grease it for his pancakes? Hadn't he installed elevators to carry pan cakes to the ends of the table, where boys on bicycles rode back and forth on a path down the center of the table dropping the cakes when called for? Hadn't he fed his men pea soup through a pipe line, and perfected a method for pulling curves out of rivers?

Yes, he had done all these things. Yet no one knows how large Paul is or ought to be. When Carl Carmer and other writers went to Hollywood to assist Walt Disney with *Melody Time*, they intended to utilize Bunyan. They had to discard him because they were unable to decide on a size that would enable him to do his tricks without turning into an implausible giant.

If *Fortune* erred in calling Paul Bunyan "a genuine American folk character," there was still a certain poetic justice in selecting this tycoon of the imagination for an exalted place among the brilliant advertisements of twentieth century America.

*   *   *

As we fight our way through the macadam jungles of our time, we are prone to feel sorry for "the folk" degenerating out in the provinces, untouched by the self-righteous blessings of technology. We yearn for the days when "yeomen" produced "folklore." We apologize for our ad men and publicists who have exploited them, copied their crafts for the carriage trade, and palmed off their own city-bred brainchildren as folk heroes.

But the folk are not as degenerate, nor as dumb, as we may think. They are quite capable of putting one over on the city slickers, even in the field of folklore. Joe Magarac proves it.

Joe has a place of honor in volumes like Carl Carmer's *America Sings*, Walter Blair's *Tall Tale America*, Anne Malcomson's *Yankee Doodle Cousins*, and B. A. Botkin's *Treasury of American Folklore*. Readers have found him in such scholarly journals as the *New York Folklore Quarterly* and *Western Pennsylvania Historical Magazine*, as well as the less aspiring *Saturday Evening Post* and the commercial comics. U.S. Steel and Carnegie-Illinois Steel advertisements have pictured him. Joe even got a governmental boost in a Federal Writers Project report. The Jinni of Steel has been adapted with equal success by class-conscious writers who have opposed corporations and capitalism; he is the hero, for example, of Michael Gold's "A Strange Funeral in Braddock." On one point the evidence is conclusive: Joe Magarac has arrived.[2]

Oddly enough, no one seems to know quite how.

Despite individual twists, there is only one basic tale about him. Since variation of theme and event is the folk's specialty, and the publicist's main device, this is noteworthy. How would the "folk" in one remote area know just what people elsewhere had said? Equally disturbing is the fact that although Joe is always presented as a Hungarian, the word *magarac* doesn't exist in the Hungarian language. Whoever picked Joe's name and nationality either didn't know better or else created a deliberate confusion.[3]

Writers have repeated, without giving any hint as to historic source, the notion that "Joe's birthplace can be traced with some certainty to the J. Edgar Thompson Works, built in 1873 at Braddock, Pennsylvania." Yet files of the Western Pennsylvania and the Pennsylvania Historical Societies, as well as those of the Pennsylvania Folklore Society, have nothing that confirms this "certainty." Nor do the newspapers, periodicals, or special collections in the region. If Joe flourished in the nineteenth century, not a shred of evidence is left to prove it.

What seems likely is that Joe Magarac was born in a magazine article done by Owen Francis in 1931, that Francis was tricked by his informants into using *magarac*, that Jules Billard, Frank Vittor, and others helped spread the story, and that Joe has endured because the steel industry needed a "folk hero" of its very own.

Owen Francis, the central figure in the Magarac story, was born in southwest Pennsylvania. After a brief schooling he went to work in the Monongahela Valley steel mills, where he stayed until World War I. There he learned the jargon and methods of the steel industry. During World War I he was a doughboy with the 18th Pennsylvania Regiment. Badly gassed, he was hospitalized for a long time. During his convalescence, he read the work of Gogol, Turgenev, and Gorki. This interest may have been related to his contact with Eastern Europeans in the steel mills. "Having breathed the literary air," Francis said, "I could not go back to slag and prune jack." After working as day laborer, cantaloupe picker, and bus boy, he went to the University of California, where he got three years of education before becoming a Hollywood press agent.

When Warner Brothers bought one of his stories, Francis decided to devote all his time to script writing. The movie didn't work out. Eventually he returned to Pittsburgh, the mills, and the common people. He was through with the super-sophisticates of Hollywood.[4] His ambition was to be back with "the Hunkies and the Polacks, who understand life." The sentimentality and condescension in the account prepares us for what happened when he turned his journalistic talent into folk hero channels.

Although Francis had no formal interest in or contact with folklore, he decided to invent a mythical steel hero. After re-visiting the mills and settlements, he introduced Joe Magarac to the world in the October, 1931, issue of *Scribners*. The motive seems plain enough. He wanted to sell a story.

Here we find the basic Magarac tale which has been only embellished by later writers. A man's man, he could outwork and outlift anyone in the mills. Born in an ore mountain, Joe was as strong and enduring as the steel he made. He lived at Mrs. Horkey's boarding house. Like all the other steel men, he admired the lovely Mary, whose father (Steve Mestrovich) offered her in marriage to the winner of a weight-lifting contest. Joe won it, but allowed Mary to marry Pete Pussick, whom she loved. Later on Joe threw himself into a furnace to improve the quality of steel for a new mill. Like John Henry, he gave his all to the job.

This martyr's death has been variously interpreted. Staff writers for U. S. Steel modified it so that, when the Depression came, Joe melted himself down to make better steel for a modern mill that would produce more. Thus Joe was made to support the industry's argument that hard times are cured by more production and lower prices. The less capitalistic Federal Writers Project had Joe realize that his great strength was actually depriving others of jobs. His solution was to quit and hibernate until prosperity and employment returned. He was an N. R. A. hero.

All this was very well; but the fact remained that the people who should have known most about Joe, and been closest to him, knew nothing. Editors of Slavic and Hungarian newspapers had no information on him. Local historians and editors of Braddock, McKeesport and Homestead (the Magarac towns) had never heard an oral story. Nor had the workers. Folklorist Richard Hyman interviewed a hundred steelmen (Swedish, Croatian, Slovenian, Polish, Russian, Hungarian, and Italian) without finding one who had heard of the steel-man's idol.

In one instance, Mr. Hyman was able to interview 42 informants, the entire supervisory staff of a large mill. They had from 20 to 50 years of steel experience, many having worked up through the ranks. Not a single one had ever heard of Joe Magarac. But they could define a magarac.

It is, in the Serbian, a word whose closest English equivalent is "jackass." Paul Blazek, Slavic publisher, said that to call a man magarac "is to lower him to dirt that is worse than after pigs pass over it." An old time steel worker in Clairton was embarrassed when Mr. Hyman used the word in front of his wife. Steve Berko, a moulder, warned him that if he called someone that he might get his head bashed in.

What probably happened is that the Slavic steel workers decided to play a joke on the tenderfoot—in this case journalist Owen Francis.[5] It was like telling him to go get a sky hook, or a bucket of steam. They must have been amazed to find a former mill worker so naive as to be deceived by something they reported in jest. Albert Stolpe, veteran steel worker, told Mr. Hyman, "Somebody played a hulluva big joke on Francis." Andrew Matta, a Braddock mill's craneman, thought they wanted to make a fool out of him. Not only Francis, but many American folk-

lorists and anthologists were fooled. The joke, and hidden profanity, stuck.

With this in mind, we can, in reading Francis' six Magarac
articles published in *Scribners* from 1930 to 1935, detect his gulli-
bility, and attitude towards his ethnic informants. He refers to
the "childlike delight" of the Slavs, in much the condescending
manner that Rudyard Kipling described the Africans in the days
of the White Man's Burden. Frequently Francis uses the work
"Hunkie," which is degrading and insulting to the Hungarians.
Never penetrating the minds of the people with whom he talked,
he came to collect their material, not to understand them. Such
a man might well accept seriously, and put into print, what he
did not recognize as a joke at his own expense.

Several years later a clever writer named Jules Billard got
hold of Francis' brainchild and decided to do an article on Joe.
Though he did not bother to acknowledge his debt, he showed it
in his phraseology and displayed it to several million *Saturday
Evening Post* readers, thus helping to increase Joe's fame. Billard
professed to be an admirer of this man of steel. It was a remote
sort of admiration, since he apparently didn't get closer to the
steel workers than Francis' article. He merely toned down some
of the lustier passages.

For example, Francis' Magarac had said: " 'My name is Joe
Magarac, what you tink of dat, eh?' Everybody laughed at dat
for magarac in Hunkie means Jackass Donkey. Dey know dis
fellow is fine fellow all right when he say his name is Joe Jackass."

Translated by Billard, the passage became, "My name's Joe
Magarac,' he said laughing. Instantly the crowd's tension snapped.
Everyone knew that a fellow with a name like Joe Jackass was an
all-right guy. It's a compliment to be called magarac."

Another man, himself an immigrant from Southern Europe, had
meanwhile seen the heroic possibilities in Joe. This was the Ital-
ian-born sculptor, Frank Vittor. It was he who headed up the
campaign on behalf of a monumental Magarac statue "worthy of
the age of steel." To be executed by Vittor, it would be placed
at the proposed Point Park where the Monongahela and Allegheny
rivers merge to form the Ohio. Thus the steel worker's idol
would look out over an America which his fortitude made possible.

In 1953 Vittor even unveiled a clap model of just what he had in mind. The severest critic had to admit it was monumental. To be made of steel and bronze, it would tower up a hundred feet in the air, cost three million dollars, and take five years to complete. No one has suggested that Vittor get started. But even if he never does, the publicity and attention he had created place him among the Magarac hero-makers. Like Joe himself, Frank Vittor sees things on a large scale.

The big steel companies have found Joe ideal for advertising purposes. "This Side of the Iron Curtain and Glad of It," which appeared in the July 1948 isue of *U.S. Steel News* found in Joe Magarac the refutation of another powerful Joe in the U.S.S.R. Hardly a month goes by that Magarac doesn't break into print on the steel front. His position as the folk hero of a major industry that ought obviously to have one, is taken for granted. Demand and logic have created what the folk didn't. Joe has come from the top down, rather than from the bottom up. The Magarac tale has not yet entered the workers' oral tradition, even two decades after Francis' work, and probably never will. It's too phony. But enough elements from the older Bunyan and Crockett traditions exist to keep the general reading public interested—and unaware of the hoax worked first on Francis, then on folk writers, and finally on the public itself.

A journalist named George Swetnam recently published in the *Pittsburgh Press* (May 2, 1954) what purported to be a pre-Francis Magarac story. It involved the Hungarian poet, George Szecskay, who claims to have heard it at New York's Hotel Metropole in 1910, shortly after he entered the country. Szecskay remembered that another immigrant, Andrew Katonah, had been so detested for spying on steel workers that he was called Magyaron (the Hunky) and even Magarac (the jackass).

Szecskay's tale did not sound like a folk tale, and no other story about Katonah has ever been collected. Yet in summarizing it, George Swetnam explained why Magarac will very likely endure:

"Maybe the common form of the Magarac legend was a fake, and maybe the others were, too, when they first started. But fake or not, they'll go on, and are now part of the Pittsburgh heritage. There will be new ones, too, as the legends grow. Nothing is harder to kill than a folk hero—especially when he's become attached to a few good stories."

Meanwhile, almost no one knows about the really impressive strong men who would have made more logical candidates for fame; men like Henny Palm, who could shape horseshoes and pretzels out of bar stock with his bare hands, or Mike Lesnovich, who made neckties out of thick bars. Stories of men who went unprotected into furnaces, broke world sprint records when a hot bar ran wild, and lifted huge weights, circulate around steel towns, where physical strength and endurance are still required. But to the country at large, if any one name comes to mind when you say "steel," it's Joe Magarac.

To think that Joe was a real folk hero might not make the student a magarac; but it certainly would show unawareness of the way in which this twentieth century American hero was born. If he has real appeal, he will stick, and people will finally overlook his shoddy credentials. Already this is the case with Joe's forest counterpart, Paul Bunyan.

As to the line between truth and fancy in all this business: let the one who really knows where it is stake out the boundary.

CHAPTER 12

The Man and the Mouse: Doug and Mickey

"My strength is as the strength of ten,
Because my heart is pure."
—Alfred Tennyson

Douglas Fairbanks was all man, Mickey all Mouse. But they found similar answers to common problems. And thereby, so far as the story of the American hero is concerned, hangs a tale.

Movie stars are barometers of contemporary taste. In films we see people and places we would like to know; Hollywood is our dream factory. Technicolor images on modern screens, like those on medieval stained glass, are windows to the soul. Doug, Mickey, and our other celluloid idols tell us what we are.

Analyzing movies is more difficult than it might seem. More than most creative efforts, films are conditioned by their special history and mode of production. The naiveté of the end product often conceals unseen complications. Movies are intricate and communal. Writers, directors, and executives have their say before the filming. Styles are set before actors appear. The casting director must meet preconceived public demands by steering available personnel into available channels. Once associated with a stereotype, a star cannot escape it easily. The result is ham for ham's sake. Hollywood has supplied us with new favorites through an art form which allows less spontaneity than any in history.

Movie heroes fall into one or two categories. The first is the lonesome good man. We have met him earlier in our history as Daniel Boone, Abraham Lincoln, or the Cowboy. He is outdoors and Western, goes through life under a spell of troubled silence, and gets his woman by saying nothing. Perhaps his name is

Gary Cooper, Henry Fonda, or Hopalong Cassidy; the personality is unchangeable.

The second is the gregarious tough guy. Belligerent and egocentric, he reminds us of Captain John Smith, Andy Jackson, or Billy the Kid. He stands for rebellion and force, and masters his gal by knocking her down and dragging her away. (She loves it.) Indoors and Eastern, he might be Jimmy Cagney, Mickey Rooney, Humphrey Bogart, Burt Lancaster, or George Raft. They are so much a part of the pattern than we can study them collectively.

Where did the two sterotypes come from? Go back to the early World War I wildcat movie days for the answer; examine simpler, less thoroughly rehearsed productions, not camouflaged with paint, pretention, and publicity. That is what you must do to find out. Before the industry turned ballyhoo into a major business of its own, there was one man who bridged the Eastern and Western types, and who made the transition his acrobatic specialialty: Douglas Fairbanks.

To study the creation of "Doug" is to touch the problem at a vital point. In him the thought and act combined. His forty-three pictures comprise the most valid case history of the making of a character in Hollywood's history—perhaps, now that many hands manipulate every phase of it, the best we ever shall have.

Born Douglas Elton Ulman in 1883 near Denver, Colorado, he showed few of his later traits at the Jarvis Military Academy or the Colorado School of Mines. He drifted to New York City. Those who saw him make his tame and respectable Broadway debut in *Her Lord and Master* in 1901 hardly thought he was up to tackling mountain lions, jiu-jitsuing Yaqui Indians, or scaling castle walls for audiences which were to break all box-office records.

After a meandering decade as order clerk, hardware merchant, and law student, he returned to Broadway. Few noticed him. Frederick Warde described his Shakespeare as a catch-as-catch-can with the immortal bard. Still Harry E. Aitken, representing the newly-formed Triangle Films picked Doug (as well as Billie Burke, Eddie Foy, and Texas Guinan) to go to Hollywood in 1914. Having persuaded D. W. Griffith, Thomas Ince, and Mack Sennett to launch the Triangle studio, Aitken first saw the heroic potential in Doug. When he secured Wall Street backing, big money discovered the movies. Doug, for example, started at $2,000 a week. "We picked him as a likely film star not because of his stunts, but because of the splendid humanness that fairly oozed out of him," Aitken said. He never made a better choice.

Bouncing smiling Fairbanks went West, like many of the screen heroes he later created. There he made movies and wrote books which document his thinking during the years when "Doug" was born. *Laugh and Live* (1917), a volume on social ethics, had a chapter on "Building up a Personality." He made it sound as easy as building up a tinker toy. Fairbanks believed in heroes, and considered Lincoln "the most shining example of the power to will victory." Though he never read Carlyle and Nietzsche, he admired strong leaders as much as they. Emphasis on physical exercise became a mania. He must have done handsprings on the typewriter before writing, "The more we exercise the more energetic we become, the surer we are of ourselves, and the farther we get in the development of our personality."

To sum it all up, Doug was enthusiastic about everything, especially the future of movies in America. "I love to go into those little music halls in out-of-way places, and see the men, women, and children packed there of an evening. The Camera has brought the world to their doors. Life is richer, happier, and better for it." His films showed he was basically a muscle-flexing crusader attacking the social problems of the Jazz Age. Doug, as he was known to his followers, was more than a mere athlete. He was an activist with a purpose, in his own eyes even a philosopher. The Great Doug was an answer to the Great Gatsby.

Making Life Worth-while and *Assuming Responsibilities* attempted to answer critical problems. While Doug's books entertained they instructed. No actor of his time better typified the strain of respectibility in Hollywood. His essential achievement was creating both a character and a type for the movies. Only Chaplin among his contemporaries did so well—and Charlie's genius for pantomine was set back by sound. Thanks to an intuitive sense of attachment to his public, Doug simplified his screen character to the point where it could be understood instantaneously. The 1920's needed him. No movie casting or typing systems had developed to stymie his strenuous and original efforts. Here was a situation in which a celluloid hero might be born.

The result was the "good-bad" man, or beneficent rogue. His
prototypes were Robin Hood and D'Artagnan; but Doug was cast
in an unmistakably American idiom. The unforgettable thing
about him was the irrepressible sparkle, the latent mischievous-
ness that made him hold up trains merely to get the conductor's
ticket-punch. Saving damsels in advanced degrees of distress
was a stock specialty. Young girls could not imagine greater
bliss than being held in Doug's strong arms.

Yet his appeal to men was an equally strong one. A life-long
gymnast and stunt-man, Doug got the maximum effect out of life
encompassed by laws of gravity. For him an ounce of fat meant
a week of starvation. He personified the red-blooded American
of whom one asked almost instinctively, "Let me feel your mus-
cle." Here was a pint-sized Paul Bunyan, a wall-scaling Will
Rogers, Rousseau's natural man let loose on America. Fairbanks
stayed on the fluctuating list of favorite film stars for a generation.

The formative years were 1917-1920. In them Doug so directed his energy and moralizing that he codified his new film personality. He worked out a plot which allowed him to do the
same things many times, always with happy results. The standard
formula pictured a dull routine life (usually in the city) and the
workaday fellow who submitted to it. Then a catalytic agent,
usually the heroine, transformed him. Off he went to the West
where he could be a man. He carried the Frederick Jackson
Turner frontier thesis to Everyman in America. Doug was
Daniel Boone minus the coon-skin hat, but plus a dapper double-
breasted suit.

His early satires were convincing because he believed them himself. They were gymnastic sermons, like those Billy Sunday rounded
off by sliding into second base for the Lord. "In many of his
comedies, the West is conceived as a source of natural virtue,"
Alistair Cooke noted. "In his first few years he was devoted to
it as to a new faith. The West was a very effective background
because it was the best one to demonstrate how he felt about the
enervating effects of modern plumbing."[1]

This "golden West" formula grew out of pictures like *American
Aristocracy* (1916), *The Americano* (1916), *Wild and Woolly*
(1917), *Down to Earth* (1917), and *Arizona* (1917). The *Wild
and Woolly* plot synopsis, printed for the first New York show-

ing said, "Our hero is a city clerk who frets along within the
confines of the crowded city in anticipation of the day when he
will sit astride a bucking broncho and shoot Indians in the wild
and woolly West." The day dawned—Doug saw to that. Sunlight
was everywhere in *The Knickerbocker Buckaroo* (1919) and *The
Mollycoddle* (1920), the scenarios of which Doug himself wrote.
He not only followed his own star; he guided it. In 1920 the
character he contrived was well enough understood for Fatty Ar-
buckle to parody it. Doug had made the grade.

His public was ready for a "great moment" off the screen. On
March 28, 1920, he married America's Sweetheart, diminutive
Mark Pickford. Movie-goers considered it inevitable; a splendid
example of divine justice; and the vicarious thrill of the decade.
Fate had given Doug Mary, and Mary Doug, to be happy ever
after. In America public endings must be happy ever after—or
at least until another public beginning catches the communal eye.
Commenting on their propitious mating, Ferri Pisani wrote: "Ce
bluff, c'est l' optimisme Yankee et Pickford-Fairbanks en est le
symbole." Never mind that in order to wed Mary, Doug had to
divorce Anna Beth Sully, his wife of thirteen years; that Mary
had to leave her husband; and that Doug would eventually in
turn divorce America's Sweetheart, to marry the high-stepping
ex-chorus girl, Lady Ashley. These were not the things featured
in the newspapers.

In Mary Pickford childhood eternally flourished. She demonstrated the charm of keeping skirts up and hair down. Like Doug,
Mary was both loved and lovable. Hadn't he written (in *Wedlock
in Time*) that "It is a pleasant duty indeed to marry the woman
of our choice?" A word-hungry public devoured Alexander
Woolcott's article on their "Strenuous Honeymoon." Dos Passos
described the popular reaction in *Manhattan Transfer*. As her
mind wandered, Anna dreamed Elmer had suddenly taken on the
form of Doug, and she of Mary. Golden curls covered her shapely
head and a little kitten snuggled in her arms. Then came Elmer,
"crushing me to him with Dougstrong arms, hot as flame."

The heat and the flame leaped into accounts of Hollywood
monthlies which explore screenland boudoirs. Because both Doug
and Mary had been married before, the ceremony itself was
simpler than one for virgins. The point here, so far as the feature

writers were concerned, was that America's sweethearts actually
led simple lives, even in the midst of trinkets and chattels that
would have affected less genuine personalities. Articles discussed
plans on the newlyweds' part for adopting children. If not this,
then there were snaps of the handsome couple feeding horses,
pigeons, or small dogs at their home, "Pickfair." Could anyone
not love them?

Mary looked definitely unlike Nita Naldi, queen of the vamps.
Sex in any eruptive sense was out of the wedding sequence, for
Mary transcended rouge, lipstick and the Charleston. Underneath the god-like figures of ideal man and womanhood was the
dim Platonic core of a visionary grinning pink-cheeked boy and a
blushing golden-haired girl, romping hand in hand up the hill,
leaving their sins behind them.

Fairbanks was his own chief hero-maker. Under the pen name
Elton Thomas he kept turning out books and scenarios. A precocious young lady named Anita Loos helped. The daughter of
a theatrical manager, she played Little Lord Fauntleroy at five,
and wrote *The New York Hat* for D. W. Griffith when twelve. At
twenty she was averaging three movie stories a month when
"Doug" hired her. The six scenarios she did in three years defined the heroic activist. Two-dimensional and satisfying, the
Loos stories portrayed Doug winning the three F's: fame, fortune,
and female. They stressed his good humor and optimism. Doug
was as bully as Teddy Roosevelt, and much more wieldy. In addition to projecting him onto America, she even wrote a book
which explained how it was done.

Her *Breaking Into the Movies* (1921) made it clear that Doug
must perceive what he was doing, but pretend that he didn't. "The
movie actor," she commented, "must know precisely how to control the reactions inside the discredited gray matter of his." Someone behind him, such as Anita Loos, had to know just what to
write: "In choosing your story be sure it has the dramatic quality.
It must not be rambling; and it must have an element of conflict,
Good and Evil. The great demand today is for the sane, wholesome stories of modern American life, wherein character is the
paramount interest rather than eccentricities of the plot or camera."

Booth Tarkington, who saw plainly what Doug was becoming

for America, commented in a national magazine: "Fairbanks is a faun who has been to Sunday School. He has a pagan body which yields instantly to any heathern or gypsy impulse. . . . He would be a sympathetic companion for anybody's aunt. I don't know his age; I think he hasn't any."

Doug's plots didn't change much, but he did try to increase his physical feats and stunts. This was notably true during 1916, when he did eleven films for Triangle Studios. In *The Lamb* he let a rattlesnake crawl over him, and manned a machine gun singlehanded. After running a car over the cliff in *His Picture in the Papers* (one of Anita Loos's scripts), he fought a professional boxer, jumped from an ocean liner far off shore, and swam back only to leap twice from swiftly moving trains.

In *Manhattan Madness,* a sort of St. Vitus's dance set to ragtime, Doug carried his audacity too far. Pursued by his enemies, he ran into an actor whose revolver accidently went off. Doctors thought the flash and burn might blind him for life. After three weeks in a dark room, however, Doug recovered. He may have been a buffoon, but he was not a coward.

Biographers have suggested that Doug's brothers, Robert and Jack, must be classed as hero-makers. "Douglas acting and supervising the writing, directing and shooting his films, Robert handling all the construction problems, and Jack managing the business end made an efficient trio."[2] But the relative whom most Americans know is Douglas Fairbanks, Jr., son and inheritor of Doug's magic name. When he grew up, he tried to perpetuate his father's image in such movies as *Exile, The Corsican Brothers, Gunga Din, Prisoner of Zenda,* and *Sinbad the Sailor.* Junior lacked the master's touch. Yet he never forgot his father's stereotype. By virtue of many speeches and some action during World War II, he managed to get a British honorary knighthood, the Cross of Military Valor from Italy, the City of Vienna medal from Austria, and Order of the Southern Cross from Brazil. All were well publicized. But Doug's boy was not a hero. He had tried to preserve the Fairbanks form without substance. Thus he passed through the American hall of fame dragging his father's name behind him.

After World War I, Doug, Sr. became a world symbol of "Americano," the Yankee worker of miracles and exemplar of the United States' faith in victory by grin power. His later movies got more pretentious, but less compact. Taken as film sermons, they revealed a growing softness. *The Mark of Zorro, The Three Musketeers, The Thief of Bagdad,* and *The Private Life of Don Juan* were lusher, but less persuasive, than the "golden West" films. Although the public remained faithful, Fairbanks gradually lost his early mastery. On March 15, 1936, he retired. Two years later he organized the Fairbanks International Company, planning to star his son in the first production. But even Doug's grins were numbered. He died quietly in his sleep in 1939.

Unlike Charlie Chaplin, Doug has enjoyed no recent revival, and some now consider him merely a personable gymnast. Yet his contribution was major, and is still affecting us. He staked out the boundaries of Hollywood's heroic tradition. He was the good-bad man, adopted to democratic mores. Like the most enduring American idols, he helped shape a new vision, turning every-day events into things of rhythm and beauty. His best films identified his own personality with his heroic function. More than any early film figure, he put into practice Louis Sullivan's pithy dictum that "form follows function". Many later favorites have adopted it.

Among those who recognized at the time of Doug's death the impact he had made on America was Frank Nugent. In the December 17, 1939, *New York Times* he explained why people had never tired of the actor:

"Doug Fairbanks was make-believe at its best, a game we youngsters never tired of playing, a game—we are convinced—our fathers secretly shared. He was complete fantasy, not like Disney's, which has an overlayer of whimsy and of sophistication, but unashamed and joyous. Balustrades were made to be vaulted, draperies to be a giant slide, chandeliers to swing from, citadels to be scaled. There wasn't a small boy in the neighborhood who did not, in a Fairbanks picture, see himself triumphing over the local bully, winning the soft-eyed adoration of whatever ten-year-old blonde he had been courting, and wreaking vengeance on the teacher who had made him stand in the corner that afternoon."

One of Doug's best roles was that of *Don, Son of Zorro.* Throughout his captivity he tapped out, "Truth crushed to earth

will rise again, if you have the yeast to make it rise." Doug was
sometimes a caricature of the American hero; he nevertheless
became one of the pivotal men in motion picture history, in a way
which he himself probably never understood.

*   *   *

One of Doug's most formidable rivals was a mouse. Although
he had his being on a drawing board, world famed Mickey Mouse
acquired a following that most flesh-and-blood beings might envy.
Mickey seems at first glance to be another Doug cavorting in a
world of special fantasy. Though acrobatic, and clownish, they
both have missions. Both go about righting wrongs and foiling
villains. Often Mickey satirizes the things Doug does in earnest;
this is the basis of his mousey humor. In his second appearance,
made before sound was introduced, Mickey was a *Gallopin'*
Gaucho doing Doug's feats the wrong way.

Walt Disney deliberately set out to parody the Fairbanks technique. His mouse took the melodrama out of the rescue scenes,
and substituted pathos. With only his spindly pencil legs and
freedom from gravity to save him from a hostile world, Mickey
somehow got along. Deeds that had caused Doug's well-toned
muscles to quiver, Mickey disposed of with a flick of one of his
three fingers. In ridiculing the cult of masculine push-ups, Mickey
won his own fame.

Although more than a thousand people now work at the film
factory known as Walt Disney Productions, Mickey Mouse owes
his existence to Walter Elias Disney's imagination. The son of
a contractor, Walt was born in Chicago in 1901, grew up in
Kansas City, and drove a French ambulance in World War I.
Back home, he took art lessons and drew illustrations for farm
magazines. His real interest became the creation of movie shorts,
and he began a series of early fairy tale films. When his distrib-
utor failed, Disney took a new tack. He devoted his time to perfecting a medium by which he could fuse infinite detail into one
single vision—the animated animal cartoon.

He did not invent it. People had seen animated pictures long
before movie days by flipping booklets in their hands. Nineteenth
century scientists, like the astronomer Herschel, had worked on
animated visions. Georges Mélies had established an animated

film studio in France before 1900. His film called *A Trip to the
Moon* (1902) was a classic of its type. Russia's Ladislas Star-
evitch did La Fontaine's *Fables* and released his full-length *Adventures of Reynard* before World War I. Winsor McCoy, in
America, turned out *Gertie the Dinasaur* in 1909. *His Felix the Cat*
amused people before Disney even began to work.

Walt's first animal was Oswald the Rabbit, a descendent of Br'er
Rabbit and Uncle Remus. He was reasonably successful, but when
his associates refused to advance Disney money for experimenta-
tion, Walt resigned and started west. En route Mickey Mouse
was created.

Here is an American hero who sprang, like Diana, full-blown
from the brow of Zeus. Naturally we want to know as much as we
can about that moment. In connection with the Silver Anniversary
of the Disney Studios, the *Saturday Evening Post* published "The
Amazing Story of Walt Disney," on October 31, 1953. Since it
had the full sanction of Disney, we may consider it an authoritative account:

"Walt resumed sketching as they whizzed westward out of
Chicago. When he was ankle-deep in rejected drawings and
getting mighty tired of it all, he began, for no explanable reason,
to sketch mice. He found himself strangely amused as each new
rodent figure took shape on his tablet. Suddenly, he shouted to
his wife, who was dozing, 'I've got him! Mortimer Mouse!'

"Mrs. Disney was amused by the drawings, but she insisted—
and even today cannot tell why—that Mickey Mouse was a better
name. Walt, who was enjoying a happy creative delirium, accepted the suggestion."

A mouse was born. Not two, but three, Disneys were responsible; for in addition to Walt's wife, his brother Roy had a hand.
As the *Post* article put it, "Aided by inspired blocking on the part
of Roy Disney, an older brother who took over as business manager
and now is president, Walt developed into one of the most spectacular broken-field runners in the history of small industry."

Whether or not it was all as accidental and inspired as the
Disneys now claim, they did hitch their wagons to a mouse. This
need not embarrass them. The mouse has a high standing in
world folklore. Stories are told of a magic mouse-skin, of mice
transformed into other animals or humans, or of town and country

mice rivalries. The little rodent's weaknesses inspire stories of mice stronger than wall, wind, or mountain; and braver than any animal in the forest.

In German tradition a mouse won fame by putting his tail in a sleeping thief's mouth and making him cough up a magic ring. Spaniards tell of one who tormented the bull who couldn't catch him.[3] There are also tales about real mice that caused Disney to think of creating "Mortimer," whose name was altered to "Mickey." In the years to come these stories will grow and take on many variations.

The early Mickey was functional, not handsome, with black dots for eyes, pencil legs, three fingers per hand, a string-bean body, and a jerky walk. When he started to talk, Disney became his voice, and has remained so ever since. From the first Mickey was concerned with heroes. In "Plane Crazy," his initial short, he parodied Lindbergh, who had just flown across the Atlantic. The second poked fun at Mickey's acrobatic rival, Douglas Fairbanks. People applauded as the Mouse imitated the Man. Mickey talked for the first time in "Steamboat Willie," a short which (said the *New York Times*) "growls, whines, squeaks, and makes various sounds that add to the mirthful quality." His first western, "The Cactus Kid," took Billy the Kid as its satirical target. By 1931 newly-formed Mickey Mouse clubs had a million membrs. Mickey now appeared in twenty foreign newspapers—and Madam Toussaud's waxworks. Then America's Sweetheart fell for the mighty mouse.

In 1933, Mary Pickford announced that Mickey was her favorite star—an admission which might have contributed to the incompatibility that made Doug seek a divorce in 1935. The same year Mohamet Zahir Khan, potentate of Hyderabad, called Mickey the leading American hero in India. *Film Daily* estimated that over 100,000 people a day saw him on the screen. Later, when the Iron Curtain proleteriat clamored for "Mikki Maus," Soviet art critics quickly pointed out that Disney was "showing the capitalistic world under the masks of pigs, mice, and penguins." In other countries the little fellow with the big eyes, known as Michel Souris, Miguel Ratonocito, Michele Topolino, or Miki Kuchi, had strong appeal. Even the conservative Metropolitan Museum of Art hung an original Mickey Mouse. English cartoonist David Low called Mickey's creator "the most significant figure in graphic art since Leonardo da Vinci."

Now Mickey left the studio and began to invade the nation's kitchens and bedrooms. Off the drawing board his guide was a former department store promotion man, Kay Kamen. Joining Disney after leaving a Kansas City job in 1932, Kamen and Roy Disney universalized Mickey, becoming middlemen between Disney and American manufacturers. By 1940 they had over 2,000 companies affiliated with Disney. One of them, Lionel Corporation, sold 253,000 Mickey Mouse toy handcars in a single Christmas season. The Ingersoll Watch Company sent its five millionth Mickey Mouse watch to Walt as a special present. Not all the items were children's trinkets. A diamond-studded Mickey Mouse bracelet sold along Fifth Avenue for $1200.00. From these schemes manufacturers grossed almost $100,000,000 in 1948, over a million of which went to Kamen Enterprises.[4] American children began to live in a Mouse-dominated world. They wore Mickey clothes, mittens, bibs, and jewelry. At home they read Mickey comics. At school they worked on Mickey desk outfits. Outside they played with Mickey toys, balls, and games, and on Saturday they went to see Mickey Mouse cartoons. At night they put on Mickey pajamas and tumbled into Mickey beds, to dream of a happy land where cats do not break through and steal.

All this helped, but Disney's cartoons continued to be the chief means of spreading Mickey's heroic image. Over a hundred of these have been made, utilizing simple plots summed up in a single line of Disney's desk. Whole films have grown from such phrases as "Covered wagon type of story—western locale;" "Mickey plays organ to skeleton's dance;" "Explorer, Mickey with cannibals, musical ending."

The actual working out of the production is more graphic than verbal. It takes sixteen drawings to make Mickey move once on the screen. Few write at Disney's, but hundreds draw. Senior animators make key drawings, and assistants sketch in those between. A ten-minute cartoon requires 14,400 pictures; a hundred minute feature, 144,000 final drawings, carefully synchronized with the sound tracks by a process called "Mickey Mousing."

Hence Mickey's reputation has been made by tons of drawings transferred to miles of film. Other centuries would have admired

him; only the twentieth century could have fabricated him. Without skilled technicians to develop, cut, and print film, and to provide for the sound and sequences, there could be no Mickey. By
a process so complex that only a few fully understand it, the deceptively simple and spontaneous antics of the Mouse reach mass
audiences.

His very existence shows that the machine is capable, when
properly directed, of producing heroes completely divorced from
biological process. This only increases our delight in seeing
Mickey satirize the machine. In the guise of a vacuum cleaner or
cement mixer, technology sets out to destroy Mickey, who is himself mechanical without being mechanized. As with all heroes,
Mickey's triumphs arise out of the desire of the human spirit to
transcend the mechanical forces of brute nature. He is a Mouse
of good will.

Mickey's war on the machines makes him a symbolic foil of
Frankenstein. Alarmed by the growing tyranny of ungoverned
production, Mary Shelley created her terrifying villain in the
novel, *Frankenstein*. Big, unwieldy, humorless, destructive, the
Monster served as a warning that man might continue things that
would wrest control from their makers. Mickey, on the other
hand, is tiny, agile, funny, and full of compassion. He releases
us from the tyranny of things, and from the fear of the very in-
tricacy and impersonality that makes him possible.

Gradually Mickey lost the stark two dimensional quality that
was the mark of his special reality. The use of technicolor, a
streamlined torso, and perspective, damaged rather than helped
him. Significantly enough, the only Mouse Disney himself can
draw is the early, flat one.

It is as if the Disney staff, determined to create a more adroit
Mickey, snatched him away from Disney: an act which could
eventually destroy Mickey. If that proved to be the case, Frankenstein would have won out after all.

Efforts at using animated and real characters in the same film
have been unsuccessful. Having Donald Duck pursue a real
girl created a jolting, even a vulgar, spectacle. Some feel that
Disney erred in dropping Mickey and his two-dimensional friends.
William Vaughan has even created the "Society to Keep Live
Actors Out of Disney Movies." It has not turned the tide. In

summarizing Disney's activities at the time of Mickey Mouse's twenty-fifth birthday, *Life* commented: "Amid the hubbub of his expanding studio, Disney has little time for Mickey Mouse, who is judged too sweet-tempered for current tastes." Such a judgment may well rule out the only thing for which the Disney studios, given now to nature studies and Jules Verne under-water documentation, will be remembered. Mickey's old friends got some, but not much, consolation from the fact that in *The Living Desert*, best of the new nature movies, mice were really the heroes, resisting successfully all the poisonous and armoured bullies in the desert.

Visitors to Disney-land also comment on the "cult of Walt" which has taken place of the earlier creative atmosphere. Everything ends up on his desk. In Ford's empire, they were afraid to call the top man Henry. In Disney's, they dare call him nothing but Walt.

But neither Walt nor anyone alse can deprive us of Mickey. Like Uncle Sam or John Bull, the Mouse has a separate existence off the drawing board. He belongs to those of us who accept him, as well as to those who create him; he is public property. One notes, in passing, how much Mickey resembles Disney. The soulful eyes, pointed faces, and gift of pantomime distinguishes them both. In discarding Mickey, Disney has helped obliterate himself.

Cast in the Aesop genre, Mickey (again like Doug) is a moralist. As with the great characters of Sophocles, Moliére, or Shakespeare, Mickey depends on oversimplification to make his points. Because his world has laws of its own, Mickey achieves an illusion of independence from his creators. He improves on nature. But the nature involved is not that of our Newtonian world. Disney's heroes arise from his ability to see little people dancing under the hedge at twilight, and to rationalize the incredible. "We just try to make good pictures, and the professors tell us what they mean," Walt once said; and again while in Ireland, "If people would think more of fairies, they would soon forget the atom bomb."

Mickey demonstrates that art and mass production aren't antithetical, and that movies appeal to all ages and levels. Using him as a springboard, Disney has created a new animated Noah's ark to ride the waves of the chaotic modern world. His skillful cartoons show that line and form can portray ideas and tensions, and that the artist can utilize technology. Disney has revitalized fantasy for our times. Mickey has lost none of his youthfulness. For a quarter century he has done the unexpected as a matter of course, and endured terrible punishment without pain. Master of his world, he is a living graphic symbol. Army intelligence officers planning the Normandy invasion quickly agreed that "Mickey Mouse" was the appropriate pass word for the whole operation. It was tribute enough to turn the average rodent's head. But then, Mickey is no average rodent.

*   *   *

A nation's pressing fears and ideals find their way into those media most readily accessible to the people. One of these, in the United States, is the motion picture. There one finds the mirror held up to America. We are naive if we think Hollywood can't make better or different movies. They make just what the people want; and if the more disillusioned producers have mottoes like, "No one ever went broke underestimating the American intelligence," others have succeeded in creating a new galaxy of heroes.

Here dwell Douglas Fairbanks and Mickey Mouse, whose activism, morality, and appeal gave them second fictional lives. In the future others will mould their stereotypes into new personalities—but they will not ignore them. The Man and the Mouse show us what we are, and what we want to be.

CHAPTER 13

Sons of Satan: American Villains

"Dere's little stealin' like you does, and
dere's big stealin' like I does. For de big
stealin' dey makes you Emperor and puts
you in de Hall o' Fame when you croaks."
—Eugene O'Neill, *The Emperor Jones*

Major American villains are scarce. There is no shortage of lawbreakers; we probably flaunt more laws than any other people on earth. Our adolescents are constantly harrying the local cops, our officials persist in parking on yellow lines, our petty thieves collect tons of loot daily. The comparatively few criminals who are convicted go quietly to their cells without changing the basic American pattern.

Lacking the dramatic flare and timing that would make them memorable, most evil-doers are soon forgotten. T. S. Eliot noted that few contemporaries err with enough purpose or awareness to land in hell. Most of them deserve no longer epitaph than that on a young gunman's grave in Arizona's Tombstone cemetery: "He done his damndest."

A real villain must be able to talk, think, and act in the "grand manner," so that defiance lends symbolic significance to his crime. He must be able to obstruct the hero, to come dangerously close to succeeding, and to descend to his deserved fate open-eyed. Villains of history are unforgettable. They tend to be divided into two main groups—the persecutors and the traitors. Herod, Goliath, Cyclops, Nero, Yoritomo, the Sheriff of Nottingham, and our Western desperadoes belong in the first category; Nessus, Hagen, Mordred, Ganelon, Delilah, Judas, Iago, and John Wilkes

Booth in the second. Cato without Nero, King Arthur without Mordred, Othello without Iago, and Lincoln without Booth are unthinkable. Heroic foils provide history with tension. Psychologically, they are as important as heroes.

No creed is successful unless someone is trying to violate it. Performers as different in technique as the professional wrestler, the traveling preacher, and the presidential candidate recognize this. Seeking out a Son of Satan to oppose is basic, if public interest is to be sustained. Every political campaign since Washington's day has demonstrated it. The oldtime frontier revivalists were more honest about the good-and-evil dualism than their smooth-talking descendants. Their first task was specified in a nineteenth century hymn:

> "I pitch my tent on this camp ground
> And give old Satan another round."

For centuries Satan has been the chief scoundrel in Christendom. The sulphur smell of his hellish dominions has been very real to many an American nostril. Satan's story is constantly revitalized by our need for equilibrium. Thus Washington had to contend with Charles Lee, Jefferson with Aaron Burr, Henry Ford with Eastern bankers, the Muckrakers with monopolies, and Mickey Mouse with the vacuum cleaner. How else could they have demonstrated their true mettle?

Whether or not John Brown, General Sherman, and Stonewall Jackson seem heroic depends on which side of the Mason and Dixon line one was born. The British opinion of Benedict Arnold and the Russian notion of Joe Hill differ sharply from America's. Moreover, historic reputations fluctuate. Jefferson, Jackson, and Wilson came up from the realm of rascals to the heroic plateau in a single generation. The tendency to revise reputations was pointed up by Willard Wallace's 1954 biography of Benedict Arnold, paradoxically titled *Traitorous Hero*. There is a definite see-saw tendency when two strong men oppose one another on public issues; when one reputation is up, the other is down. This certainly applies to Jefferson and Hamilton, Calhoun and Webster, Hoover and Franklin Roosevelt.

Americans tend to turn abstractions into personalized villains.

Most of us agree that "robber barons," "the idle rich," "big-time lobbyists," and "international bankers" are wicked fellows. Those who sit on the other side of the big mahogany desks feel the same way about "labor agitators," "left-wing dreamers," "socialists," and "traitors to their class." Applied freely and indiscriminately, such clichés are convenient, but they have little direct bearing on genuine villainy.

The evil "someone" need not be an individual or a group; it may be, and in the case of the American Indian actually has been, a whole race. For generations all Indians were barbaric savages whose only aim in life was to detach the scalps of white men. Actual Indian massacres and atrocities, especially during the Revolution, increased the bloody accusations and legends. By 1840 an elaborate American morality play, with many local variations, had come into being. In it the forces of light, the white settlers, invariably struggled with the forces of darkness, the Indians. All the trials of the early saints and the colors of medieval tapestries were part of the backdrop. The moral tone was summed up by the frontier dictum, "The only good Indian is a dead Indian." Arthur Guiterman aptly satirized it in his "Ballade of Dime Novels":

> *"Take up the long neglected pen*
> *Redeem its valiant steel from rust*
> *And write those magic words again:*
> *Another redskin bit the dust!"*

The battle between the white hero and the red villain was viewed as a thing of beauty and the Nordic triumph as a joy forever. By a sort of symbiosis, the two rode through history together. The American hero's specialty, ever since Boone illustrated it, has been saving beautiful blond heroines from swarthy Indians — snatching them metaphorically from the very gates of hell, just as in medieval morality plays.

In our time, the movies mass-produce this stereotyped story. Its endless reiteration is welcomed by countless young Americans via yells, foot-stomps, and whistles. For many of them Saturday has become a day of ritual, much as Sunday was in past centuries. In ten thousand darkened motion picture houses or TV-equipped

living rooms, they sink back for two hours of reverent attention
and devotion.   Before their credulous eyes appear spotted ponies,
naked bodies smeared with war paint, and deadly arrows whizzing
at beleaguered wagon trains.   Then the cowboys or cavalry appear. The orgy of lust and violence is averted. With Old Testament swiftness punishment is meted out.   Here is effective teaching
of a basic American myth; here is the most familiar type of
villainy in our whole culture.

Since Daniel Boone's time most bad men have come from the
West.   That region, with its short history, has created legends and
folklore with extraordinary fertility.   There have been courageous
soldiers, like Fremont and Custer, but they were not uniquely
Western.   Marcus Whitman and Brigham Young were colorful,
but somehow they lacked universal appeal.   Western scouts and
trappers were of a breed similar to that of the Canadians.   The
job of Western glorifiers was to find a unique heroic type indigenous to the region.   They found the answer in the open-range
cowboy and the two-gun killer who opposed him.   Almost overnight untamed horses, bewildered women, unshaven rustlers, ruth-
less killers, and uninhibited sheriffs made life one roaring, bloody
crisis after another.   Western villains created the medium in which
the hero could function at his best.

Tough hombres have been anything but fictional in American
history.   Billy the Kid got a man for every one of his twenty-one
years, and had other prospects in mind when Sheriff Pat Garrett
shot him in a dark room.   The Daltons, Wild Bill Hickok,
Cherokee Bill, Geronimo, and Chochise were not docile fellows.
The James boys robbed real banks.   These desperadoes, and others
like them, have long had faithful followings.   Although they were
the persecutors and not the persecuted, and as tough a group as
one could find anywhere, they were and are still thought of as
men who performed brave deeds with skill.   Bandits are apt to
acquire cults similar to those of saints.   They are venerated and
celebrated in song and legend.   Their very tombs can become (as
with Billy the Kid) places of pilgrimage.

Jesse James is a case in point.   The second son of a Baptist
minister, Jesse was raised on a Missouri farm.   During the Civil
War he served with Quantrill's guerrillas.   He embarked early

on his career of lawlessness. By holding up a Rock Island Railroad train in 1873, he added a spectacular crime to the American records. Once he rode with a posse in his own pursuit; he lived for fifteen years with a huge reward on his head. Finally he was shot in the back by one of his own gang. Robert Ford, "that dirty little coward that shot Mr. Howard, and laid poor Jesse in his grave," has become the fall guy. By shooting Jesse (alias Thomas Howard) from behind, Ford violated the code of the west [1]—to the great relief of the railroads, banks, and Pinkerton men whom Jesse had terrorized for years.

Resurrected, Jesse became a Robin Hood who helped poor squatters, oppressed farmers, and widows. Since it was Yankee money he had stolen, Southerners undertook to deify him. Ballad-makers waxed maudlin:

> "Jesse was a man, a friend of the poor,
> He never would see a man suffer pain;
> And with his brother Frank he robbed the Chicago bank
> And stopped the Glendale train."

Novelists and playwrights eagerly took up this theme. A "James Boys Series" appeared in 1900, beginning a widespread James fad in popular literature. One publishing house, Street and Smith, published six million copies of some 121 James novels between 1901 and 1903: probably the all-time record for bandit-glorifying.

Interest in Jesse James lives on. *The Missouri Legend*, a successful 1938 drama, romanticized him; the next year saw Tyrone Power and Henry Fonda in movie roles justifying the murderous James brothers as misunderstood victims of railroad infamy. Jesse was a crusader, tender to his mother and loved ones, relentless in his noble endeavors. In a sequel made several years later, Frank James got the villainous Robert Ford and avenged his brother's death. Movie goers from coast to coast were satisfied. That Frank had actually spent his last years selling shoes in Dallas and forgot about Ford did not inhibit the Hollywood version. The code had become more important than the truth.

Each outlaw's saga differs according to his own personality and satanic kink, but all of them have what might be called the Tender Spot. Under his tough exterior, the killer is a "good guy" who took the wrong turn in the road. We can say of no American criminals, as it is said of England's King John, "He was a thoroughly bad man." Admittedly they have carried rugged individualism a bit too far; they get what's coming to them. But when they get it, Ma or "the girl he left behind" do what we should like to do too. They cry.

*   *   *

In a twentieth century concerned with social legislation and the Common Man, robber barons of the last century have been "exposed," especially by muckracking journalists. Tycoons like "The-public-be-damned" Vanderbilt and "God-gave-me-my-dimes" Rockefeller have been copiously attacked. John Pierpont Morgan, human symbol of Wall Street arrogance and amorality, has been a favorite target. Though he controlled 72 directorships and dozens of corporations, brought on the panic of 1863, bested the federal government during the 1895 financial crisis, and often worked against the public interests, he fell short of the character portrayed in John Winkler's *Morgan The Magnificent*, Gustavus Myers' *History of the Great American Fortunes*, and Lewis Corey's *The House of Morgan*. Morgan has been charged with villainous acts in just the same manner in which Washington or Lincoln have been credited with heroic ones. The legendary process works cumulatively for the bad as for the good.

Proof may be found in Gordon Wasson's *The Hall Carbine Affair: A Study in Contemporary Folklore* (1939). Wasson dissects, sinew by sinew, a living legend, born in our own generation and palpitant with the vitality of unchallenged acceptance. The story held that J. P. Morgan personally took delivery of certain Hall carbines at a federal arsenal during the early days of the Civil War and refused to ship them to Union troops until an exorbitant price had been paid. To put it more directly, he held up Uncle Sam. Yet documents show that Morgan, far from being involved, was not even aware of the transaction.

The real value of Wasson's work lies not in his revelation of the actual facts, but in laying bare the process by which the truth was perverted. He provides us with one of our few case studies on outright misrepresentation. That two writers, unsympathetic to Morgan and his class, should have made the distortion does not seem strange; that it could so infiltrate American historical thought as to be reproduced in the authoritative *Columbia Encyclopedia* and *Dictionary of American Biography*, indicates that villains too are made, not born.

The Hall carbine legend was first fostered either by the careless research or the careful contrivance of Gustavus Myers, whose distortion of Morgan in his *History of the Great American Fortunes* (1910) is revealed by Wasson.   Lewis Corey picked up the legend and strengthened it in *The House of Morgan* (1930).   Later accounts have been based on these two sources.   John Winkler, Matthew Josephson, H. C. Engelbrecht, and George Seldes repeated the story without checking it.   Huey Long stressed Morgan's carbine deal in a nationwide broadcast on February 10, 1935. Bertrand Russell accepted and reproduced it in *Freedom vs. Organization*.   The list of perpetuators includes Harry Elmer Barnes, John Dos Passos, Upton Sinclair, H. G. Wells, and Carl Sandburg. When Morgan died in March 1943, the obituary in the Communist *Sunday Worker* and news broadcasts from Nazi Germany elaborated on the carbines.

Where the will to believe exists, "facts" become inconsequential. The blackness of our villains depends at least in part on what the public wants to see.   Legends that take hold are those that gratify potential believers.   In this way fact is supplanted by fiction, and fiction becomes history.   A little incident, released by uncorking the bottle of fancy, grows until it becomes incontestable historical truth.   The heroic process applies equally to the good and bad; only the nature of the end product differs.   No matter how many Wassons discover facts which exonerate Morgan, "J. P." will symbolize economic gluttony and irresponsible use of power.

*   *   *

Some bloodthirsty feuds—the Mafia and Camorra of Italy, the Molly McGuire fights among the Irish-Americans, and the squabbles among Scottish clans—have attracted world attention.   For most Americans, however, feuding means the Hatfields and McCoys.   The mountainous country of Kentucky and West Virginia has been a feuder's paradise; and the Hatfields and McCoys excelled at family slaughter. From their respective sides of the Tug River they shot themselves into distinction of a special sort.

Leading one clan was Anse Hatfield, six foot of devil and 180 pounds of hell. Firm in his belief that the God who watched over the hills was first of all a God of vengeance, he inspired his side to bloody acts. Opposing him was Randolph McCoy, a bitter man who saw three of his sons fall on one day, and a seasoned killer himself. The animosity had its beginning long before the family feud broke out. During the War Between the States, the Tug River marked not only the boundary between Virginia and Kentucky, but also the line between the North and South. Kentuckians favored the North and Virginians the Confederacy. Skirmishes took place and ill feeling grew between the participants. As a matter of chance, Virginia Hatfields had some scrapes with McCoys from Kentucky, and it is thought that Harman McCoy, brother of Randolph, was slain by a Hatfield.

Another account attributes the feud's outbreak to a pig. In 1873 Floyd Hatfield found an extra pig with his own. Times being bad, he took it to town to sell. There he met Randolph McCoy, who claimed the animal for his own. A trial ensued. The jury, heavily loaded with Hatfields, awarded Floyd the pig. Not many years later, the argument took the form of hot lead. When Johnse Hatfield took Rose Anne McCoy home to live with him, both families were scandalized; the McCoys took Johnse prisoner, leaving Rose Anne at the cabin. Ballad-makers made up such verses as this:

> "Come and listen to my story
> Of fair Rosanna McCoy.
> She loved young Johnse Hatfield,
> Old Devil Anse's boy.
> But the McCoys and Hatfields
> Had long engaged in strife;
> And never the son of a Hatfield
> Should take a McCoy to wife."

Shouting that his own flesh and blood had been seduced by a no-good Hatfield, Talbert McCoy rushed in with a knife to carve up Ellison Hatfield. Assisted by two younger brothers, he managed to stab the unfortunate Ellison twenty-seven times. The constable took the three McCoys into custody. "Devil Anse" and his clan recaptured them from the peace officers. On the bank of the Tug River the captives were tied to paw-paw bushes and riddled with bullets. For a decade, open warfare between the two families, and almost between the two states involved in the border killings, raged. Not until after the 1888 Battle of Grapevine Creek did it abate. Anse Hatfield died in 1921. Randolph McCoy held on until he was 103, determined not only to outshoot but outlive all his enemies.

There is no official record of the deaths which the feud caused. The lowest estimate is 27, the highest 200. Hatfield-McCoy stories have spread everywhere. Songs, stories, and movies have publicized the feud, the press has featured the present descendants, and Virgil C. Jones has done a scholarly study called *The Hatfields and the McCoys* (1948). In short, the Hatfield-McCoy saga has become part of our national heritage.

*   *   *

That 14-year orgy, Prohibition, sired the American gangster. An individualist like the cowboy, he traded six-shooter for submachine gun and tooled leather belt for bullet-proof vest. That he was resisting a national law which most people opposed gave him a romantic sanction. Gangsters became public idols as well as public enemies.

The individual who epitomized the type was Al Capone, alias Boxcar Tony, Scarface, and the Big Fellow. Born in Naples in 1899, and brought to America as a child, he became involved in a Brooklyn pool-hall fight, and fled to Chicago. He specialized in the vice business until bootlegging became more profitable. His syndicate's income became so great that others began to horn in. The result was nine years of gang warfare and over 500 violent deaths. From Cicero, where Capone ran his intricate business, orders went out that affected the lives of thousands.

Al was no punk. He had a London tailor, a French cook, and a fine library. In his own eyes he was practically a public servant. "I've spent the best years of my life giving people the light pleasures, and all I get is abuse," he complained. "Well, tell the folks I'm going away now. There won't be any more booze. You won't be able to find a crap game, let alone roulette, or faro. Public service is my motto. Ninety-nine per cent of the people of Chicago drink. I've tried to serve them decent liquor and square games. But it's no use. I'm going."

Of course, Al didn't go. When his friend Lombardo was killed by North-siders, he directed the machine gun execution of seven Moran men in a beer truck garage on Saint Valentine's Day, 1929. "Bugs" Moran retaliated; after murdering three Capone men, he ordered several attempts on Capone's life, all unsuccessful. They only furthered the myth of Scarface's invincibility. Much impressed, Yale seniors in the class of 1931 voted him the "second most interesting personality of the present age." Sensational newspapers described his trips about the country as "Capone's Odyssey." A French best seller called *Une Grande Figure: Al Capone* enhanced his European reputation, and he became a minor hero in Hitler's Reich. Such was his importance that in 1930, F. D. Pasley published *Al Capone: Biography of a Self-Made Man.* Even Horatio Alger would have found it hard to extol Scarface's rise to fame.

The movie *Scarface* (starring Paul Muni) was a success, painting the killer's life in bloody but thrilling hues and leaving the impression that he was a martyr to his principles. A folk hero was definitely shaping up. *True Detective, Harpers, Newsweek, New Republic,* and *North American* heralded his daring. The federal government finally convicted him of income tax evasion and shipped him off to Alcatraz. The Al Capone who died peacefully in 1947 was but a shadow of the once invincible Big Fellow; but his imprint on the American mind was deep and lasting.

Al's closest rival for gangster notoriety has been John Dillinger, "Public Enemy Number One" and a front-page character for several years before he was betrayed by "the girl in a red dress." As a result of this, he was mowed down by G-men in a Chicago alley in 1934. Souvenir hunters have chipped off much of his tombstone in the Indianapolis Cemetery. One scholar has predicted that Dillinger will eventually be moved up with the heroes. "I've heard some pretty complimentary things said about him at cross-roads filling stations in Dillinger's (and my own) native Morgan County, Indiana," he reports. "Too bad his folks didn't

name him something flossier or more mellifluous—I never knew a
really top-flight folk hero named John." [2]

The persistence of the gangster type in the popular mind long
after the repeal of Prohibition shows that real cities produce criminals, and imaginary cities gangsters.   Or, as Robert Warshow
put it, "The experience of the *gangster as art* is common in
America, even though most Americans have never seen a gangster."[3]
Only in an ultimate sense does the movie gangster invade our own
experience of reality.   Much more immediately, he appeals to our
previous and no less vicarious experience of the type itself.   The
type has created its own field of reference.

Nervous, enterprising, skillful, the gangster moves like a dancer
among the crowded dangers of the city.   His story is a nightmare
inversion of the traditional success story.   He is doomed to be
punished because he has succeeded by his own unsocial Darwinian
standards.   Gangster films invariably resolve the dilemma by
making sure the hero is disposed of relentlessly. Thus, in *Scarface*,
outside the gangster's bullet-proof apartment is a big neon sign
reading, "The World is Yours."   It is the last thing we see after
the protagonist's death.   The world is *not* his, any more than it is
ours.   By dying, he pays for our fantasies, and even releases us
for the moment from the concept of success.   His death seems not
so much punishment as defeat.   Lonely and melancholy, he "has
to do" what he does, just like the heroes of Greek tragedy.   He
is perhaps the closest approximation to a tragic hero our urban
folklore has yet produced.

*   *   *

The robber baron in his day, and the gangster in his, symbolized
theft and corruption.   But presently a man who was not after our
money, but our tolerance and integrity, came closest to being the
star villain.   This deceptively simple fellow was a product of the
"poor white" Southern strata, of indignation turned to malice, and
of the Great Depression.   His name was Huey P. Long.   It can be
said of him, as it can of few Americans, "He might have wrecked
our democratic form of government."   The Kingfish almost did.
His career demonstrates that we are never immune from dictatorship.   We have Huey's own word for it that should dictatorship

come to America, it will come disguised as super-democracy.

In Louisiana's bleak, Bible-fearing Winn Parish, Huey Long grew up on his father's farm. Later he became a traveling salesman. Unsuccessful on the road, he attended law school when he was 21, and finished a three-year course in eight months. "I came out of the courtroom running for office," he wrote. In 1928 he was governor, in 1932 United States Senator and boss of his native state. This spectacular iconoclast snuffed out the democratic process in Louisiana, and was concentrating on the 1936 Presidential nomination, when a young dentist named Carl Austin Weiss shot him in a corridor of the Baton Rouge Capitol. Long's bodyguards riddled Weiss with 61 bullets. Weiss' one shot killed Long. Seldom has a single bullet burrowed so deeply into American history.

Impudent, forceful, venomous, forgetting nothing and forgiving no one, Huey Long projected the demagoguery of the "Kingfish personality" upon America. With his genius for words and drama, his shrewd understanding of the depression psychology, and his alluring slogan of "Every Man a King," he attained national importance. Not wealth goaded him on, but power, revenge, and the accumulation of force.

An exhibitionist who walked about hotel lobbies reading dispatches, he often called his secretary on the long distance telephone to give insignificant orders in the presence of onlookers. His private instructions to his followers at home were far from trivial, however. He personally dictated the appointment of every state officer. The legislature met only to rubber-stamp his dictates. He bought representatives the way he bought sacks of potatoes. "Lots of fellows would like to stand up the way I do, but they haven't fixed things up back home the way I have," Huey bragged. So confident was he that he shouted out all the secrets of the Senate cloakroom, and even shook his fist at the President of the United States. "You can continue to oppose me in the Louisiana political arena with all the weapons and resources which your public treasury now affords to my enemies," he yelled at Franklin Roosevelt. The very freedom of speech, which he squelched in Louisiana, was a weapon he wielded ruthlessly. Long had calculated the crassness, ignorance, and resentment of certain followers very closely;

they were the only factors he never disregarded. Otherwise he was prone to play the game without the rule book.

The figure of Huey Long, which he himself left in bronze to face the new skyscraper state capitol at Baton Rouge, has been the basis of John Dos Passos' *Number One* and Hamilton Basso's *Sun in Capricorn*. Basso said Long appealed to him as a stripped-down example of the dictatorial idea, "whose only equipment other than an animal-like cunning was a brutal energy and the ability to sway thousands of people by the sound that rhetoric makes." Other writers who treated the Kingfish type were Adrian Langley, who wrote *A Lion is in the Streets* (1945) and Robert Penn Warren, author of *All the King's Men* (1946). Mrs. Langley's hero, Hank Martin, weeps for his people and never forgets the cozy little tenant's shack in which he educated himself. He is a lion who, in his own words, "comes a-trumpetin' loud 'n' in no way uncertain." Warren's hero is called Willie Stark. Jack Burden, a reporter who tells Willie's story, is convinced that Stark is a great man. "What happened to his greatness is not the question," Burden says. "Perhaps he could not tell his greatness from ungreatness and so mixed them together that what was adulterated was lost."

Huey "Kingfish" Long is the one Luciferian American villain of our generation. Despite all his buffoonery he was tragic, for he could have been a statesman and interpreter of America. In 1935, when asked if he were a Fascist, Long replied with a characteristic quip: "I'm Mussolini and Hitler rolled in one. Mussolini gave them castor oil. I'll give them tabasco, and they'll like Louisiana." The Kingfish who set out to control the Democratic party and prevent Roosevelt's 1936 re-election was, however, hurled down by a simple citizen of Louisiana; the dentist Weiss.

To Huey's followers his assassination was his martyrdom. On April 25, 1941, officials unveiled a bronze statue of the Kingfish in Statuary Hall of the National Capitol. Each state is entitled to two statues. Long was the first man Louisiana ever nominated. With raised arm, the bronze figure stood between Wisconsin's LaFollette and Nebraska's Bryan. Long's former henchmen spoke at the dedication. One called him "the greatest humanitarian in history." Even this tribute was outdone. "When he was shot,"

said another orator, "the Maker looked down and saw little children crying." What he did not say was whether they were tears
of grief or of relief.

Traitors, assassins, robbers, feuders, gangsters, deceivers—the
forms of villainy are many. The fascination they have over Americans remains constant. They are as necessary to our thinking
and our culture as the heroes whom they oppose. There could be
only one thing worse than having villains. That would be not
to have them.

CHAPTER 14

Don't Fence Me In: The Cowboy

"There's still hundreds of miles of country where there's plenty of cattle and no fences, where the cowboy wears his boots out in the stirrup and not in irrigation ditches . . . where a man's a man."—Will James, *The Drifting Cowboy*

Rousseau's "natural man", that romantic symbol of freedom which captivated the eighteenth century, triumphantly entered the American forests as the buck-skin clad hunter, only to emerge on the Great Plains a century later as the American cowboy. Somewhere between the Alleghenies and the Rockies the followers of Daniel Boone traded coonskins for sombreros, long rifles for six-shooters, and moccasins for spurs—without losing their fascination for the hero-loving American public.

The two symbolic figures, hunter and cowboy, made similar appeals to the trait valued above all others in American culture: freedom. The hunter wasn't happy unless he had what Daniel Boone called elbow room; which translated into the twentieth century terms became a popular cowboy ditty, "Don't Fence Me In." There was something nostalgic about it. For only two decades had the cowboy roamed hundreds of miles with no fences to hamper him or his herd. By 1954 those days were as distant as speculation over the morals of Grover Cleveland or the feasibility of eating tomatoes. With the coming of barbed wire and homesteaders in the 1870's, the open range quickly disappeared in fact, but not in fancy. On the back of Old Paint, the Cowboy has ridden through whole libraries of serious literature, hundreds of

203

light novels, box-car loads of pulp paper, and miles of celluloid (mostly grade B, alas), a world symbol of twentieth century America.

Today, with much less freedom but much better publicity than cowboys who went before him, he rides through the fictional world. No other occupation in America has developed so virulent a tradition. The American G. I.'s found this out during World War II. In remote places they discovered they were expected not to shoot the way the sergeant had taught them, but from the hip; to abandon their jeeps if a horse of any description were available; to ignore posture drills, and let their legs assume a normal bowed position; and to toss army tactics aside and track down enemy bad men in posses. The popular magazines and movies had done their job well. The cowboy legend preceded the American army around the world. This is even more noteworthy since the west's open ranges were gone forever before the turn of the century. Conditions have altered radically, but not the notion of the prairie paradise.

In analyzing the cowboy we are dealing not so much with individuals as with a recognizable type; not with an historical reality, but with a fictional ideal. This was precisely the case, in the age of the Enlightenment, with Rousseau's natural man, and the trailblazer on the early American frontier. Most Americans feel that the west is governed by a compelling and unwritten code, a "spirit" unlike that east of the Mississippi. The cowboy eptomizes this code and spirit. That this is an oversimplification is beside the point; that many Americans believe it is central.

During the American Revolution, "cowboy" was a term applied to the Tories who organized raids on the Whigs' cattle. It was spoken in scorn rather than admiration. In the 1830's hired workmen called cowboys, much closer to current conceptions of the word, began to round up stray cattle in the Rio Grande county, and drive them to interior market towns. Some of the more daring ones drove their herds overland to Shreveport, Louisiana, there to be shipped down the river on flatboats to New Orleans. Thus their feats became widely known.

Major expansion in the cattle business came after the annexation of Texas in 1845. The number of cattle increased about 30% annually, with an equivalent increase in the herders. By the time of the 1849 California gold rush there was a less spectacular but more solid one underway on the Texas plains. There the gold was on the hoof. The editor of *DeBow's Review* noted in 1850 that these Texas herds were "happier and prettier than those pastured by Virgil in his pastoral, enlivening the otherwise oppressive loneliness of the scene."

Most Easterners did not share this writer's enthusiasm for the little-known topography of the West. On many maps the plains appeared as the Great American Desert, which made the deeds of those who thrived there seem even more heroic. No less a figure than Daniel Webster, speaking in 1838 against a bill to establish a mail route between Independence, Missouri and the mouth of the Columbia River, asked in the Senate: "To what use could we ever hope to put these great deserts or the endless mountain ranges, impregnable and covered to their very base with eternal snow? What use have we for such a country? Mr. President, I will never vote one cent from the public treasury to place the Pacific coast one inch nearer to Boston than it now is."

John C. Frémont's widely-read reports of his western exploration (actually written by his wife, and incidentally serving to make a hero of Frémont's scout Kit Carson) helped dispel the notion that the plains were an uninhabited desert; of course the dramatic exodus caused by the gold rush increased America's knowledge about the west enormously. The development of the cattle business, and popular interest in the cowboys who made it possible, stopped abruptly with the Civil War. In April, 1861 Lincoln declared a blockade on Southern ports and prohibited all commercial dealing with the rebels. During the war the open range could not compete with the firing range. Young Texans who had mastered the art of rounding up cattle went off to round up Yankees.

In 1861 the total number of cowboys was small, and there was still no recognizable stereotype. Most of the early men on the range had been Mexicans, admittedly skillful horsemen, but (according to Anglos in the Southwest) untrustworthy and hard on the stock. Since the standing of Mexicans in Alamo-obsessed Texas was not far above that of the longhorns which were coming into prominence, Mexicans had not been considered very heroic. The cowboy grew in stature after Appomattox; the two decades that followed were his golden years. Herds too vast to be counted grazed on the open pasture which extended from the Rio Grande to Canada, and from Kansas to the Rockies. Here was the famous sea of grass. The cowboys who drove their herds northward to be marketed were masters of it. If their lives were far from romantic, their duties and exploits brought them suddenly and dramatically into their own.

With relatively light rainfall, high summer temperatures, violent winters, and fine grained soils, the Great Plains constitute an area in which a few inches of rain can make the difference between a thriving region and a dustbowl. A major wet period on the plains coincided with the post-war expansion. Abnormally good grass and crops enticed the new adventurers westward. Few thought of what might happen in the dry years; no one had any way of telling when, if ever, they might come.

The result was a major cattle boom. Between 1860 and 1880 the human population tripled in Texas, and jumped from 107,000 to nearly a million in Kansas. The increase in cattle was even more spectacular. In the 1870's the number of head soared from 11,000 to 520,000 in Wyoming; 26,000 to 430,000 in Montana; and 71,000 to 791,000 in Colorado. This was the Great American Barbeque.

Tycoons and combinations appeared equaling in magnitude those of the Robber Baron East. The Prairie Land and Cattle Company grabbed off 790 square miles of land. Charles Goodnight's J. A. Ranch got over a million acres. The Capitol Freehold Company, in return for a promise to build a state capitol, was given 3,000,000 acres on which to graze 160,000 head of cattle within 1500 miles of barbed wire. The range cattle business was king-size from the first.

Unadorned truth would have been sufficient to start a boom. After western editors and boosters, (never noted for understatement) had had their say, the notion that fortunes in beef were plentiful had moved on past the east coast to the other side of the Atlantic. All over Europe, drawing rooms buzzed with cowboy stories. Club members who scarcely knew the difference between a steer and a heifer discussed it. The flow of wealth from across the Atlantic encouraged overstocking and brought the day of reckoning nearer.

Across the roads and trails west went caravans of covered wagons headed for the New Promised Land—which was gradually moving from the wet to the dry years of its cycle. "This is it, Ma! We'll be big-time cattlemen before you know it!" gloated the men who held the reins. They could not know that they were destined to turn the grassy plains into the Dust Bowl; to drive their children's children, the future Ma and Pa Joads, to a land where the grapes of wrath were sown.

We are not concerned here with the 1873 panic and the economic, physical, and social factors which brought disaster to the boom land, littering the plains with the bones of cattle.[1] Despite this collapse, the saga of the American cowboy gripped the American imagination. Writers, executives, and directors have dedicated themselves to the remunerative principle that old cowboy tales and deeds shall not die, nor even slightly fade away. They have added to the glory and guts of the historical cowboy, making him into what Omar Barker calls a "fictitious hero," a guitar-strumming, movie set outdoors man, a pale imitation of the man who was once content to punch cattle.

Everyone (but especially 25,000,000 juvenile Americans) knows what the cowboy looks like. Physically he is tall, tanned, sinewy, a man at home in the great outdoors. Weatherbeaten and rough, this child of nature is innately handsome, despite eyes squinted from work in the glaring sun and legs bowed from a life in the saddle. He is never far away from his horse, who has almost human intelligence. The two of them form the most enduring team in American mythology. This helps explain the growing horse cult in a highly mechanized American. Details of his uniform vary little. On his head is a broad-brimmed felt hat, white if he's a good guy, black if he is shady. Tied around his neck is a colored silk handkerchief, to be pulled over his face during a dust storm. A handsome loose flannel shirt (elaborately embroidered if a technicolor movie camera is lurking nearby) covers his manly chest. To his pants, which fit him not like trousers but a glove, might be attached leather chaps, to ease the strain of continuous riding. Since he must carry the law with him on his hip, a gun and holster are standard equipment. If he intends to make a place for himself with he-men, he will have two guns, symbols of quick and decisive action. These six-shooters, of heavy caliber, can be depended on to open a path for daylight through the body of any hostile critter, man or beast. On his feet are tight-fitting, high-heeled boots which go into the stirrups. They make him out of place when walking like the lowly pedestrian. On these boots are spurs, which guide his horse while his hands are occupied with lasso or revolver.

All these things are functional for the cowboy, his best solutions to daily problems. But to the outsider, who has little use for any of them, they seem bizarre and dangerous. They put the cowboy in a different world. They mark him as a man who can cope with the lonely, grieving plains; with the shotlike sleet and smothering snow of winter; or the blistering heat and searing dryness of summer. Here is a real he-man dressed for the part, called by an awed Englishman "a species of centaur, half horse, half man, with immense rattling spurs, tanned skin, and dare-devil, ferocious face."

You will find him, (say his admirers) modest, truthful, brave, enduring, democratic, fun-loving, and highly individualistic. He is the model of all who believe that life in God's outdoors, close to the "real" things, is desirable; a good man to have with you, and demon when against you; a man to be tampered with only when you are reconciled to picking lead slugs out of your carcass on short notice.

As a class, cowboys have always presented a discouraging field for missionaries. For years there was "no Sunday west of the Kaw and no God west of the Pecos." A traditional specialty, once the long drive was over and the long-earned rest won, was raising hell. Naturally some excuse had to be advanced for such carryings-on in a nation where blue laws endured and the ghost of Calvin still stalked the land. An ample one existed in the effects of isolation and solitude upon the cowboy. If they did not condone, they at least explained his lawlessness. The unbroken quiet of the plains, a sort of perpetual solitary confinement, could be oppressive, almost unbearable. Like a heavy weight, the silent space bore down upon the mind. A man felt like crying aloud to break through the wall of padded loneliness surrounding him, but knew it would do no good. Not everyone could stand it. Some went mad.

So the cowboys shot up the town when they could get there and turned pleasure and vice into synonymous terms. To the usual sins were added as many new ones as conditions would permit. In his *Sketches of the Cattle Trail* (1874), McCoy pictured the cowboys reveling in pockets of iniquity with "men who lived a soulless, aimless life, dependent upon the turn of a card for a living; blear-eyed and dissipated, life had long since become for them worse than a total blank." What could seem more shocking, and actually more enticing, to the sedate, law-abiding, urban East? The West's "beautiful bibulous Babylons of the Plains," as one writer called them, became symbols of escape. Many a tourist dollar was, and is, spent in order to indulge in a little authentic western revelry, no holds barred. Such towns as Las Vegas, Tombstone, and Reno, have capitalized on it for years.

This fascination of the wide-open land is no new thing. On January 1, 1878, the editor of the Washington *Star* reported that "those nomads of regions remote from the restraints of normal life"were actually laws unto themselves. There cowboys "loiter sometimes for months, and share the boughten dalliances of fallen women." How many readers could attribute trips or moves west to such editorials as these, can never be computed. Oh, for a life on the distant plains, where a man can let off a little steam without ending up in a police court!

In his own bully way Theodore Roosevelt was as good a publicist for the strenuous life, and the cowboy who lived it, as anyone. He admired the cowboy, as his book on *Ranch Life and the Hunting Trail* (1888) showed. Roosevelt called him "the grim pioneer of our race," who "'prepares the way for the civilization from before whose face he must disappear. Hard and dangerous though this is, it has a wild attraction that strongly draws to it his bold, free spirit." Such passages, repeated in many twentieth century books, established the general picture of the cowboy. None of them succeeded in making historical individuals into cowboy heroes. No Daniel Boones or Kit Carsons of the range emerged, and none exists in our heroic portrait gallery.

Heroic cattlemen were plentiful. Nelson Story, Oliver Loving, Ike Pryor, and Charles Goodnight led lives that would make a Hollywood executive have technicolor dreams. In 1866 Story, with a handful of cowboys, drove a thousand cattle all the way from Fort Worth to Montana, right through the heart of the Indian

country, despite stiff opposition from the Sioux, Cheyennes, and
contingents of the United States Army.   But what Easterner knows
these early cowboys' names?   What politician or publicist eulo-
gizes them?

In cowboy fiction there is no single hero who rides successfully
through a series, to match the exploits of the Deerslayer in
Cooper's forest tales.[2]   Even in Hollywood, which has made
cowboy movies an indispensible part of the juvenile diet, the turn-
over in "stars" is large.   The widely acclaimed Tom Mixes and
William S. Harts are forgotten after they have passed from the
screen.   True enough, the first man to utilize the cowboy in the
dime novel had a single individual as a model.   This author was
Prentiss Ingraham, Buffalo Bill's ghost writer.   The cowboy was
Buck Taylor, who performed in Cody's Wild West Show for years.
In 1887 Ingraham finished the first cowboy novel to appear in a
popular series.   Buck Taylor was a youngster living in a Texas
Ranger camp.   He eventually "won his spurs" with the famous
outfit.   Afterwards Taylor indulged freely in his favorite outdoor sport of tracking down Mexicans.   The hero was a Nordic
who carried the White Man's Burden with him as he galloped
through Texas.   This racialism in the American cowboy stereotype has persisted up to the present day, and has even become
more pronounced.   Answering an inquiry as to the cause of the
Western story's popularity, an editor of a cowboy pulp magazine
replied:

"It is understood by us, and should be understood by everyone,
that we are dealing with the popularity of Western stories as con-
cerns readers who are white, who may be called Nordics, using
that term advisedly.   The white race has always been noted for
being hard-drinking, hard-fighting, fearless, fair and square.   The
heroes of Western stories have these characteristics." [3]

Yet there was nothing like 100 percent Americanism among
the real cowboys on the open range.   They were an international
crew, with such nicknames as "Mex" Garcia, "Nigger" Jones,
"French" Bareau, and "Kamuk" Simons—names taken from
Wyoming ranch life in the 1880's.   Considering that the first
American herds were Spanish in origin, and that much of the
American cowboy's technique and equipment was of Mexican
origin, the Nordicism in cowboy stories is difficult to explain.   So

is the chauvinism. American money did not turn cattle raising into big business. The headquarters of the major outfits and investors were in London, Aberdeen, and Edinburgh. The stock cowboy is as much a fiction in America as the Self-Made Man, *homo economicus*, Uncle Sam, Pecos Bill, or John Q. Public.

* * *

In order to " escape from civilization's school room," a sickly 1885 Harvard graduate sought better health and adventure in the Rockies. He was able to return after a while and set himself up as a Philadelphia lawyer. The drabness of the city depressed this young man who had breathed the clear dry air of the west, and who rode the range with cowboys. On his next summer vacation he had himself photographed in the outfit of a cowboy. Then he began to write stories about the ranch life he loved.

Owen Wisters' (1890-1938) first collection of stories (*Lin MacLean*) was followed in 1900 by the *Jimmy-john Boss*. But his masterpiece came later. "I left some good company at a club dinner table one night to go off to a lonely library and begin work on a story," he recorded later; the result was *The Virginian* (1902). Reprinted fifteen times during the first year, it has remained a much-imitated best seller, the model for western novels.

The cowboy novel presents a peculiar difficulty for the author. He must write about a pastoral and half-nomadic group for a body of settled and usually urban readers. *The Virginian* was the first novel which, despite its romantic gloss, solved this dilemma. It thereby set the tone for the realistic western libel which is the standard fictional version.

Wister's chief triumph was the portrayal of his hero, a gallant latter-day knight, spiritual descendent of such earlier cavaliers as John Smith and Jeb Stuart. He could ride a horse, solve a mystery, entertain a crowd, and infatuate a girl with equal facility. Wister, whose mind dwelled often on heroes, enjoyed creating such a paragon. In 1900 he had done an uncritical life of Grant. Even while working on *The Virginian* he was beginning to collect material for his biography of Washington, publishd in 1908. His work on Theodore Roosevelt, which appeared in 1930, reaffirmed his belief in great men. None of these have the significance of *The Virginian*, which depicted life on the open range of the 1870's, and made the little-known and much-maligned cowboy a respectable, even intriguing, character for serious literature.

Though none of his sixty novels was as influential as *The Virginian*, the extent of his writings and popularity made Zane Grey (1875-1939) one of the most successful cowboy writers. Generally considered sub-literary by his critics, Grey's formula-ridden and poorly constructed novels have had much effect on America. By 1950 over 24,000,000 copies of his cowboy books had been sold.

Born in Zanesville, Ohio, he began his career as a dentist, but became a writer in 1904. Prolific and methodical, he turned out 100,000 words a month for years, always in longhand. No one had written so much that was read so eagerly since the days of Ned Buntline and Horatio Alger. More than anyone else, Grey is the heir of the nineteenth century dime novel writer in America.

He wrote too fast, and followed conventions too closely, to achieve literary distinction. His brawny, blameless hero was "a bronzed, strong-jawed, eagle-eyed man, stalwart, superb of height."[4] He tangled time and again with villains, with inevitably happy results. There was an untarnished but willing heroine at the end of the trail. While few readers remember the names of his heroes, they do not forget the type he portrayed, nor the things the character always did. The cowboy and Zane Grey made a wonderful combination; the former existed, and the latter thought, in terms of a pattern. Grey had only one story to tell—that of the brave cowboy surmounting human and natural obstacles, and living happily ever after. In 1939, just before he died, he published *Knights of the Range*. The title indicated that things had not changed much as stories poured out. So did the description of the cattle baron, whose blue eyes "lingered long before shifting round to the west, where a splendour of range empire unfolded to his gaze" and the invocation to the "wildspirited knights who slept in unmarked graves, out on the lone prairie."

A third major cowboy glorifier was Charlie Siringo (1855-1928), who spent years in Hollywood transferring the cowboy to celluloid. We have already discussed his life and writing in the chapter on Billy the Kid. Siringo's pose was much admired and imitated, particularly by Will Rogers, Oklahoma's famed lariat twirler.

Though he claimed he was only "a dumb comedian," Will Rogers was much more. W. H. Payne's *Folk Say of Will Rogers* and Jack Lait's *Will Rogers' Wit and Wisdom* reveal the acuteness of his chatter. The placing of his statue in the Nation's Capitol, beside those of Franklin and Jefferson, demonstrates the extraordinary reputation he achieved. For a generation of Americans, he was Mr. Cowboy. Europeans, Eastern dudes, and highbrows were his special targets; a lariat and chewing gum his only props. Never so dumb as he tried to look, Will proved that the only thing more attractive to a New York theatre audience than a Ziegfeld girl was a Ziegfeld cowboy. If his personal fame came from the stage, his general appeal sprang from a newspaper column, "Slipping the Lariat Over." By 1931 according to one estimate it had over forty million readers.

No other writers rank with Wister, Grey and Siringo as cowboy hero-makers, although men like Will Rogers, Emerson Hough, O. Henry, James Oliver Curwood, Eugene Manlove Rhodes, William McLeod Raine, Clarence Mulford, Stephen Payne, and Omar Barker are important. The central thread which binds all their work is adventure—action by men on horseback, external stories concerned with doing and not thinking, stories which perpetuate a simple myth for a complex culture.

*   *   *

Being "western" is, for thousands of writers, real estate men, restaurant owners, tourist specialists, and showmen, not only a preference but a vocation. One wonders where genuine love of the region stops and mere concern with the pocketbook begins. The greatest western publicist that ever lived was a man who died debt-ridden and harrassed by creditors—"Buffalo Bill" Cody. By living so dramatically the role of plains hero, he convinced people that the west, and the cowboy who set its tone and pace, was heroic.

In order to bolster up this notion a good many towns annually stage an Old West Week and get their regional trappings out for the stereotyped saturnalia. It is, in effect, an open season—on tourists. Commenting on the way the local burghers whoop it up, Bernard DeVoto writes: "The realtor, the bank cashier, and the soda jerk sport big hats, chromatic shirts, short neckties painted with longhorns, and high-water levis.   They pitch about on the high heels of unfamiliar riding boots and trip over three inch silver spurs that match their belt buckles.   For the duration of Old West Week they are going to be cowpokes, bronzed horsemen, cattle barons.   And that is what in fantasy they tend to be all year long.   Here is make-believe on a national scale." [6]

Those who cannot go to see the elaborate pageant can get in via radio, television, or motion picture instead.   The Western generally considered the ancestor of all others was made in the East, near Dover, New Jersey.   Called *The Great Train Robbery* (1903), it featured "Broncho Billy" Anderson, a protége of Buffalo Bill.   A decade later Thomas Ince was making Westerns out West, using real cowboys and Indians.   In this locale William S. Hart rode "Pinto Ben" into stardom, as movies usurped the place of the dime novel in America.

The Covered Wagon (1923) was the first cowboy epic.   It was based on a novel by Emerson Hough, whom we have already met among Billy the Kid's hero makers.   Directed by James Cruze and filmed near Snake Valley, Nevada, *The Covered Wagon* was free from staginess, and was much praised as a uniquely American production dramatizing the idea of Manifest Destiny.

Since then thousands of Westerns have come from Hollywood. Many have been "oaters," designed for friendly Saturday runs in little towns.   Others, like *High Noon, Yellow Sky, Shane, The Gunfighter*, and *Hondo*, have been much more.   The better ones reveal artistic conventions as rigid as those in a Greek temple, a classical sonata, or a medieval morality play.

The Great American horse opera involves rapid action, the struggle of right and wrong, and the triumph of justice.   It bristles with violence, which allows the hero to show his caliber.   The actual drama and setting, though important, are always subordinate to the cowboy; they simply present opportunities for the definition of his code and character.   Like a sacrament, the drama is repeated *ad infinitum* to reaffirm the audience's child-like faith in its idol.

The setting is Hangman's Hill or Go-to-Hell Gulch.   The time is invariably about 1870; everyone prepares to do what he or she "has to do."   The villain is very bad, the heroine very good; the hero must see that the twain never meet.   In this he is ably assisted by his horse, a hero in his own right. Good and Evil finally clash head on. Everybody on and off the screen holds his breath. Guns blaze. The smoke clears. Destiny is suspended for a fleeting instant.

The hero wins—he must. Defender of the purity of his own image, he is unconquerable. He fights not for laws or women or property, but to prove what he is: the last gentleman. In him not only the code of the Old West, but that of the Old South, flowers.

Only when one understands this can he explain the national appeal of the cowboy in a nation with the Mason and Dixon line drawn across its middle. The ranch is really a duplication of the plantation, without slaves. Free of this stigma, the Southern dream was purged and revitalized on the grass frontier. It is no accident that the novel that best explicated the modern cowboy ideal was called *The Virginian*.

The regenerated myth of the ante-bellum South, as David Davis has noted, could and did take advantage of certain western features: "It could focus all energies on its former role of opposing the peculiar social and economic philosophy of the Northeast. This took the form of something more fundamental than mere agrarianism or primitivism. Asserting the importance of values beyond the utilitarian and material, this transplanted Southern philosophy challenged the doctrine of enlightened self-interest and the belief that leisure time is sin." [7]

The most important thing that the South contributed, however, was a foundation for the cowboy's code which basically is nothing more than a democratic version of the Southern gentleman's "honor."

The cowboy movie is the only American art form in which the notion of honor retains its full strength. "The Westerner," Robert Warshow comments, "seeks not to extend his dominion but only to assert his personal value . . . Since he is not a murderer but a man of virtue, and since he is always prepared for defeat, he retains his inner invulnerability. His story need not end with his death (and usually does not); but what we finally respond to is not his victory but his defeat." [8] Most good westerns are seemingly comic but basically tragic.

If there were one archetypal movie, it was *The Virginian*, made in 1929 and starring Gary Cooper. Taken from Owen Wister's novel, it depicted the adventures of a chilvaric cowboy who wooed and won Molly Wood, a pretty schoolteacher from Vermont. He would not violate the accepted forms of western combat. To the villain's taunts he merely replied, "When you call me that— smile!" But he knew, as do we, that sooner or later Trampas would "ask for it." The hero would then see that he got it. That was the whole point of his being there.

A quarter century later, Gary Cooper played in another important horse opera, *High Noon*. Now there were some greys among the black and whites. The pattern, as well as Cooper himself, was maturing. Slower moving, a less handsome and sprightly figure now, the heroic marshal was about to hang up his guns and begin a new life. But news came that a killer (whom he had sent to prison) had been pardoned, and would come to town on the noon train; with three friends he would hunt down and kill the marshal. Cooper was forced to play out the drama and do what he "had to do;" but unlike the Virginian, he realized that he could never achieve an absolute triumph. He no longer thought in terms of bringing Law and Order to the West; all he wanted to do was stay alive in the dusty street of a jerkwater cowtown.

The portrait of this two-dimensional and stylized hero so kind to "good girls" and horses and so mean to "bad girls" and villains, is fostered not only by the movies and magazines, but also by reality. People living in the West have adopted the myths, manners, and even the drawl which was invented in cowboy fiction. This is something worth noting. Instead of life imposing itself on literature, literature is here imposing itself on life.

Thus it is that dude ranches thrive not only beyond the Mississippi, but on Long Island, in the Berkshires, and throughout Pennsylvania. The Eastern visitor, no less than the Western cowpoke, is determined to turn back the clock, and enjoy once more the two decades after the Civil War when ranges, bars, and women were open.

The nearest thing to a national institution which the cowboy culture has developed is the "rodeo." No one is certain when the first one was held. The Cheyenne, Wyoming *Daily Leader* complained in 1872 about an exhibition of Texas steer riding which the editor found "unnecessarily cruel, suited to the prairie." Later editors took a considerably different stand towards the rodeos which became Cheyenne's major source of income. Other western towns, noting how the Cheyenne Frontier Days (begun in 1897) prospered, now have rodeos of their own. The towns have sensed the chance to establish a "tradition" in a region which, by seaboard standards, is devoid of much history, pomp, and symbolism.

Guy Weadick produced the first western rodeo which played a steady engagement to Broadway sophisticates, and sent parents of New Yorkers out after guns and lassoes for their apartment-dwelling kiddies. Known as the "New York stampede of 1916," the show's stars were Prairie Lilly Allen, Dorothy Morrell, and Leonard Stroud. While they did not stand up well against Cody's Wild Bill Hickok, Annie Oakley, and Pawnee Bill, they captivated New York, and were proclaimed "world champions" by Weadick. Since there was no central organization to coordinate rodeo rules, standards, and claims, champions cropped up like prairie grass. In 1929 the Rodeo Association, and later the Cowboy's Turtle Association came into being, the first to organize the rodeo business and the second to secure a fair deal for the cowboy. Rodeo was fast becoming big business as managers organized and workers unionized.

Cowboy idols of Hollywood, especially those able to ride a horse, have been quick to cash in on the rodeo fad. Gene Autry, who so impressed his neighbors in the town of Berwyn, Oklahoma, that they changed the town's name to Gene Autry in 1942, got together the Flying A Ranch Stampede. It was the feature attraction of the 1942 Houston Fat Stock Show. Gene and his Hollywood-wise "Champion" were in the vanguard. The performers' costumes were treated with fluorescent dyes, so that they glowed when the concealed violet ray lights were turned on them. All in all, it was enough to make a veteran of the Chisolm Trail rush for the closest swinging doors.

Roy Rogers, Republic Picture's singing cowboy, has also developed a rodeo that is smooth and streamlined. Even in this sugar-coated and commercial form, the dramatic appeal is strong enough to keep Americans coming back when the cry of "Pour 'em out" opens still another rodeo. Also effective as a medium of cowboy action and heroic valor is the television screen, which is in many

American homes the scene of a new daily ritual.   Just how the
cowboy and television might mix to create a potent cultural weapon
was indicated by a New Jersey elementary school teacher's report
made in the spring of 1950.   Mrs. Allison Palmer, in a protest
which received national attention, stated: "During class the
students strained and fidgeted, just waiting for the time to go home
to the television set again.   You know what they talk about? Hopalong Cassidy, over and over.   Just cowboys and Indians and
Hopalong Cassidy.   It's no wonder they are bored by school. How
can I compete with Hopalong Cassidy?"[9]

The rhetorical question dramatized the fact that the cowboy
hero was making the most of technology.   The rise of Hopalong
Cassidy, in real life William Boyd, indicated that ether waves,
television grids, and movie reels were effective devices for creating
new American heroes.   Just how much more so they would be than
the mere printed word, or what effect they would have on the
nation, no one could predict.   Boyd's success story was a good
clue.

Born in Ohio in 1896, he left home in 1915 to try Hollywood.
As a romantic star in the '20's, Boyd got himself a mansion in
Beverly Hills, a beach house in Malibu, and (in rapid sequence)
four wives.   Coming upon hard times during the Depression he
took roles in class "B" Hopalong Cassidy westerns.   Scripts were
prepared by Clarence E. Mulford.   He had shot his way through
54 Hopalong movies by 1943, when rising production costs caused
producer Harry Sherman to abandon the series.   After doing
another dozen Hopalong movies on his own, Boyd too conceded
defeat.

In 1947 he gambled all his remaining credit on the television
rights of the Hopalong pictures, at a time when television was
experimental.   He was able to acquire them.   When television
expanded, he became the TV cowboy hero for young America.
Appearing on 63 television stations, 152 radio stations, 155 newspaper comic pages, and the wares of over a hundred manufacturers of western specialties, Hopalong had by 1954 not only
become a hero; he had become a large-scale enterprise making a
million dollars a year.

The creator of long-lasting Hopalong fortunately left for us a
detailed description of his idol's character.   Unlike the Horatio

Alger hero, Hoppy is not motivated primarily by ambition. Despite his fine horse and saddle, he values his code and his friends more than his possessions. Basically he is a paradox. Sometimes he seems to do things just for the hell of it: "Humorous, courageous to the point of foolishness, eager for fight or frolic, nonchalant when one would expect him to be quite otherwise, curious, loyal to a fault, and the best man with a Colt in the Southwest, Hopalong was a paradox, and a puzzle even to his most intimate friends. With him life was a humorous recurrence of sensations, a huge pleasant joke instinctively tolerated, but not worth the price cowards pay to keep it."[10]

Forty years later another writer, Tex Burns, pulled the strings that made Mulford's hero hop along; but it was the same fellow, who still didn't give a hoot for fences or women.

"But you can't always move on, Hoppy!" Lenny protested. "Someday you must settle down! Don't you ever think of marriage?"

"Uh-huh, and whenever I think of it I saddle Topper and ride. I'm not a marrying man, Lenny. Sometimes I get to thinkin' about that poem a feller wrote about how a woman is only a woman but—"

The woman in the Hopalong stories, and most Westerns, is a *dea ex machina*. She must be rescued and protected. She brings out the cowboy's gentler side. For this reason, the aging William Boyd is ageless as a ladies' man.

He is, of course, a matinee idol, and cannot in any sense be considered a cowboy folk hero. Oddly enough, there is none, even though some call Pecos Bill one. The evidence presented to justify this claim is not convincing. Cowboy fiction and legend have never congealed around a single historical or imaginary figure, but Pecos Bill is America's nearest approximation.

Under the guidance of Professor Ernest Baughman, University of New Mexico folklorist and editor of the *New Mexico Folklore Record*, a survey of the Estancia Valley was made in 1951 to determine whether any oral stories of knowledge of Pecos existed there. The results were entirely negative; none of the old time ranchers, many of whom had been there as long as 40 years, had heard of Pecos Bill. The results are significant since Pecos is Anglo-Saxon and this is an "Anglo" area of New Mexico. Another indication of the lack of any oral tradition is that when the detailed study of Texas was produced by the Writer's Project of the W.P.A., Pecos Bill got slight mention in what is supposed to be his home state. Omar Barker, who has written of New Mexico for twenty-five years, admits that he had never heard an oral folk tale about Pecos Bill.

Yet as a purely literary hero Pecos Bill has done well. Getting into print in 1923, he has in three decades driven off his less virile legendary rivals. He is today the best-known literary hero of the cowboy country. Primarily the brainchild of Edward ("Tex") O'Reilly, publicist and author of the Southwest, Bill dates from O'Reilly's 1923 article in the *Century Magazine*.[12] The article reveals in what pattern O'Reilly intends to construct this oversized literary cowboy; for he judges it "highly probable that Paul Bunyan and Pecos Bill, mythical cowboy of the Southwest, were blood brothers. At all events, they can meet on one common ground: they were both fathered by a liar."

His model was Paul Bunyan. The reader also confronts a number of the episodes usually recorded as the exploits of a real-life Texas hero, Bigfoot Wallace. Pecos does humorously what Bigfoot did in deadly earnest, and with less of a flair for the spectacular and Bunyanesque. There is also something of the Crockett and Fink sagas in the Pecos stories that O'Reilly and others have constructed. Pecos Bill is a prefabricated hero, put together with parts from many other American sources and traditions. Like Bunyan, whom he meets and fights, Pecos Bill depends heavily on his retinue, which includes such fascinating creatures as Alkali Ike, One Lung Lyon, Bean-Hole Brown, Bullfrog Doyle, and Bronco Jones. Essentially Pecos Bill is a knavish blusterer, a picaresque hero who (like Davy Crockett, Mike Fink, and Paul Bunyan) passes from place to place, adventure to adventure. He has the cowboy's steel-grey eyes, sense of humor, weather-beaten countenance, quick trigger finger, and outdoor psychology. There must be a horse, naturally, and O'Reilly named it Widow Maker. An educated critter, Widow Maker has twenty-seven gaits (twenty-three forward and four reverse). Unlike most old-time cowboys, Bill also has a regular girl; Slue Foot Sue, who rode down the Rio Grande on a catfish, demonstrating that she was "a true girl of the west".

One of Pecos' great moments came when he appeared in Walt Disney's 1948 movie, *Melody Time*. The effort won him many new admirers who had not heard of Pecos before going to the theater. Simultaneously, but not accidentally, various advertisements featuring Pecos Bill appeared in *Time*, *Newsweek* and the *Saturday Evening Post*. If the hero-makers continue to concentrate on him, his reputation will grow in the years ahead. He will benefit from his connection with Paul Bunyan and from the fine writing which O'Reilly lavished on him as a birthright. After all, a hero who wants to join "not one of these ordinary cow-stealin', Mexican-shootin' bunches of amateurs, but a read hard herd of hand-picked hellions that make murder a fine art and take some proper pride in their slaughter," is not to be dismissed. We would not rank him in importance with Paul Bunyan, the nearest American approach to a folk hero. "The virility of the Bunyan legend," observes Frank Shay, "has so choked out the other heroes that today not one in a hundred old-time cowboys ever heard of Pecos Bill."

The radio, movies, ad men and television might revise things. We shall have to wait and see. Watch out Paul—Pecos is coming!

*   *   *

"If we could dispel the haze," writes Walter P. Webb in *The Great Plains*, "we could view western life as it was in reality— logical, perfectly in accord ultimately with the laws laid down by the inscrutable Plains." We can never get rid of the romantic haze that has settled permanently on the western horizon; and most of us wouldn't want to, even if we could. We like to conjure up our untarnished knights roaming about in their domains, where they make the laws and punish the wicked. We like to read about it, see it on the screen, describe it to our children. It is a world in which none of our little problems and dissatisfactions occur. There everyone knows what he is supposed to do, and does it. We have never permanently lost the tranquility and finality of the Medieval Synthesis as long as the tradition of the cowboy's west exists. Thus the editor of *Ranch Romances* writes, "We aim to lead our readers away from the complexities of civilization into a world of simple feeling and direct emotion." The formula sells millions of pulp magazines each month.

The American cowboy symbolizes a freedom, individuality, and closeness to nature which for many has become a mirage. He is a safety valve for our souls. When things get too bad, we slip into a movie house, or into a chair with the latest cowboy magazine or novel, and vicariously hit the trail. We become free agents in space and time, and for a while leave our world behind. "As I sat in the movie house it was evident that Bill Hart was being loved by all there," wrote Sherwood Anderson in *A Story Teller's Tale*. "I also wanted to be loved—to be a little dreaded and feared, too, perhaps. Ah! There goes Sherwood Anderson! Treat him with respect. He is a bad man when he is aroused. But treat him kindly and he will be as gentle with you as any cooing dove."

The cowboy legend, so appealing to mechanized and urbanized America, is spreading rapidly. Every fourth Hollywood movie deals with it, and many reach foreign audiences. Cowboy interpreters are receiving academic recognition. A few years ago the Texan historian J. Frank Dobie was called to Cambridge University to explain life on the range. After his year's visit the faculty solemnly awarded an honorary M.A. to this *Petastus inter togatas homines*: "sombrero wearer among the men with togas."

The cowboy is holding up well under all this admiration and examination; he makes an excellent hero. He is a horseback man, always the breed of heroes throughout history. As wholesome as a glass of Grade A pasteurized milk, he boasts a virile code and outlook. He has those virtues our culture most admires, and displays them on all occasions. With him the love of freedom is a passion, and the willingness to accept his responsibility a dogma. To his code, his horse, and his cattle, he is always faithful.

He quickens young America's belief in personal strength and ingenuity. The western movies are little courses in citizenship; modern morality plays. Parents send junior off to the Saturday matinee, knowing that virtue will triumph and the forces of darkness will be squelched. Like knights of old, cowboys seek combat for fair ladies. With so sound a function, they need not fear extinction.

The open range has gone forever. Only an imaginary trail winds its way through what was once the unbroken sea of grass.

All that is left of the golden moment is a group of names on the land: Bitterroot, Rawhide Creek, Whoopup, Chugwater, Tensleep, Wounded Knee, Tombstone, Medicine Bow, and Horse Thief Creek.

Heartfelt and descriptive, they endure. So does the memory and the dream.

CHAPTER 15

The Emerging American Hero

"The historic memory goes back through long defiles of doom."—Herman Melville.

"Every historical change creates its mythology."
—Bronislaw Malinowski

Being a modern hero is difficult and perplexing. "It is not only that there is no hiding place for the gods from the searching telescope. There is no such society any more as the gods once supported. The social unit is not a carrier of religious content, but an economic-political organization."[1] Corrado Alvaro finds *The Hero in Crisis,* and Ortega y Gasset, a century suffering from the intervention of the mass man into everything. Harrison Smith ascribes the woes of contemporary fiction to the disappearance of the hero, who is really nothing more than a victim. Technology and science are said to have withered up our grass roots, and capitalism our sense of community. "There is no culture where economic relations are not subject to a regulating principle to protect interests involved," Gasset claims.[2] We are told that once America had a culture without a civilization, and now a civilization without a culture.

Others bewail the fate of mythology. "Myths are construed simply by the hard Occidental mind—they are lies," writes John Crowe Ransom in *God Without Thunder.* "They are not nearly good enough for the men in our twentieth century generation, brought up in the climatic blessedness of our scientific world." With many words contemporary critics repeat what Nietzsche said in five: "Dead are all the gods."

They are wrong. Mythology cannot be superceded or elimin-

224

ated. It can and does assume every conceivable form, depending
on the culture. Like Proteus, as described by Homer in the
Odyssey, it "takes all manner of shapes of things that creep upon
the earth, of water likewise, and of fierce fire burning."

American history, in its several periods and on its various
levels, confirms this view. We have been as sure as any people
in the past that we are the Chosen People; that (to quote Abraham
Lincoln's line) "this nation, under God, shall have a new birth
of freedom." Under God, and the guidance of the heroes whom
He sends down to lead us. The military idol still thrills us. In
the 1952 presidential election, as in many others, we put one in
the White House. We swoon as readily for the television idol as
grandmother did for her favorite vaudeville star, or the Greek for
the most fashionable tragic actor. In our fiction the hero seems
lost in a labyrinth of despair; but he will come back. He always
has.

Just as certainly we have not lost our faculty for myth, which
is innate in the human race. "It seizes with avidity upon any
incidents, surprising or mysterious, in the career of those who
have at all distinguished themselves from their fellows, and in-
vents episodes to which it then attaches a fanatical belief," Som-
erset Maugham observed in *The Moon and Sixpence*. "It is the
protest of romance against the commonplace of life."

Not the scholar, but the doctor, is the current master of the
mythological realm. Like the Wise Old Man in the ancient sagas
and fairy tales, he is the knower of secret ways and formulas; the
one whose potency can kill modern dragons, apply healing balm
to the almost fatal wound, and send the heroic conqueror back
into the world to do wonderful deeds. Myths supply the power
which carries the human spirit forward. The modern psycho-
analyst has only reaffirmed the timeless wisdom of the myth-
making witch doctors. The goddess of fertility smiles at us from
beneath the thick make-up of the latest screen heroine. Ulysses
puts out to sea with the United States Marines. The grasping
Midas, the ever-searching Parsifal, the new actors in the romance
of Beauty and the Beast, stand this very moment on a busy New
York street corner, waiting for the traffic light to change.

How could it be otherwise? We simply must have heroes.
They give us blessed relief from our daily lives, which are fre-

quently one petty thing after another. Hemmed in by our little horizons, we hear the hero's voice, clear and confident. It releases us, telling us where we go and why. He gives meaning to all we do, and we gladly praise him. He helps us to transcend our drab back yards, apartment terraces, and tenements, and to regain a sense of the world's bigness.

This is especially true in the United States, which is long on heroes and short on symbols, myths, and rituals. We are so proud of our material achievements that we underestimate and even belittle our psychic ones. "America? I sometimes think she does not have a corner in her own house," commented Walt Whitman.

Like most of the world's heroes, ours have usually been physically attractive, strong, and fearless. A note of fatalism has dominated their lives, in which some catalytic experience has set the popular imagination to work, and kept it going. Episodes involved are not always true. We remember Captain John Smith's head on the block, but not his histories. The image of Washington chopping down a cherry tree has stuck more firmly than the names of all his victories. Just as the pier holds up the bridge, so does the hero support society. A moral materialist, he is concerned with both ideas and matter, never with one to the exclusion of the other.

Beyond that, all his fellow Americans demand of him is that he be able to look any man in the eye and tell him to go to hell.

We love to exaggerate, as the literature of our heroes and their adventures proves. To exaggerate is essentially to simplify. Subtle shades are removed, leaving only the bold ones in the composition. When we go in for rough-housing, we go whole hog, with such results as those described in a poem which appeared in the Galveston *Weekly Journal* some years ago:

> "They fit and fit, and gouged and bit
> And struggled in the mud;
> Until the ground for miles around
> Was kivered with their blood,
> And a pile of noses, ears, and eyes
> Large and massive, reached the skies."

Funny and even consciously preposterous, our legendary heroes are cockalorum demigods, exhibiting bold and grotesque imaginations, contempt for authority, and limitless optimism. As Josh Billings said, "They love caustick things; they would prefer turpentine to colone-water, if they had tew drink either. So with their relish of humor; they must have it on the half shell with cayenne."

Debunkers who say heroes are men with the ability to fool most of the people all of the time, have not been important in America. Nor have lady bone-worshipers, who unite under high-sounding titles to preserve the trappings of greatness. These modern vestal virgins make an easy target for parody and scorn. Real heroes resist both the venomed darts of the debunkers and the sugary epithets of the adulators.

Heroes tend to come in bunches. The Revolution and Civil War produced bumper crops. When our writers or movie-makers look back at those dramatic times, they concur with Wordsworth:

> *"Bliss was it in that dawn to be alive*
> *But to be young was very heaven."*

Both decades were military-dominated. The saddle of a white horse remains the best seat for the aspirant. In this respect the democratic hero is like any other. What democracy offers is the opportunity for every man to get on the horse. It attempts to elevate the aristoi, or naturally superior, rather than an aristocracy, or blue bloods.

This proposition thrilled Thomas Jefferson, Andrew Jackson, Ralph Waldo Emerson, and Horace Mann. Walt Whitman wanted *Leaves of Grass* to "transpose the reader into the central position," where he could become the living fountain." From our indigenous traditions and landscape must come our heroes and myths. Henry Thoreau perceived this, and was confident that it would occur. "Who knows what shape the fable of Columbus will assume, to be confounded with that of Jason and the expedition of the Argonauts?" he wrote. "And Franklin—there may be a line for him in the future classical dictionary. 'He aided the Americans to gain their independence, instructed mankind in economy, and drew down lightning from the clouds.'"

Our heroes have exonerated our faith in them and in democracy. With a strong belief in the land, institutions, and society of the new world, they have piloted us skillfully through rough waters.

The ship of state has rolled and pitched; sometimes it has taken on water. The short-sighted have shouted, "Abandon ship." But it has sprung no deep leaks, has never gone aground, and has weathered every blow.

Behind every hero is a group of skillful and faithful manipulators. We have tried to discover some of them and examine their motives and techniques. Even when their talents and goals were limited, they did well. Often, as with John Burke, Walt Disney or Charles Siringo, they were not intellectuals. Horatio Alger, Harry Bennett, and Ned Buntline demonstrate that they were not always virtuous. John Filson, W. B. Laughead, and Charles Francis Adams engineered the rise of major figures without even being aware that they were doing so. Owen Francis and Jules Billard were duped by the people they set out to fool. The trait which these hero makers all share is faith in their subjects. They believe, and make us believe, that their candidate's purpose is our own. His greatness seems so real that we equate his lengthened shadow with destiny itself.

Certain great men emerge as heroic pattern makers. John Smith in colonial times was such a figure; his buoyant optimist and audacity opened the brave new world. The Revolution produced our first demigod in Washington; our national motto, *E Pluribus Unum*, is a tribute to him. Daniel Boone, assisted by James Fenimore Cooper and others, came to personify the trailblazer and the trek west.

The nineteenth century brought bitter sectionalism and civil war. A second demigod, Abraham Lincoln, appeared to reunite us. The South dreamed of the Confederate victory that might have been and of the General who might have made it possible—Robert E. Lee, symbol of the Lost Cause. Out west men were carrying justice around with them on the hip. A young upstart named William Bonney supposedly killed a man for every one of his twenty-one years. Billy the Kid, as he was called, set the desperado prototype, while Buffalo Cody domesticated the Wild West for the tame east. And the Self Made Man took over as industry boomed. If we knew just how and why Smith, Washington, Boone, Lincoln, Lee, Bonney, Cody and the Self-Made Man became heroes, we would be well on the way to understanding the American hero.

We are too close to the twentieth century to say which of its candidates will endure. Because he took the tycoon's path and dramatized modern American know-how, Paul Bunyan has become capitalism's darling. More romantic is the American cowboy, our prime contribution to the world's mythology, whose fame is growing in a world cluttered by fences and macadam roads.

Most of them were built to accommodate the cars which Henry Ford taught America to mass-produce. Our chief mechanical hero, he chugged up Olympus in a model T. Motion pictures created new patterns of leisure, and new opportunities for heroes. Douglas Fairbanks the man, and Mickey the mouse, exemplified the activism, ingenuity, and pluck so highly valued in our culture. They pioneered in celluloid. Bunyan, the Cowboy, Ford, Doug, Mickey Mouse—five quite different figures which illuminate twentieth century America.

Our heroes' path, so silvery and apparently so solid, has usually turned out to be quicksand. These men are finally symbols of the transcience of American culture, fighting their way not into an established hagiography, but into a pinwheel. When the pinwheel loses its initial fire, then out with the pinhead and up with the new.

Were this not true, this book could not have been written at all; for otherwise we should have been satisfied with what heroes the good Lord gave us at the first settlement of his favor, or at the initial granting of independence. New generations have demanded new faces. "There's nothing as humiliating as being a has-been," observed Doug Fairbanks. Despite his almost impenetrable vanity, even he finally saw that the man of the hour goes down a one-way street. His biographer shows us Doug at the moment he learns a luxurious four months' cruise has cost him $100,000:

"Douglas was amazed. 'I spent a fortune on that damned trip and didn't get a nickel's worth of fun out of it.'

" 'You paid the piper, all right," Robert agreed.

" 'Apparently that's all I'm good for. And the worst of it is, *I've got to keep on doing it.*' " [4]

*   *   *

Heroes are not born. They are the products of their time, their insight, and the work of their devotees, who create a mythical image and a second life for them. The key to the hero's existence is function; his province is both history and folklore.

Heroes do not make history. They are the products of historic times. No combination of factors can fabricate a hero of the wrong man at the right moment, or the right man at the wrong moment. Only when there is a genuine need for a particular type, and when the qualifying candidate thinks and acts in the heroic manner, is there a culmination. Some who have tried hardest have failed. Others, like Washington, succeeded "without seeking any indirect or left-handed attempts to acquire popularity." One must have the inspired ability to do important and dramatic things memorably. Rehearsing is futile, since no one knows when the moment will come—if at all. The man's character, rather than his action, is critical. General Lee's victories jeopardized our Union; he is today a national hero because he was a man of great character. We are not concerned with Washington and Lincoln's frequent defeats. Knowing what these men were, we know that final victory had to be theirs.

Potential heroes, living and dead, are always competing. As in a horse race, one can choose his favorites; but the race must be run before anyone knows who will win. To say that the outcome is unpredictable does not mean that the course has no pattern. We can't tell which individual will become a hero. Yet in emerging he will follow one of several set formulas. It is like a mathematician figuring out a life-insurance curve. He cannot predict when a certain individual will die. However, he can tell what percentage of the population will die at what ages, over a long period.

American history does not lend weight to the great man theory, or demonstrate that heroes dominate events and institutions. It does not substantiate the wave theory, which holds that men get fame effortlessly because of historical chance. "Here is a hero who did nothing but shake the tree when the fruit was ripe," wrote Nietzche. But he added, "Do you think that was a small thing to do? Well, just look at the tree he shook!"

The firmest ground seems to lie in between these two extremes. More important than man's acts or fate's turns is the common will. Reformers follow individual visions, heroes follow communal ones. "So help me God, I can take no other course!" said Martin Luther. "The greater the man, the less is the province of his will,"

said Napoleon.   "My master is pitiless, for that master is the nature of things."

The study of heroes takes on to a point where various academic
disciplines cross.   Creating heroes seems as simple as sunlight;
it is as difficult to explain.   Twentieth century scholarship and
pedagogy tend to splinter human knowledge into fragments.   The
broad implications of many things, among them the heroic, elude
us.   Only by studying wholes can we hope to understand the world
about and within us.   We must explore the twilight area where
fact and fancy meet; where myth and reality become so intertwined that no thoughtful man would claim he could separate
them.

The old gods have gone; but we shall have new ones.   Heroes
and myths will emerge from our particular culture, just as they
have from all others.   They may not fit perfectly the old patterns
and definitions—but then, why should they?   Despite certain
universal qualities which they share with heroes of earlier times,
ours will eventually acquire a style and manner of their own.
Despite   differences of mannerisms and techniques, there is a
definite heroic relationship between the Homeric hero and the air
force "jet jockey" who travels faster than sound to meet individual
enemies far up in the heavens.   Good or bad luck, mechanical
failure, or a sudden change in the weather are so critical that
chance takes on all the aspects of a personal intervening power.
As with Ulysses or Aeneas, this man's life and reputation are in
the hands of the gods.

Eventually America will have a developed mythology and
Olympus of her own; such things come slowly.   We are, after all,
very young, and still close to Mother Europe.   Stories have to
mellow, and legends grow, before enduring myths and heroes
result.   The time-unit involved is not months or years, but generations.   We must have patience.   Our technology can modify,
but it cannot destroy nor speed up, the heroic process.   A writer
will appear who can work as successfully on film as Homer did
on papyrus or Shakespeare on paper.   The hero is not disappearing in America.   Like many things in our dynamic culture, he is
simply getting a new look.   Our literature, our pageants, and
especially our movies hint as to what he will be like when he reaches full stature.

"I have imagined," wrote Walt Whitman, "a life which should be that of the average man in average circumstances, and still grand, *heroic*." George Washington Harris gave us in *Sut Lovingood Yarns* a detailed picture of the type developed by the American frontier: "The mussils on his arms moved about like rabbits under the skin which was clear red an' white; and his eyes a deep, sparklin,' wickid blue, while a smile fluttered like a hummin' bird round his mouth all the while. When the State-fair offers a premium for *men* like they now does fur jackasses, I means to enter Wirt Staples, an' I'll git it, if there's five thousand entries."

Another democratic American hero was Bulkington, in *Moby Dick*. "From his fine stature." wrote Herman Melville, "I thought he must be one of those tall mountaineers from the Alleghenian Ridge in Virginia." When we read this line we remember another by Emerson: "America begins west of the Alleghenies." Bulkingtons are the hope of the new world. When the *Pequod* sets sail, he is appropriately at the helm. The reader and the author know the ship must follow the evil White Whale to the bottom of the ocean. Consequently we have Melville's memorable exhortation to the helmsman: "Bear thee grimly, demigod! Up from the spray of thy ocean-perishing—straight up leaps thy apotheosis!"

The American historian who best understood the emerging American hero was Frederick Jackson Turner. In his 1893 essay on "The Significance of the Frontier in American History," he asserted that "the true point of view in the history of this nation is not the Atlantic coast, it is the Great West." The advance of the heroic settler westward explained American development. His special idol was Daniel Boone, who "helped to open the way for civilization," and whose family "epitomizes the backwoodsman's advance across the continent." Turner even felt that the striking characteristics of the American intellect could be traced directly to the frontier: "That coarseness and strength combined with acuteness and inquisitiveness; that practical, inventive turn of mind, quick to find expedients; that masterful grasp of material things, lacking in the artistic but powerful to effect great ends; that restless, nervous energy; that dominant individualism—these are traits of the frontier, or traits called out elsewhere because of the existence of the frontier.[3]

Since Turner's day his ideas have been a focal point for historical speculation and controversy. "The frontier hypothesis," Frederick L. Paxson wrote, "presents the most attractive single explanation of the distinctive trends of American history"; and, he might have added, of the American hero.

Across the ocean the hero-worshiping Thomas Carlyle also conjured up a vision of the man who could conquer and control the New World. "How beautiful to think of lean tough Yankee settlers, tough as gutta-percha, with most occult unsubduable fire in their belly, steering over the Western Mountains, to annihilate the jungle, and bring bacon for the Posterity of Adam. There is no *myth* of Athene or Herakles equal to this *fact*."

Significantly, for Whitman, Harris, Melville, Emerson, Turner, and Carlyle, the common points about our emerging hero are his appearance, his attitude, and his westward trek. Masculine, full-sized, and golden, he believes in the future; he is looking for something beyond the next range of mountains.

The vision of such a man, and the democratic society which produces him, is a thrilling thing. Those who see it feel no longer that they must apologize for our many acknowledged shortcomings, and defer to older nations. Instead, they can take the offensive, as did Stephen Vincent Benét when he wrote "American Names":

> *"You may bury my body in Sussex grass,*
> *You may bury my tongue at Campmedy,*
> *I shall not be there. I shall rise and pass.*
> *Bury my heart at Wounded Knee."*

Sources

CHAPTER 1

[1] See Chapter II of W. G. Agard's *Classical Myths in Sculpture* (Madison, Wisconsin, 1951).

[2] See D. Riddle's *The Martyrs, A Study in Social Control* (Chicago, 1931).

[3] A full analysis appears in J. M. Mecklin's *The Passing of the Saint* (Chicago, 1941).

[4] See Joseph Campbell, *The Hero with a Thousand Faces* (New York, 1949); David Malcomson, *Ten Heroes* (New York, 1939); and Otto Rank, *The Myth of the Birth of the Hero* (New York, 1914).

[5] See F. R. S. Raglan, *The Hero: A Study in Tradition, Myth, and Drama* (London, 1936).

[6] Arnold Toynbee, *A Study of History* (London, 1934), III, p. 243.

[7] See A. J. Guerard, *Reflection on the Napoleonic Legend* (New York, 1924).

[8] See John Galbraith's "Perils of the Big Build-Up," *New York Times*, magazine section, March 7, 1954, p. 12 f.

[9] See *The Autobiography of Eva Peron: My Mission in Life* (New York, 1954)

[10] These lines are quoted with the permission of Mr. Stevens and his publisher, Alfred Knopf.

CHAPTER 2

[1] Lindbergh's subsequent reputation has fluctuated widely. Because of his work with the America First group that tried to keep the United States out of World War II, the Lone Eagle was discredited, and called a "Copperhead" by President Roosevelt. In 1953 his book, *The Spirit of St. Louis*, helped restore him; and in February, 1954, President Eisenhower made him a reserve Brigadier General.

[2] See David Dewitt's *The Assassination of Abraham Lincoln and Its Expiation* (New York, 1909) and Lloyd Lewis' *Myths After Lincoln* (New York, 1929).

[3] See Robert A. Theobald's *The Final Secret of Pearl Harbor* (New York, 1954).

[4] Donald Davidson, "A Note on American Heroes," in Brooks, Purser, and Warren's *An Approach to Literature* (New York, 1939), p. 137.

[5] Peter Cartwright, *Autobiography* (New York, 1856), p. 477.

[6] David Riesman, *The Lonely Crowd* (New Haven, 1950), Chapter 4.

[7] See *School and Society* for July 22, 1950.

CHAPTER 3

[1] See Jarvis M. Morse, "John Smith and his Critics: A Chapter in Colonial Historiography," in the *Journal of Southern History*, Vol. L, 1935. The main source for the life and exploits of Smith is to be found in his own works; his prose was almost as colorful as his actions. The first complete edition of his work was edited by Edward Arber and published in England in 1884; it was reprinted, with an additional introduction by A. G. Bradley, in 1910.

[2] For a full discussion of the Smith-Pocahontas plays and novels, see Albert Keiser's *The Indian in American Literature* (New York, 1933).

[3] Charles Poindexter, *John Smith and His Critics* (Richmond, 1893), p. 61.

[4] An idea of the tone of the volume may be had from this sentence: "Cheating, robbing, breaking promises—these three are clearly things which must cease to be

done; and we must extend protection of the law to the Indian's rights of property, 'of life, liberty, and the pursuit of happiness.' " Even the policy of the Hollywood movie industry towards the Indian has altered in recent years. In such post-World War II movies as "Broken Arrow," "Ranger of Cherokee Strip," "The Big Sky," "Across the Wide Missouri," and "Devil's Doorway," the cinema Indian was a noble savage.

[5] See the author's *Virginia, 1902-1941: A Cultural History*, unpublished doctoral thesis on file in the Sterling Memorial Library, Yale University.

[6] History has repeated itself, and given Virginia another Pocahontas to cherish—Lady Astor. Born in Pittsylvania County and christened Nancy Langhorne, she, too, was wooed by a high-born Englishman and taken to the Court of St. James. The English people were as enthusiastic about this Virginia belle as they had been about Pocahontas, and she became the first woman to sit in the House of Parliament.

[7] James Branch Cabell, *Let Me Lie* (New York, 1947), p. 55.

CHAPTER 4

[1] The best study of Washington's reputation is William A. Bryan's *George Washington in American Literature, 1775-1865* (New York, 1952).

[2] This is the official tabulation in the *Report of the United States George Washington Bicentennial Program* (Washington, D. C., 1932) V, p. xii.

[3] Stewart Holbrook, *Lost Men in American History* (New York, 1946).

[4] John S. Bassett, *The Middle Group of American Historians* (New York, 1917), p. 100.

[5] Edward O'Neill, *A History of American Biography* (Philadelphia, 1935), p. 164.

CHAPTER 5

[1] J. W. Lake, ed., *Complete Works of Byron* (Paris, 1825) Vol. II, p. 403-4.

[2] Clarence W. Alvord, "The Daniel Boone Myth," in *Journal of the Illinois State Historical Society*, 19:16-30, April, 1926.

[3] Reuben G. Thwaites, editor, *Early Western Travels*, 1748-1846 (New York, 1904-7), vol. 18, p. 27.

[4] Timothy Flint, *Biographical Memoir of Daniel Boone, the First Settler of Kentucky*, (Cincinnati, 1883), p. 263.

[5] Daniel Bryan, *The Mountain Muse* (Harrisonburg, Va., 1813), p. 136.

[6] The question of Cooper's use of Boone material, and of Leatherstocking's significance, is discussed in Henry Nash Smith's *Virgin Land* (Cambridge, Mass., 1950), Chapter VI.

[7] William B. Hesseltine, *Pioneer's Mission, The Story of Lyman C. Draper* (Madison, Wis.), 1954.

[8] Dan Beard, *Hardly a Man is Now Alive—The Autobiography of Dan Beard* (New York, 1939), p. 353.

[9] Letter to the author from James Taylor Adams, Big Laurel, Virginia, dated September 7, 1948.

[10] William Carlos Williams, *In the American Grain* (Norfolk, Conn., 1925), p. 137.

CHAPTER 6

[1] Talbott Sweeney, *A Vindication From a Northern Standpoint of General Robert E. Lee*, (Richmond, 1890), p. 47.

[2] Edwin Alderman, *Virginia, A Memorial Address*, (Charlottesville, 1909) p. 10.

CHAPTER 7

[1] Alfred Adler, "Billy the Kid: A Case Study in Epic Origins," in *Western Folklore*, X, No. 2, pp. 143-152.

[2] The lady was Mrs. Wallace. See Lew Wallace's *An Autobiography* (New York anl London, 1906), II, p. 920.

[3] Letter from Upson to his sister in Connecticut, dated May 6, 1882. Quoted in William A. Keleher's *The Fabulous Frontier* (Santa Fe, 1945), p. 125.

[4] J. Frank Dobie, "A Note on Charlie Siringo, Writer and Man," in Siringo's *A Texas Cowboy* (New York, 1951), p. 173.

[5] B. A. Botkin, *A Treasury of American Folklore* (New York 1944), p. 97.

CHAPTER 8

[1] See *Report of the Adjutant General of the State of Kansas* (Leavenworth, 1867), I. p. 625. Cody was a private when discharged, although he later claimed to be a sergeant.

[2] Richard J. Walsh, *The Making of Bufflo Bill; A Study in Heroics* (Indianapolis, 1928). Much unpublished material on Cody is on file in the Denver Public Library, and is used with permission. Don Russell, who is working on a life of Cody, has also supplied information.

[3] See Jay Monaghan's *The Great Rascal*, (Boston, 1952). Chapter I, "The Discovery of Buffalo Bill," of his meeting Buffalo Bill.

[4] Quoted by Richard Walsh, *op. cit.*, p. 355.

[5] See Albert Johanssen's *The House of Beadle and Adams*, (Norman, Oklahoma, 1950), 2 vols.

[6] Helen Cody Wetmore, *Last of the Great Scouts* (Duluth, Wisconsin, 1899).

[7] Henry Llewellyn Williams, *Buffalo Bill* (London, 1887), p. 191.

[8] Dan Muller, *My Life with Buffalo Bill* (New York, 1948), p. 142.

CHAPTER 9

[1] *Life*, vol. 34, May 25, 1953, pp. 134-150.

[2] Harry Bennett, *We Never Called Him Henry* (New York, 1951) p. 47.

[3] Such matters are discussed in Keith Sward's *The Legend of Henry Ford*, (New York, 1948.)

[4] Bennett, *op. cit.*, p. 156.

[5] Allan Nevins (with Frank Ernest Hill), *Ford: The Times, the Man, the Company*, (New York, 1954).

[6] *Time*, vol. 61, May 18, 1953, p. 102.

CHAPTER 10

[1] See A. Whitney Griswold's unpublished doctoral thesis on *The American Cult of Success* in the Sterling Library at Yale University.

[2] Quoted in Herbert R. Mayes' *Alger, A Biography Without a Hero* (New York, 1928), p. 226.

[3] Leo Gurko, *Heroes, Highbrows, and the Popular Mind* (Indianapolis, 1953), p. 188.

[4] See Richard Morris' "Rags to Riches—Myth and Reality" in the *Saturday Review* for November 21, 1953.

[5] James Thurber, in *Saturday Review of Literature*, 15:6, January 30, 1937.

CHAPTER 11

[1] R. E. Banta, "Folk Heroes Can Get Out of Hand," *American Heritage,* Spring, 1954.

[2] See Hyman Richman's "The Saga of Joe Magarac," *New York Folklore Quarterly,* Winter 1953. Mr. Richman has generously assisted in supplying material for this chapter.

[3] See F. J. Kern's *English-Slovene Dictionary* (Cleveland, 1919), P. A. Hrobak's *English-Slovak Dictionary* (Middlton, Pa. 1944), and A. B. Yollan's *Dictionary of the Hungarian and English Languages* (Budapest, 1905).

[4] Owen Francis, "A Prodigal Returns," in *American Mercury,* April, 1929.

[5] Mrs. Owen Francis, who lives in New York City, feels that her husband (now deceased) was in on the joke all the while. In light of what he wrote, this does not seem probable.

[6] Jules Billard, "Ever Hear of Joe Magarac?" *Saturday Evening Post,* Feb. 22, 1947, p. 41 f.

CHAPTER 12

[1] Alistair Cooke, *Douglas Fairbanks: The Making of Screen Character,* (New York, 1940).

[2] Ralph Hancock and Letitia Fairbanks, *Douglas Fairbanks: The Fourth Musketeer,* (New York, 1953), p. 152.

[3] See Stith Thompson's *Motif-Index of Folk Literature,* (Bloomington, 1936), Vol. VI, p. 377 ff.

[4] *Life* magazine for Oct. 16, 1953, carried a picture of Roy Disney "sitting proudly among some 3,000 of the 3,500 items which have been allowed to use Disney trademarks."

CHAPTER 13

[1] By 1954 the Code was so universally understood that Hollywood could produce an extravagant technicolor movie (*Red Garters*) parodying it.

[2] R. E. Banta, *op. cit.* The year after his death Dillinger had a sort of apotheosis as Duke Mantee in Robert Sherwood's *The Petrified Forest.*

[3] Robert Warshow, "The Gangster as Tragic Hero," *Partisan Review,* February, 1948, p. 242. See also Mr. Warshow's article on "The Westerner" in *Partisan Review,* April, 1954.

CHAPTER 14

[1] Anyone interested in this American tragedy should read *The Future of the Great Plains: Report of the Great Plains Commission* (Washington, Government Printing Office, 1936).

[2] Alfred Henry Lewis' series of Wolfville novels (which began in 1897) is more of an obstacle than the average reader can surmount. If Clarence E. Mulford's Hopalong Cassidy series is more palatable, it remains to be seen if it is enduring, or if the figure (portrayed by the matinee idol William Boyd) will hop right out of the picture.

[3] This anonymous editor's reply is quoted in Walter P. Webb, *The Great Plains* (Boston, 1936), P. 467.

[4] Zane Grey, *The Light of Western Stars* (New York, 1914), p. 88.

[5] Quoted by Frank Dobie in his "Note" to Siringo's *A Texas Cowboy* (New York, 1950), p. 154.

[6] Bernard DeVoto, "The Wild West," in *Holiday*, July 1954, p. 35 f.

[7] David B. Davis, "Ten-Gallon Hero," in *American Quarterly*, Summer 1954, p. 114.

[8] Robert Warshow, "Movie Chronicle: The Westerner," in *Partisan Review*, April, 1954, p. 196.

[9] Account in *Time*, May 22, 1950.

[10] Clarence E. Mulford, *Hopalong Cassidy* (Chicago, 1910), p. 65.

[11] Tex Burns, pseud. (Louis L'Amour), *Hopalong Cassidy and the Trail to Seven Pines* (New York, 1951), p. 187.

[12] Edward O'Reilly, "The Saga of Pecos Bill," in *Century Magazine*, October, 1923.

CHAPTER 15

[1] Joseph Campbell, *The Hero with a Thousand Faces* (New York, 1948), p. 387.

[2] Ortega y Gasset, *The Revolt of the Masses* (New York, 1950), p. 52.

[4] Ralph Hancock, *op. cit.*, p. 256.

[5] F. J. Turner, *The Frontier in American History* (New York, 1920), p. 31.

Bibliographical Note

As a necessary preliminary task, the author prepared a *Bibliography of the American Hero*, which the Bibliographical Society of the University of Virginia published in 1950. It lists about five hundred works classified in terms of the classical modern literature, and the hero considered from a philosophic, literary, historical, social science and folklore viewpoint. Anyone especially interested in the literature on the American hero is referred to this bibliography.

For the general reader, these books are highly recommended: F.R.S. Raglan, *The Hero: A Study of Tradition, Myth, and Drama* (New York, 1937), Dixon Wecter, *The Hero in America* (New York, 1943); Sidney Hook, *The Hero in History, a Study of Limitation and Possibility* (London, 1945); Stewart Holbrook, *Little Annie Oakley and Other Rugged People* (New York, 1949); and Leo Gurko, *Heroes, Highbrows, and the Popular Mind* (Indianapolis, 1953).

The articles and works cited in the references will also be found useful.

Heroes All: A Synopsis of Case Studies

Hero	Type	Hero-Makers	Key Date and event
Smith	Knight-errant	Henry, Robertson Poindexter, Cook	1907 (Tercentennial)
Washington	Father	Weems, Marshall, Stuart, Bloom	1932 (Bicentennial)
Boone	Pioneer	Filson, Cooper Draper, Beard	1934 (Bicentennial)
Lee	Aristocrat	Sweeney, Adams, Benet, Freeman	1907 (Centennial)
Self-Made Man	Go-Getter	Franklin, Alger, McGuffey, Carnegie	1929 (Great Depression)
Billy the Kid	Avenger	Upson, Siringo, Hough, Burns	1926 (Burns' revival)
Cody	Matinee Idol	Buntline, Burke Ingraham	1890 (close of frontier)
Bunyan	Tycoon	Laughead, Auden Stevens	1914 (adoption by Red River Lumber Co.)
Magarac	Immigrant	Francis, Billard, Vittor	1931 (Francis' article)
Cowboy	Natural Man	Wister, Grey, Siringo, Cody	1910 (first western movie)
Ford	Mechanic	Sorenson, Cameron, Bennett, H. Ford II	1953 (Ford Motor Co., 50th Anniversary
Fairbanks	Activist	Loos, Pickford, John and Doug Fairbanks, Jr.	1920 (Fairbanks-Pickford wedding)
Mickey Mouse	American Boy	Walt and Roy Disney, Kamen	1932 (Kamen Enterprises started)

Index

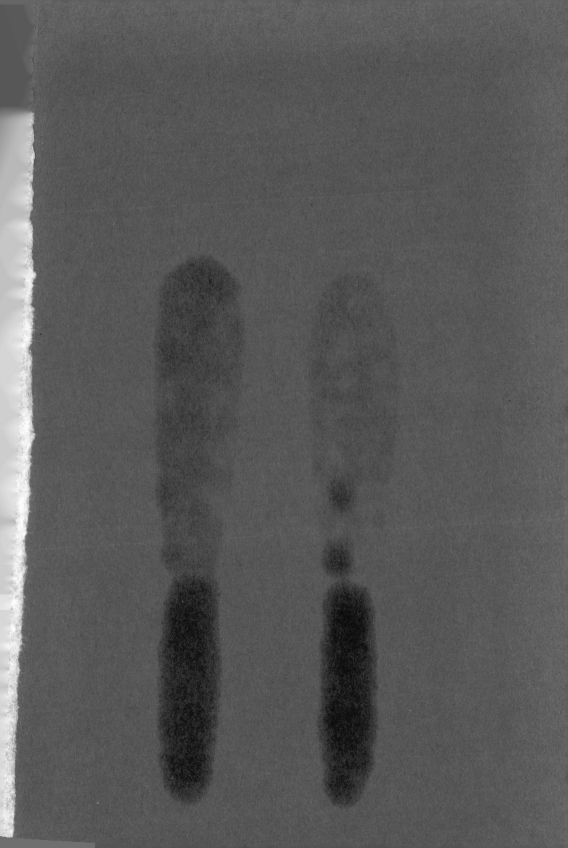

DATE DUE	
MAR 1 9 1997	
DEC 1 2 2003	